HEALING WISDOM FROM THE BIBLE

From bringing out your hidden talents to standing up for yourself, from getting angry to getting ahead, the Bible's teachings cover all aspects of our busy lives. This unique book sheds light on these timeless issues, covering such topics as:

Ridding Yourself of Anxiety: When Jesus said, "Therefore I tell you, do not be anxious about your life," he urged his followers to live in the present, and to be free of the *what if's* in their minds.

Facing Human Suffering: The Book of Job teaches us that we can discover our challenge in life, and find meaning in the pain we feel.

Sex: Sexuality is a divine gift. While the Bible does warn against promiscuity, Jesus was quick to forgive sexual mistakes and soothe the suffering that such mistakes cause.

How to Stop Trying to Control Others: Pharaoh asked, "Who is the Lord, that I should heed his voice and let Israel go?" Real human strength is the acknowledgment that our own happiness depends on giving freedom to others.

Coping with Fears: The greatest fear is of the unknown. Jesus counseled that "nothing is covered that will not be revealed," and that we should turn our fears into the first steps toward understanding.

Healing Wisdom from the Bible

Spiritual Guidance, Inspiration, and Comfort for Everyday Life

JAMES E. GIBSON, Ph.D.

A Dell Book

Published by
Dell Publishing
a division of
Bantam Doubleday Dell Publishing Group, Inc.
666 Fifth Avenue
New York, New York 10103

The Bible text in this publication is from the Revised Standard Version, copyright 1946, 1952, 1971, by the Division of Christian Education of the National Council of Churches of Christ in the USA, and is used by permission.

The names of any persons mentioned in this book are fictitious, and any resemblance to the names of persons living or deceased is unintentional.

Book design by Glen Burris

ISBN: 0-440-21016-X

Reprinted by arrangement with Rodale Press

Printed in the United States of America

Published simultaneously in Canada

June 1992

10 9 8 7 6

OPM

To my father,
Reverend Robert E. Gibson

Contents

Acknowledgments

Every book has a thousand authors. Only a few can be recognized and thanked. First, my deep appreciation to Charles Gerras, who conceived this book and shepherded it with consummate editorial skill; to Dominick Bosco, who brings the Spirit when darkness threatens; to Ann Marie Bahr, Rev. John Pritchard, and the other students and faculty of the Religion Department of Temple University, who showed me what a true community of scholars can be; and finally, to my wife, playmate, and friend, Deborah.

Introduction

I will always remember watching Aunt Viola take her tattered old family Bible from the top shelf of her bookcase and disappear into her "study room," as she called it. She was a mystery to us. She never preached or moralized. She never really talked about religion much at all. But she always seemed to be able to bring the family together during a crisis. She always knew how to calm a conflict or end a misunderstanding.

When her son, Charles, died in an accident at work, Aunt Viola was the strongest among us. When I asked her how she could bear this tragedy, she told me she gained all her strength and wisdom from the Bible. That strength sustained her till she died at the age of ninety-one.

Today's psychologists are rediscovering the value of the Bible's wisdom and insight. In many universities therapists are returning to study religious thought and theology because so many of their patients suffer from a kind of spiritual anguish. The patients seek ways to confront the universal issues that have always faced mankind, and therapists find themselves ill-equipped to deal with these issues themselves, so more and more of them are turning for help to traditional sources of wisdom and inspiration, notably the Bible.

This is not at all surprising. The stories and sayings of the Bible have survived thousands of years because generation upon generation found in them a practical wisdom.

It was a wisdom that helped to solve everyday problems as well as to resolve theological and spiritual issues.

Much of the insight offered by contemporary psychotherapy has its root in spiritual practice. Carl Jung, Erich Fromm, Abraham Maslow, Victor Frankl, and many other renowned psychotherapists have consulted the Bible for ideas on solving human problems. The word "psyche" means "soul" or "spirit." Psychology is the study of the soul. Few sources are better than the Bible.

In the Christian Gospel, Jesus was seen as a wonderful healer of physical diseases and crippling handicaps. He also dealt effectively with the common complaints that stem from sorrow and discontent. Jesus was, in fact, a master teacher and therapist. His genius was in transforming situations into astonishing lessons that can clarify and help to heal the problems and pains life can bring.

To find this therapeutic message we must read carefully. The Bible is not simplistic. It is not a collection of outdated aphorisms that placate us or indulge our neuroses. Nor is it a sugarcoating of reality. The Bible is a tough book. It looks squarely at life as we know it and live it. Often, its prescription is stronger than we would expect. However, the Bible was *not* written to make us feel guilty or sinful. Nor are we to use it as a weapon to make others feel low and outcast. The Bible was intended to bring us a sense of joy and peace, a sense of energy and life. The Bible is not just a guide to the afterlife. It was written as a guide to everyday life.

Often, the wisdom in the Bible needs to be restated in modern terms. The book you have in your hands is designed to act as a guide from a modern perspective. It asks you to take an active role, put yourself in the place of the characters in the biblical stories. Look for a part of your inner identity—your soul—in each of them. This is challenging and can even be painful, like any therapeutic process. But the result is a healing self-understanding that can sustain any of us through the most difficult times. Use this book to help search for and experience the healing wisdom of the Bible.

KNOW YOURSELF

Where to Find Yourself in the Bible

 But an angel of the Lord said to Philip, "Rise and go toward the south to the road that goes down from Jerusalem to Gaza." This is a desert road. And he rose and went. And behold, an Ethiopian, a eunuch, a minister of Candace, the queen of the Ethiopians, in charge of all her treasure, had come to Jerusalem to worship and was returning; seated in his chariot, he was reading the prophet Isaiah. And the Spirit said to Philip, "Go up and join this chariot." So Philip ran to him, and heard him reading Isaiah the prophet, and asked, "Do you understand what you are reading?" And he said, "How can I, unless someone guides me?" And he invited Philip to come up and sit with him.

ACTS 8:26–31

Like the Ethiopian official, we all want a knowledgeable guide to help us understand the Bible. What is the right way to get the most from this glorious gift from the past?

There is no single way to understand all the Bible has to teach us. Its depth is infinite. It tells us about the

4

beginning and the end of time. It shows us the full range of human emotion, from the deepest suffering to the highest joy.

No one approach can encompass the Bible's full message. However, there are two basic ways to tackle it. One is to read the Bible objectively and scientifically, for information about the text or about the people and culture the text describes. The other is to search the wisdom of the Bible, so to speak, and hear the Bible's healing message as it applies directly to us.

The second approach is the one we take in this book. We enter the stories in a personal way and explore the psychological and spiritual insights we find there. Then we apply them to our lives, thoughts, and feelings.

Reading the Bible this way may be a bit frightening at first. But the potential rewards in self-understanding are well worth any risk.

Once we understand ourselves, we start to recognize parts of our behavior and thinking that can cause us pain and sorrow. At the same time, wonderful opportunities for a more joyful and satisfying life become apparent. Seeing the truth about ourselves and our world makes healing inevitable.

Where do we find self-understanding in the Bible? How can we find ourselves there?

The first step is to become sensitive to the symbols of the Bible. Symbols point to the depths of the human psyche, parts of us that are so deeply personal that we fear to express them even to ourselves. Yet the Bible helps us discover that these parts of us we consider so deeply personal are actually universal—the pain, the longings, the mistakes, the deep regrets, the broken resolutions. This is why we can read Genesis and Job and Ecclesiastes and find that they speak directly to some hidden part of our minds, even though they were written thousands of years ago.

Consider the people we read about in the Bible. Their lives are significant to us in ways far different from ordinary historical figures. They speak so strongly to us because they represent something deep in us. Their lives reflect our own soul in fundamental ways.

This may not be immediately apparent. We may resist the idea that we could ever be as heroic as Moses, or as jubilant as David. We hope we would never be as mean as Pharaoh or as vindictive as Herod.

But think a bit. What truly touches you when you read the Bible? Isn't it the spark of recognition, the inner voice that says, "Yes, I have felt that way myself at times"?

Like Job, we have all been victimized by tragedy. We have all felt shame like Adam and Eve. We have all yearned for the Promised Land, like the people of Israel. We have all felt the desperation of lapsed faith like Simon Peter, when Jesus called him to walk on the water during the storm.

But we have also had our spirits lifted by the Psalms of David, by the courage of the Israelites, and by the faith of Paul in organizing the new Church.

These inner feelings, these movements of our spirit in resonance with the story, are all effects of the power of the Bible's symbols. They are the ways these stories touch our lives.

Once we see how the symbols of the Bible can affect us, we become aware of that bit of infinity each of us has within us, some indefinable divine spark. Then we glimpse the limitless possibilities of our spirit. Without it, our vision of who we can be and what we can do is too narrow. We come to believe that the surface, the mask we allow ourselves and others to see, is all we are.

The secret of entering the stories of the Bible and finding the healing wisdom hidden there is to see that the Bible reflects and reveals hidden and infinite parts of ourselves to us. We can find ourselves on every page of the Bible. We can read the same passage time and again, and with each reading learn a wider and deeper truth about ourselves. Then we see that the power of this magnificent book is that we can't help but find ourselves in it, ready for undreamed-of opportunities for a better, more satisfying, more joyful life.

What It Means to Be a Man

Then the Lord God said, "It is not good that the man should be alone; I will make him a helper fit for him." So out of the ground the Lord God formed every beast of the field and every bird of the air, and brought them to the man to see what he would call them; and whatever the man called every living creature, that was its name. The man gave name to all cattle, and to the birds of the air and to every beast of the field; but for man there was not found a helper fit for him. So the Lord God caused a deep sleep to fall upon the

**man, and while he slept took one of his ribs and
closed up its place with flesh; and the rib which the
Lord God had taken from the man he made into a
woman and brought her to the man.**

GEN. 2:18–22

Here is one set of questions sure to awaken every drowsy
male student in my classroom: What's the difference between
a man and a woman? What does it mean to be a man? How
can you know you are no longer a boy?

Unlike women, most men find it difficult to respond.
They rarely discuss the questions among themselves. They
seem to have a code of silence about the doubts and
insecurities that surround their sexual identity.

The silence reflects the confusion men feel about
their role in the world. The aggressive and combative
stereotype so dominant in the first half of this century is
now uncomfortable for many, if not most, men. So who
are they? What are they supposed to do to be "real" men?
They can turn to the book of Genesis for the answers.

In the story of the Creation, we come upon the male
hard at work naming all the animals.

Giving a name was a symbolic task of great importance in biblical times. A name created an identity. A name
held the essence of a thing. (The name of God was too
sacred to be spoken or written.) A name was so special that
a person undergoing a major spiritual transition or revelation,
took on a new name to mark the change.

Perhaps while learning so much about the world of
animals, Adam became curious about himself. "What kind

of animal am I?" he might have asked. "What is my name, my essence?"

The Bible tells us that man could not answer this question alone. To truly understand himself he needed a helper, or he would be incomplete and without an identity. So God created woman from Adam's body, while Adam slept. She was and is, in many ways, man's deepest self—truly his "other half."

This story is especially appropriate today, when women struggle to find their identity. They explore their emotions and learn new ways to communicate and celebrate their feelings. Men can take a lesson in how to express who they are, what they feel, what they can be. Too often men pretend to feel nothing at all. They tend to hide their feelings at the risk of stress and tension. In fact, many men become ill because they bottle up their emotions.

Women are more likely than men to speak to each other about their identity, and to younger women about what it means to be an adult woman.

Men often distance themselves from their family and other men because of their exclusive attention to their roles as protectors and providers. They rarely communicate their feelings to other men because they see even close friends as potential competitors. The result is a common loneliness, insecurity, and confusion about identity I see among my male students.

If the fear of self-expression dominates family relationships, the results can be even more damaging. Men need to talk to their sons and daughters about themselves. They must tell the story of their life: how they met and came to love their wife; how they chose their career; how they dealt with danger and triumph. Children love to hear these stories.

Just as important, children have their own story to tell, and fathers need to listen to it and understand. This exchange of stories can provide a foundation of love and understanding that will last the child's lifetime.

Finally, women can teach men an awareness of their link with nature. This is especially true concerning the body. Women seem to be more attuned to the signals their bodies send, and they take action more quickly when something goes wrong. Men, on the other hand, tend to hide pain and ignore the distress signals the body sends.

The Bible provides a clear model for the fundamental relationship between the sexes. We are helpmates. Men and women need each other for support and love. It's through this relationship we learn who we are and who we can be.

What It Means to Be a Woman

And the rib which the Lord God had taken from the man he made into a woman and brought her to the man. Then the man said,

> "This at last is bone of my bones and flesh of
> my flesh;
> she shall be called Woman,
> because she was taken out of Man.

Therefore a man leaves his father and his mother and cleaves to his wife and they become one flesh. And the

**man and his wife were both naked and were not
ashamed.**

GEN. 2:22–25

Both sexes are in a struggle for identity in the modern
world. But, as my college classes show, women have made
far more progress in this struggle than men.

It is difficult and uncomfortable for males to confront
the question of what it means to be a man. When I ask my
female students, "What does it mean to be a woman?"
however, they speak out with little or no hesitation.

Though women, like men, may be confused about
who they are and what they can be, it is a confusion of a
different kind with a different source. The pride women
feel in themselves and in their accomplishments is well
earned. They have escaped the confines of old stereotypes
that were unfair and oppressive. Women have fashioned
new roles and new possibilities for themselves in modern
society. They have become aware of themselves and their
power, and this has changed the world for the better.

But these gains have exacted a price. For the modern
woman, it is increasingly difficult to find satisfying and
fulfilling relationships with men. She faces difficult decisions concerning career and children. She is exhausted
from trying to live up to the "super woman" ideal she has
set for herself. She feels cheated because her success doesn't
match her expectations.

Many modern women reject the Bible because of the
subordinate role it describes for women. Their reaction is
understandable—but hasty, too. Certainly, the biblical

The need to Love + Dot not to be loved, also is important.

writers were heavily influenced by their cultural norms, which were frankly sexist. But the Bible has a deeper wisdom about male and female that transcends such failings.

The Bible tells us that women and men are made of the same flesh and bone. Whatever the differences between the sexes, both face the same basic challenges in life—the need to be loved, the search for understanding and companionship, the ache of despair. But both are also capable of joy and creativity; both also possess a potential for wonder and intimacy.

While men may need women to teach them openness and intimacy, women can learn from men about the pitfalls of power and material success—the terrible toll of stress and tension. Men can teach women about the fear and vulnerability that can lead to drug and alcohol addiction. These are important lessons that men have paid dearly for—women need not experience the same horror for themselves.

The biblical term for physical intimacy is "to know." The phrase reveals the basic goal the Bible sets for male and female relationships. Only through each other can we truly know who we are. Only through each other can we reach our highest potential for understanding and love.

How to Like Yourself

You have heard that it was said, "An eye for an eye and a tooth for a tooth." But I say to you, Do not resist one who is evil. But if any one strikes you on the right cheek, turn to him the other also; and if any one would sue you and take your coat, let him have your cloak as well; and if any one forces you to go one mile, go with him two miles. Give to him who begs from you, and do not refuse him who would borrow from you.

You have heard that it was said, "You shall love your neighbor and hate your enemy." But I say to you, Love your enemies and pray for those who persecute you, so that you may be sons of your Father who is in heaven; for he makes his sun rise on the evil and on the good, and sends rain on the just and on the unjust. For if you love those who love you, what reward have you? Do not even the tax collectors do the same? And if you salute only your brethren, what more are you doing than others? Do not even the Gentiles do the same? You, therefore, must be perfect, as your heavenly Father is perfect.

MATT. 5:38–48

We often expect too much of ourselves. We know we're not perfect. We make mistakes. However, we sometimes feel so angry and frustrated when we don't measure up that we make ourselves unhappy. We all need to learn to like ourselves more. The Bible tells us how.

Jody was an example of a person much too self-critical. She was a competent and efficient secretary. She kept her department running smoothly. We all depended on her in crisis situations, and she usually came through. Still, she constantly criticized herself. "I'm just not good enough," she once told me. "I've been able to pull through so far. But if you really knew how little I know and how incompetent I am, you would just hate me."

I tried to reassure her, pointing out how grateful we all were to have her with us. It didn't seem to help.

"Doesn't the Bible tell us to be perfect?" she responded. "I know how imperfect I am. I am just hopeless."

"Let's turn to that passage," I said. "It teaches a worthwhile lesson, and it will make you feel much better."

We all get down on ourselves at times. But when we make a habit of self-criticism, we can make ourselves sick. Some of us, like Jody, are perfectionists. We drive ourselves crazy insisting on flawless performances, and we make life impossible for our friends and family as well.

The Bible has an important lesson for us on this matter.

In the passage from Matthew, Jesus presents a startlingly new idea of perfection. He begins by reciting a familiar Jewish law: "An eye for an eye, a tooth for a tooth." This is the rule for justice. It is a rule most of those listening agree with. They all want to see people punished for their crimes. It is only fair that criminals get what they deserve.

Surprisingly, Jesus wants to replace this rule. We should love our enemies, he says. We should pray for those who persecute us. In giving this new rule, Jesus presents a formidable challenge. It is easy to love our friends. It is easy to love the lovable. Loving unpleasant people is a challenge. Loving people who mean to do us harm seems impossible. We would rather have justice. We want the satisfaction of seeing our enemies punished.

Like most of Jesus' teachings, this lesson works on many levels. We can apply this message to our inner life as well as to social situations. Here, too, it is a challenge.

Many psychologists believe each of us has a "dark

side." We have hidden within us desires and impulses we feel are wrong. Like Jody, some of us tend to exaggerate our imperfections and faults. We see only our darkness and ignore the goodness that also lives within us. We become our own worst critic. Sometimes we even become our own worst enemy.

If Jesus' teaching applies to our inner life, then he is asking us to love our inner enemy. He is asking us to love our dark side, the side of us that is unpleasant and perhaps even nasty. He wants us to be kind to that part of ourselves that makes mistakes and leaves us feeling foolish or guilty.

What a challenge! It is easy to love ourselves when we are successful and strong. It is easy to be our own best friend when we've done something heroic. But how can we love ourselves when we are weak, when we are failing or messing up our lives?

Jesus' lesson is a great relief. He demonstrates that love differs from justice. If we were to apply the rule of "an eye for an eye" to ourselves, we would always be condemning our actions and thoughts. But this is not the rule to use. Instead, we must learn to love our inner enemy, just as we must love our outer enemy.

Jesus' message is clear—love allows imperfection. God sends his refreshing rain on all the people of the earth. The perfection of God's love comes to us even when we do not deserve it.

Jesus' call is to this same perfection. We can be spiritually perfect by loving ourselves even though none of us is perfect in the objective sense.

Of course we do not condone injustice. Loving an enemy either within or without does not mean allowing that person to hurt others. We must treat an enemy as we would a friend. If a friend were doing wrong, we would ask him or her to stop. We would try to understand the reason for the action. We would offer to help. We would try to help correct the wrong, rather than ignore it.

In just the same way, we must treat our inner enemies. We must try to understand and confront our faults rather than ignore them or cover them up. We must also learn to forgive the imperfections we have and resolve to do better.

Identifying and Overcoming False Ideals

And the scribes and the Pharisees watched him, to see whether he would heal on the Sabbath, so that they might find an accusation against him. But he knew their thoughts, and he said to the man who had the withered hand, "Come and stand here." And he rose and stood there. And Jesus said to them, "I ask you, is it lawful on the Sabbath to do good or to do harm, to save life or to destroy it?" And he looked around on them all, and said to him, "Stretch out your hand." And he did so, and his hand was restored.

LUKE 6:7–10

Society couldn't go on without rules and standards. Learning to observe these rules is part of being a healthy adult.

In fact, many of society's rules can be traced directly to the Bible—a perfect source for perfect rules. Obey them without question and be a perfect person.

Too pat. Life isn't that predictable. It's possible to make yourself miserable, even emotionally ill, by following rules that no longer fit the situation.

We try to live up to standards and ideals chosen for us by our parents or our friends and neighbors. But what if ideals are not realistic for you as an individual. Do you doggedly live by them, even at the expense of your well-being? And if you'd give up on the rules, is it a sign of weakness, or of good sense?

How can we know the difference between rules and ideals we should follow, and those that can lead us into trouble? The Bible helps us sort it out.

Lisa is one example of a person who was the victim of false idealism that nearly ruined her health and her life. Lisa had grown up in a wealthy family with a sure sense of the proper standards and goals. She was sent to the finest prep schools and then to one of the best women's colleges in the nation. She knew what the family expected of her. When she met Dan, a promising corporate lawyer, Lisa saw in him the fulfillment of the dream her parents had for her future.

At first, the marriage was nearly perfect. At least it seemed so to others. But Lisa saw that Dan's behavior while they were in public was far different from the way he acted privately. When they were alone Dan would become suddenly abusive and irrational. He would threaten violence, then sulk for days without speaking.

Though Lisa came to live in constant fear, she tried to

manage her life so that others would not suspect the truth. She didn't want to speak to anyone about her problems. They might not understand. Besides, it would smash the illusion of propriety and perfection she was trying to project.

Finally, Dan began to act on his violent threats. Lisa's life became a living hell. When she could stand her pain no longer, she separated from Dan, took a job as a secretary, and began to attend law school at night.

But Lisa's separation did not eliminate her pain entirely. She was bound by a deep sense of guilt. "I should have tried harder," she told me. "I might have saved the marriage somehow. If I had been a better wife, perhaps he would not have changed into such a monster. I should have done what he wanted more often."

I reminded Lisa of the passage in Luke. It offers a healing answer to her problems.

Jesus is dogged by Pharisees trying to lure him into making a serious mistake. He has a sick man before him, a man paralyzed from a physical deformity in his hand. Jesus knows it is against the formal religious law to heal on the Sabbath. He also knows that the man before him needs his help.

Everyone comes up against similar situations in life. The old rules that worked for us once are no longer valid. The old pictures we have of how our life should be are out of focus.

Giving up old standards and rules is difficult, and it should be. Such steps are not to be taken lightly. The difficulty may come because others in our lives—family or friends—may not understand why we're making the changes. Nor are they willing to consider our reasons.

But the real problem usually comes from within. We're challenged by our own inner Pharisees, who, like the ones baiting Jesus, accuse us of faults and crimes. These voices rise from our own fear and insecurity. But we interpret them as self-accusations of wrongdoing.

For Lisa, her inner Pharisees were blaming her for not living up to her family's standard of being a good wife. Her parents had given her the picture of an ideal marriage. Unfortunately, hers did not match it and she blamed herself for that.

Jesus demonstrates that standards and rules, even from the Bible, must never inflict or prolong suffering of any kind. And workable law (the U.S. Constitution is a good example) needs to be adapted to the situation at hand. Applying the law properly requires knowledge of the underlying purpose and meaning of it. Jesus knew that the rest we take on the Sabbath is one which heals and restores us psychologically and spiritually. To heal and restore a man's hand is consistent with that underlying intent.

In this passage, Jesus shows us how to make decisions concerning the rules and standards that govern our lives. We must often ask ourselves, "Who made this rule? Why do I follow it—only because I have been taught to by my parents, or told I must by my friends? What good result is intended by this standard?"

The ideal of a strong and lasting marriage is an important and valid one. But it was never intended to force us to live in a situation that is physically or emotionally damaging.

If we can seriously and prayerfully conclude that obedience to the rule will hurt rather than benefit us or someone we love, then it's right to consider that higher values may be at stake in this situation.

We must reflect on whether we are following this rule only because fear, our inner Pharisees, is blocking us from a life change we need to make. Sometimes we cling to old standards and rules only because we cannot see clearly what a new course of action can do to benefit us and those we love.

Lisa came to see her self-critical voices as unspoken fears about her ability to succeed in law school. She realized she had not given up on marriage. She began to look forward to the day when she would meet a partner who could provide the ideal marriage she wanted. Now it was clear to her that she could not force a rigid standard on a situation that was flexible and changed beyond the intent of the rule.

Learn to Deal with Your Mistakes

Woe to the world for temptations to sin! For it is necessary that temptations come, but woe to the man by whom the temptation comes! And if your hand or your foot causes you to sin, cut it off and throw it from you; it is better for you to enter life maimed or lame than with two hands or two feet to be thrown into the eternal fire. And if your eye causes you to sin, pluck it out and throw it from you; it is better for you

**to enter life with one eye than with two eyes to be
thrown into the hell of fire.**

MATT. 18:7–9

Jonathan was a warehouse shipping manager for a multi-national corporation. He came to me on a recent Friday evening to discuss a serious problem.

"I don't know how this happened. Somehow we accidentally shipped nearly a boxcar load of materials to our factory in Italy instead of to our German plant. I know it was my fault. We were rushed and I accidentally switched the forms."

"Sounds like you have quite a mess to clean up," I said.

"Well, I'm afraid I won't get the chance," Jonathan replied. "Once they find out, I know they'll fire me. But I just can't afford to lose my job right now. My assistant pointed out that I could pin the blame on clerks in the records department. They should have caught the mistake anyway and they can take the heat instead of me. I know doing this isn't right, but it's a way out. I'm considering it. Besides, what else can I do?"

Learning how to handle our mistakes is fundamental to good mental health. If we can learn to face our mistakes, we can open the door to spiritual and emotional growth. When we hide from our mistakes we dig ourselves deeper into destructive behaviors and emotions. The Bible shows us the important steps to take in keeping our minor slip-ups from becoming major blunders.

In this passage from Matthew, Jesus teaches his disciples how to cope with their defects and errors. He uses strong and dramatic images to impress his disciples and us with the seriousness and importance of his lesson.

First, he emphasizes something we all need to know: Temptation comes to all of us. We all make mistakes. A problem we all have in facing our mistakes is the sense that we are the only ones who fail.

Mistakes are inevitable because we are all limited. Often we are forced to make decisions and act with incomplete knowledge. Later, when we have more information, we might find out that our decision was wrong. At times we feel confused in our decisions, and only discover later that the better path lay before us all the time. This happens to everybody. So don't feel alone when you make the wrong choice. And don't allow others to convince you otherwise.

Jesus' second lesson is central. He makes his point with vivid symbols. "If your hand or foot causes you to sin, cut it off and throw it from you. . . ." He repeats the point with emphasis, "And if your eye causes you to sin, pluck it out. . . ."

Jesus is not telling us to hurt ourselves physically. He is speaking symbolically, as he does so often. He means that dealing with our mistakes is one of our most painful tasks. It is painful because our first impulse is always to deny our mistakes and pretend to others—even to ourselves—that they never occurred.

It's the worst thing we can do. It can result in a life based on a lie. Our deceit and dishonesty might become the foundation of our image in the eyes of others. We can become trapped by a false image. In extreme cases, we would be so torn by fear and hopelessness that our psychological state could only be described as "hell."

Jesus' healing wisdom is that we must learn to admit our mistakes. We must acknowledge to ourselves and others, as soon as possible, that we have made a wrong choice. When we do this we feel a sting at first. Our pride is hurt a bit. Our vanity may be wounded. But in the end these pains are minor compared to the torment of a life of concealment.

The positive side of this teaching is that once we have admitted our errors, we have taken a significant and courageous step toward spiritual and psychological growth. The initial pain is followed by a wave of elation. We suddenly realize relief from the weight of the burden. We are ready for a new and healthier life.

Jonathan discovered this for himself after that long, painful weekend. He returned to work on Monday and spoke honestly with his superiors. His company was angry about the delay. But luckily, Jonathan's confession was in time to prevent the shipment from being loaded at the docks. Jonathan was seriously reprimanded. But he offered to work with his boss to develop a set of new procedures to make sure the same mistake could not happen again in any department of the company. Jonathan clearly saw that confessing his mistake was far less painful in the long run than living with the knowledge that he had lied and jeopardized the livelihood of others to save his job.

Feeling "Down" Sometimes Is Natural

All things are full of weariness;
  a man cannot utter it;
the eye is not satisfied with seeing,
  nor the ear filled with hearing.
What has been is what will be,
  and what has been done is what will be done;
  and there is nothing new under the sun.
Is there a thing of which it is said,
  "See, this is new"?
It has been already,
  in the ages before us.
There is no remembrance of former things,
  nor will there be any remembrance
of later things yet to happen
  among those who come after.

ECCLES. 1:8–11

Life is the same old thing over and over again! Nothing really changes! What is a passage like this doing in the Bible? Shouldn't life be eternally positive and rosy? Shouldn't our outlook be cheerful and happy? The answer, of course, is no. The Bible shows us that moments of sadness and depression are natural.

You may be lucky enough to know one or two people who are congenitally happy. They hold a reservoir of excitement and energy that never runs dry. They have the innate ability to put aside the dark and gloomy thoughts. They weld their emotions securely to the positive side of life, and never break from that strong attachment.

These wondrous souls can be a healing ray of sunlight on an otherwise cloudy day. But they are rare. Most of us get grouchy, frustrated and bored. At times we may even be unhappy for no identifiable reason. Such occasions may appear to be nothing but moments of useless pain. But they can serve a useful and even healing function. A healthy psyche requires moments of activity and rest, tension and relaxation, wakefulness and sleep. These rhythms appear to have a biological basis, although it is extremely complex. Sadness and happiness are part of the emotional side of this life-rhythm.

Without these rhythmic changes in our lives, we couldn't function well. They may be ways for the body and the psyche to replenish themselves.

We need moments when we can retreat from the bustle of everyday concerns and think about our lives. Sadness sometimes signals us to make room in our lives for deep and healing reflection.

Finally, the Bible shows us that moments of sadness and gloom can serve to deepen our appreciation of life. A life filled with nothing but sunlight and roses would soon lose its flavor. There is a bitter sweetness to existence that adds depth and wonder to our time spent here.

Don't Expect a "Golden Calf" to Solve Problems

When the people saw that Moses delayed to come down from the mountain, the people gathered themselves together to Aaron, and said to him, "Up, make us gods, who shall go before us; as for this Moses, the man who brought us up out of the land of Egypt, we do not know what has become of him." And Aaron said to them, "Take off the rings of gold which are in the ears of your wives, your sons and your daughters, and bring them to me." So all the people took off the rings of gold which were in their ears, and brought them to Aaron. And he received the gold at their hand, and fashioned it with a graving tool, and made a molten calf; and they said, "These are your gods, O Israel, who brought you up out of the land of Egypt!"

EXOD. 32:1–4

I could hardly believe my ears! A young woman, about to be married, was talking: "I have to admit," Ellen said, "I am not madly in love with William. As a matter of fact, I really don't love him at all, I am not even sure I like him."

"Then why, in heaven's name, are you thinking of marrying him?" I asked. "Well, here I am, twenty-seven years old. The biological clock is ticking away, and I want

26

a family. I am not happy with my career. I don't have any better offers. And William is available. Who knows what will happen to me if I break this off?"

"Watch out!" I said. "You are about to carve a golden calf."

One of the great battles in life is to resist easy solutions to our problems. We can get so desperate to overcome our fears and frustrations that we'll try any remedy even when we know it's not the answer to our real needs. The story of the golden calf is a warning against accepting such easy solutions.

God had led the people of Israel out of the bondage of Egypt, and the new nation made a covenant with God. God summoned Moses to the top of Mt. Sinai to receive the laws of this covenant. The people of Israel, camped below the mountain, became impatient for Moses to return. They demanded that Aaron, Moses' brother, make them a god. And he fashioned a golden calf from their jewelry to satisfy them.

When we read this story, we are astonished. How could the people of Israel have been so stupid? They must have known it was ridiculous to try to replace God with a hunk of carved metal. Did they really think it would answer their needs? And why did Aaron give in so easily to the demands of the mob? He must have suspected that the consequences would be disastrous. It's all so obvious.

Is it? Consider how accurately this story pictures human nature. How often are we like the people of Israel in the desert, facing a crisis and feeling lost and alone? In these moments we are highly vulnerable. Our impulse is always to look for some immediate solution to try, some quick course of action to take, even if we suspect it won't do any good.

That's how the people of Israel must have felt, alone and without their beloved leader. They were desperate to resolve their overwhelming problems. Any solution, even one that risked total disaster, seemed better than continuing with the current situation.

Like Aaron, we often surrender to the pressure for a quick fix—anything for some kind of relief. This "golden calf solution" may be a marriage of convenience like the one planned by Ellen. It may be a compromise career; it may be alcohol or drugs. But whatever it is, we know, deep down, that it is a false god we choose to worship because we need a tangible and immediate way out.

The story of the golden calf goes on to show us how disastrous the consequences of following this impulse can be. God was furious and threatened to abandon his new nation. Moses was so angry, he broke to pieces the tablets that held the new law. Only through a terrible retribution could the mistake be purged from the nation.

The message is clear. Temporary and easy solutions too often result in a disaster far worse than the original difficulty.

The story shows us that patience is often the most important quality we can adopt in times of crisis. While a quick and easy remedy may, like the golden calf, look wonderful at first, it can lead to trouble in the long run.

Patience need not mean inactivity. Use the time to discover more about the problem and yourself. Ellen saw that she needed more time to know William better, and to learn more about what she wanted from marriage and her career. She explored their relationship more deeply, and eventually realized that her patience had saved her from a disastrous marriage—a "golden calf solution."

Learn to Face Your Faults

Judge not that you be not judged. For with the judgment you pronounce you will be judged, and the measure you give will be the measure you get. Why do you see the speck that is in your brother's eye, but do not notice the log that is in your own eye? Or how can you say to your brother, "Let me take the speck out of your eye," when there is a log in your own eye?

MATT. 7:1–4

When Robert walked into the restaurant, I could tell immediately he was in another bad mood. He had been brooding for nearly two weeks now, ever since he lost the promotion he was shooting for. As soon as he sat down with me he started to complain. "Everyone is down on me today. My boss is angry. My wife left in a huff this morning without even saying good-bye. Even the cashier at the grocery store was surly. What is wrong with people? You know, I think this world is doomed. No one cares anymore. I'm ready to pack it in and go to a desert island somewhere."

Clearly, Robert needed a strong dose of medicine to

shake him up. I quoted Jesus' saying from the book of Matthew about the speck and the log.

"Are you trying to tell me that all this is my fault?" Robert said. Now he was becoming angry with me. But he let me explain why I quoted this passage.

I pointed out to Robert that we usually read this passage as ethical advice. Jesus is saying that before we charge someone else with a fault we should make sure that we do not have that failing ourselves.

On another level, however, Jesus is giving healing counsel as well. Jesus is gently pointing the way for each of us to use our negative feelings about other people and the world as an aid to self-understanding and insight. In this passage, Jesus is calling our attention to what psychologists refer to as "projection." In the same way a movie camera projects images onto a screen, psychologists say we project attitudes and ideas onto people and things in the world. If we see the world as sad, miserable, and unhappy, it's probably because we feel that way ourselves.

Jesus wasn't thinking about the mechanics of movie cameras, but he was concerned about the mechanics of the human mind. He warns strongly against projecting our negative emotions onto others. Jesus is telling us that the faults we see in someone else are often a reflection of our own troubles.

Projection is really a way to avoid coming to terms with painful emotions of our own that we don't want to acknowledge. We imagine instead that they are outside of us in the world. Admitting our troubles, even to ourselves, is often disturbing. It's so much nicer to blame someone or something else.

Jesus insists, in dramatic fashion, that this is not a healthy or productive way to live. He provides the way to turn our unhealthy projections into a healing force for ourselves and the world.

First, Jesus redirects our attention from the world around us to our inner feelings. He shows us that when we project our emotions and attitudes onto the world, we forget that they really belong to us. If we are to conquer our negative projections we must recognize the emotions and thoughts as our own. They are the "log" in our own eye.

A good way to understand this is by paying close attention to those occasions when your emotions run high. Watch your thoughts, for instance, when you become angry at another person. Ask yourself if you are attributing emotions or motives to them that they may not have. Remember, you cannot see into their mind. Perhaps the negative feelings you perceive in them are really your own.

A sure sign of projection is making general assumptions about the world that are just not true. If you think to yourself "No one likes me," or "Everyone is out for himself," you can be sure you are projecting.

Once we have learned to recognize our projections, Jesus asks us to direct our attention to the inner world. This is the way to heal, by making use of our projections. If projection is really a way of avoiding or hiding from our troubled feelings (and it is), then admitting to ourselves that we are sad or unhappy is the beginning of the healing process.

Admit to your feelings, and you can use the inner

power you have to change. Events in the world are often beyond your control, but you can do something about the way you feel inside.

This inward journey is not all unpleasant. Jesus knows that there is a surprise waiting for us if we are willing to examine our inward life. Hiding within us are reserves of happiness and joy that we may never have imagined. This is the promise the Bible gives us. The peace and joy of life are already ours, if we only look for them in the right place. We think we'll be happy if the world outside is set right, but true happiness comes from within.

For those who have this inner peace, projection becomes a wonderful healing force. Their inner joy radiates and affects everyone they meet. The world truly responds to inner happiness. It is infectious, and can change the world.

How to Stop Repeating Your Mistakes

 Now Peter was sitting outside in the courtyard. And a maid came up to him, and said, "You also were with Jesus the Galilean." But he denied it before them all saying, "I do not know what you mean." And when he went out to the porch, another maid saw him, and she said to the bystanders, "This man was with Jesus of Nazareth." And again he denied it with an oath, "I do not know the man." After a little while the bystanders came up and said to Peter, "Certainly you are also one of them, for your accent betrays you." Then he began to invoke a curse on himself and to swear, "I do not know the man." And immediately the cock crowed. And Peter remembered the saying of Jesus, "Before the cock crows, you will deny me three times." And he went out and wept bitterly.

MATT. 26:69–75

Do you find yourself solving the same life-problems, over and over? Do you resolve never to get caught in some miserable entanglement, then discover that you're in it again, with different people and in a different place, but the very same issues?

This frustrating phenomenon is familiar to nearly everyone. Our deepest problems tend to recur throughout life. The outward circumstances may change, but the real issue remains the same.

Scott, a middle-aged professional, had a tendency to repeat the same unfortunate pattern in his friendships. "I always find people who take advantage of me," he said. "I'm always the person stuck with cleaning up after the party. I always pay the tab when someone forgets his wallet, and I never get paid back. You know, even when I was a kid, I nearly got arrested because a so-called friend broke a car window and left me to take the blame. I have made the same poor choices in friends all my life. I try to watch out. But I always end up holding the bag."

I told Scott his frustration and anger with himself was a good sign. He was well on the way to solving his problem already. He only needed a bit more insight. I suggested the story of Peter's denial of Christ as the path to a broader perspective.

Jesus knew the weaknesses and strengths of his disciples. Peter had steadfastness and courage, but his resolve seemed to weaken in tense and anxious moments. Jesus realized that Jesus' imminent arrest and confrontation with Roman authorities would be a test more severe than any Peter had ever faced. Peter needed to become aware of his weakness and learn to overcome it, if he were to become the leader in Jesus' church.

Jesus' therapeutic method was to make Peter see for himself that these negative patterns of behavior were habitual. Jesus warned Peter far in advance (Matt. 26: 31–35) that his behavior here would be an echo of the past. It had happened before. It would happen again, unless he made the effort to change. But Peter had to be aware of his failings if he were to improve himself.

A crucial first step in healing our self-destructive patterns is to recognize that we have a problem. Just as important, we need to become aware of the damage our behavior is doing to us and those we love.

Scott had made this first step. He saw, very clearly, how he repeatedly chose insensitive friends and how it was making him dissatisfied, often miserable. He knew he needed to change.

Jesus' next therapeutic step was to prepare Peter. Jesus told Peter that his weakness would show itself again before the morning. Jesus knew this warning would not prevent Peter from crumbling under the stress of the coming test.

It would, however, set the stage for an inner transformation that would strengthen Peter for his life's work.

We need to make this same preparation in our own lives. No matter how seriously we promise ourselves never again to repeat our mistakes, it rarely works. Time and again we fool ourselves into thinking we have conquered a problem, when in reality, we have only hidden it away. It will reemerge when we least expect it. But if we prepare ourselves, we can face the situation in a new way.

The trick is to watch ourselves closely as we begin to reenact the pattern; observe what happens inside and around us. We should pay close attention to our emotions and ask ourselves what sets off this pattern of behavior. How do our own responses lead us into trouble? Where could we have made different choices that would lead to healthier results?

Because of Jesus' preparation and warning Peter saw clearly that the denial of his friend and teacher was part of a larger pattern of behavior. At the end, Peter wept with pain and anguish. The weeping shows that he was finally healed. Then Peter knew that he would never fall into this trap again. His full realization of the depth of his weakness strengthened Peter. He would never "forget" again.

As I discussed with Scott the details of his problem, he saw more clearly how he created situations in which he allowed himself to be exploited. He prepared himself to watch closely what happened when he was with his friends.

Soon it was clear that he himself frequently encouraged their exploitation by what he said and the way he acted. Eventually, he learned to spot the early signs of the problem and end it before it began. Like Peter, Scott had found a healthy insight that would serve him well for the rest of his life.

Dismissing Problems Doesn't Solve Them

> So when Pilate saw that he was gaining nothing, but rather that a riot was beginning, he took water and washed his hands before the crowd, saying, "I am innocent of this man's blood; see to it yourselves."
>
> MATT. 27:24

Some years ago I visited with Sam, a college friend. I stayed with him and his family for a few days while on a business trip. During my visit, it became apparent that Sam was an alcoholic. His drinking had escalated from occasional binges in college to all day, every day boozing. His wife came to me in tears asking for help and advice. She was on the verge of leaving the marriage. I knew I was risking Sam's anger for interfering. But I also knew it was important for me to say something.

"Is it that obvious?" Sam asked. "You know, I really have it under control. I don't let it interfere with my work. Marge doesn't mind. We just don't speak about it. I do get a little plowed occasionally. But, hey, who doesn't? What harm can a few drinks do? I'm not hurting anyone."

I told Sam bluntly he was only fooling himself. He

needed to get help for himself and his family. Instead, he was acting like Pilate washing his hands. I could see he was annoyed. But the remark about Pilate sparked his curiosity.

When Pilate was confronted with Jesus, the Roman governor found himself in the middle of an explosive controversy. Outside his door was a raging mob, rallied by the challenges Jesus had introduced to their lives. Pilate's wife had warned him against having anything to do with Jesus. Her dreams had told her Jesus was innocent. Pilate saw nothing dangerous in Jesus. In fact, he thought Jesus was a fascinating man, perhaps even wise.

Yet, Jesus said nothing to vindicate himself of the charges against him. The mob refused to accept Pilate's ploy: the choice of releasing either Jesus or a convicted and brutal murderer. Pilate was responsible for keeping the peace and governing this small colony. He had to resolve the problem.

Pilate decided on the easy way out. He pretended the situation was beyond his control, and abdicated all responsibility for what was about to happen. His excuse was that he wanted to avoid added trouble for the tortured country. The price for such stability was the execution of an innocent man. Pilate washed his hands of the whole matter.

Like Pilate, in the face of conflict and pain, we tend to paper over the problem, and placate everyone. We pretend we can't change things. We assume we have no power to improve the situation. So we gain temporary calm and a short-term solution. But in the end, evading the problem is bad for us and those we love.

Sam knew his drinking problem was tearing his family apart. He knew it was embarrassing for his children and his wife when he became drunk at parties or in front of guests at his house. Sam knew his children were afraid and his wife was angry. Yet he simply washed his hands of the problem: He pretended he was innocent, incapable of ~~quitting; he convinced himself that no one minded.~~ In his mind, Sam created the myth of a stable family, when in reality, the family was disintegrating.

Pilate's story shows that stability, when won through refusing to face real issues, is fragile and fleeting. Pilate's pronouncement quelled the mob for a time. But we know the nation did not remain quiet. The people rebelled openly a few decades later. Jesus' followers eventually became so powerful that they overwhelmed the empire Pilate served.

In Sam's case, the facade was cracking. He was close to losing all he loved, as well as the business he worked so hard to build. The loss was not inevitable. But by washing his hands of his trouble, he showed willingness to substitute false appearances for facing and solving problems.

In Matthew's story we find the healing answer to Sam's problem. Remember, Pilate controlled the full power of the Roman Army in his district. He could have defied the mob and acted justly. He could have released Jesus on legal grounds. Jesus was innocent and Pilate knew it. Pilate could have faced the crowd and insisted on a proper resolution of the conflict. His hand washing was an act of weakness. He capitulated to the mob.

The Bible assures us that we have the power to settle our problems. The path may be rocky, for it requires facing reality and acknowledging our role in bringing unhappiness to those we love. But in the end, it is the only way.

Sam had the resources he needed. His family still loved and supported him. He entered a rehabilitation program and joined Alcoholics Anonymous.

Sam realized that washing his hands of his problems only made them worse. He used his power to face his true situation and to change it.

Standing Up for Yourself

> But Moses said to the Lord, "Oh, my Lord, I am not eloquent, either heretofore or since thou has spoken to thy servant; but I am slow of speech and of tongue." Then the Lord said to him, "Who has made man's mouth? Who makes him dumb, or deaf, or seeing or blind? Is it not I, the Lord? Now therefore go, and I will be with your mouth, and teach you what you shall speak." But he said, "Oh, my Lord, send, I pray, some other person."
>
> EXOD. 4:10–13

When I heard that Eva's husband had been taken to the hospital, I phoned her immediately. Her voice told me how worried she was. "I'm not convinced Fred is receiving the kind of care and attention he needs," she told me. "The doctors seem so busy. Sometimes I feel they're ignoring me. I want them to explain what is wrong with my husband so I can make the right decisions. I don't even know what to ask. I don't want to seem stupid. They seem

39

to know so much. Sometimes I feel so useless. I guess I'm being a bit irrational."

I offered to drive Eva to the hospital that night. Obviously, she was intimidated by the doctors. But it was important that she stand up for herself and her husband at this time, even though the white coats and clinical atmosphere of the hospital unnerved her.

If ever you're in a situation like Eva's, think about Moses when he was summoned by God. Moses knew he was called to free his people from the oppression of the Egyptian Pharaohs. But he did not welcome the task. Moses asked God to "send someone else." We know how he felt. We all shrink from confrontation. Even when we're right, we often allow ourselves to be treated badly rather than face an uncomfortable conflict.

In the biblical story, Moses learned to stand up for himself and his people against the full strength of the Egyptian empire. We can apply the same lesson to our own lives.

First, the Bible teaches us to be sure of our cause in standing up for ourselves. Before a confrontation, review the case for a moment. Be confident that what you are fighting for is right. Moses was able to take on the Egyptian rulers because he knew their oppression of God's people was unjust. Moses knew his cause was righteous, and that gave him the strength he needed to succeed.

Second, we learn from the Bible to trust our inner resources. Moses complained that he could not speak eloquently enough to appear in the royal hallways. God knew Moses' limitations, and he guaranteed that Moses and his brother would know what to say when the time came. We all have more resources at hand than we know. In fact we often surprise ourselves at how well we react to a challenge. God rarely asks us to face situations we are incapable of handling.

Third, be simple and direct. Moses' words to Pharaoh are exquisite. We need no university diploma to understand them: "Let my people go."

This demand for justice and freedom has moved generations of oppressed people to stand up for themselves in the face of overwhelming odds. Remember this lesson when you argue for yourself. The most effective communication is uncomplicated and plain. Say what you need and what you want. Your message will be heard if conviction lies behind your words.

Finally, the Bible teaches us that we must speak for ourselves. We cannot depend on others to fight our battles. God rejected Moses' plea that he send someone else. Not because there was no one available, but because God knew that the confrontation was important for Moses as well as his people. Not only would it result in freeing the Israelites from oppression, it would also transform Moses. Remember, Moses started out as a frightened farmer. In the end he became one of the world's greatest leaders. The message is that in standing up for ourselves we can gain an inner strength that comes in no other way.

Eva learned this lesson. We discussed the story of Moses and I reminded her that she had the right to know every detail of treatment. That night at the hospital she questioned each of the staff who had treated her husband. And she insisted on getting the answers she needed. At the end of an exhausting evening, she felt equipped to decide what was best. Like Moses she had insisted on her rights and gained the satisfaction of knowing she had demanded what was rightfully hers.

Finding Your True Identity

🌿 Now a man from the house of Levi went and took to wife a daughter of Levi. The woman conceived and bore a son, and when she saw that he was a goodly child, she hid him three months. And when she could hide him no longer she took for him a basket made of bulrushes, and daubed it with bitumen and pitch; and she put the child in it and placed it among the reeds at the river's brink. And his sister stood at a distance, to know what would be done to him. Now the daughter of Pharaoh came down to bathe at the river, and her maidens walked beside the river; she saw the basket among the reeds and sent her maid to fetch it. When she opened it she saw the child; and lo, the babe was crying. She took pity on him and said, "This is one of the Hebrews' children." Then his sister said to Pharaoh's daughter, "Shall I go and call you a nurse from the Hebrew women to nurse the child for you?" And Pharaoh's daughter said to her, "Go." So the girl went and called the child's mother. And Pharaoh's daughter said to her, "Take this child away, and nurse him for me, and I will give you your wages." So the woman took the child and nursed him. And the child

grew, and she brought him to Pharaoh's daughter, and he became her son; and she named him Moses.
EXOD. 2:1–10

Who am I—really? It's a tough one. But unless we find the answer, find a sense of identity, we are lost and directionless. Robert, a young and successful stock broker, is an example of what can happen without this crucial step in our development. Robert's parents were divorced and both were remarried. Robert had lived part of his life with each family. The two households differed greatly in lifestyle, cultural outlook, and religious commitment. Growing up, Robert felt torn between the more religiously oriented and conservative beliefs of his natural mother and the more flamboyant outlook of his father. When he was finally on his own, he threw himself into his work. That way he avoided dealing with the conflicts burning in his mind.

By the time Robert reached thirty-five, he knew his life was missing something essential. "I want to know who I am and why I'm here. I'm just not satisfied with identifying myself with my job. Certainly, I am not here just to collect cars and boats. I want to see more meaning in my life. But how can I do that? One part of me wants to go back to church. Another wants to quit this job and find adventure in some South American jungle."

The story of Moses in the bulrushes provides a blueprint for finding our way through a crisis like Robert's.

No character in the Bible had more trouble deciding his true identity and place in the world than Moses. The problem began in his infancy. Fearing the Egyptians' murderous slaughter of the Hebrews' firstborn males, his mother set Moses out in the Nile River in a reed basket when he was only three months old. Pharaoh's daughter found him and raised him as her own son.

Today we have few stable points of reference for our lives, so Moses' experience of being set adrift, adopted by a stranger, and raised far from his family strikes a somewhat familiar note. Our modern lifestyle often takes us away from family and friends, into new cultures, without any sense of roots or belonging. We are faced with so many options we can hardly find any grounds for choosing one identity over another.

Many of my students have this problem as they move from adolescence to adulthood in their college years. Often they make painful mistakes and try many paths before they find their way. Like Moses, they feel adrift, with little control over where they are headed or what will happen to them.

But none of us ever really finish formulating our identity. Periodically we may find ourselves having serious doubts about the lifestyle we have chosen or the kind of person we have become. At times, this concern becomes so severe we must step aside from the path we currently walk and take stock of our goals. When our doubts and fears overwhelm us in these situations, psychologists say we are having an "identity crisis."

But how do we thread our way through this kind of crisis? What force remains steady and meaningful enough to serve as a guide in a world where things change so rapidly? Use Moses as a model. Moses, a Hebrew, was raised as a son by the Egyptian princess. But he was constantly aware of his roots. He also knew of the suffering and oppression afflicting his true mother's people. He must have been torn between rage over the oppression of his people and love for his adopted mother. His anger found violent expression when he discovered an Egyptian overseer beating a Hebrew slave. Moses furiously attacked and killed the Egyptian. Because others had witnessed the deed, Moses' fate was sealed. He could no longer stay within Pharoah's household.

Like Moses, we often feel the frustration and anger that come when we cannot decide on a path to follow. We can't fit into life lived before, yet the path before us is dark and uncertain. No wonder we feel like two different people, one choosing one path, the other deciding on another way. Sometimes, we too lash out in anger and have to pay for our rashness.

After the episode of violence, Moses fled into exile. But he could not escape his inner conflict. Moses' crisis was resolved only when God spoke to him in the burning bush and told him to free the Hebrew people. Though Moses resisted, eventually he realized that his identity lay in accepting the seemingly impossible mission God had assigned.

Of course we cannot expect to receive a direct message from God in the same way. But the story suggests the way to come to terms with our most basic problems.

Through God's message, Moses found a calling to meaningful and fulfilling duty as liberator of his people. In a world where identity is so often a matter of prestige or wealth, it might seem strange to think that our identity can be found in service to others. But it often happens that way. Sometimes a crisis of identity occurs because the time and effort we put into tasks and goals have lost their importance for us. We have all the comfort and security that success can bring—now what? Like many, we might find the answer to that question by turning away from private concerns to the problems we see in the world. Like Moses, we will find many people in desperate need of help. We can renew our sense of worth and find our true identity by answering this call.

GLORIFY YOUR GIFTS

How Best to Use Your Talents and Gifts

He also who had received the one talent came forward, saying, "Master, I knew you to be a hard man, reaping where you did not sow, and gathering where you did not winnow; so I was afraid, and I went and hid your talent in the ground. Here you have what is yours." But his master answered him, "You wicked and slothful servant! You knew that I reap where I have not sowed, and gather where I have not winnowed? Then you ought to have invested my money with the banker, and at my coming I should have received what was my own with interest. So take the talent from him, and give it to the one who has ten talents. For to everyone who has will more be given, and he will have abundance; but from him who has not, even what he has will be taken away."

MATT. 25:24–29

We are often surprised at Jesus' stories. Some of them portray situations that seem paradoxical, unfair, and even mean. But often, these are the parables that contain the most powerful lessons. Jesus gently shocks us to attention. He wants to be sure we don't miss his real message.

The parable of the talents is one startling example. Here Jesus provides the solution to a problem we all have wrestled with: how to make the best possible use of the many internal resources we are given in this life? But he is not speaking only about our spiritual existence. He is also showing us how to use our many gifts to live healthy and productive lives here on earth.

From the very beginning this parable strikes us as somewhat strange. A master entrusts his servants with large sums of money, a symbol of the resources and gifts each of us are given to help us through life. But the allotment in the story seems unfair. Some servants are given more than others. Why doesn't the master give each servant the same amount of money? Would the Master of the Kingdom of Heaven be so inequitable?

Certainly this is not Jesus' point. Instead, Jesus is telling us a simple but disappointing truth of our existence. Some people do have greater gifts than the rest of us. Some are brighter, more energetic, more gifted in the arts. Some have more money or better connections in business. This may seem unfair. But Jesus is being realistic. He is never a teacher who sugarcoats reality. He is not about to pretend that the world is better than it is.

As Jesus tells the story, the master makes a journey and leaves his servants free to do with their money as they choose. The lesson is really about responsibility. When we ~e children our parents watched over us, making sure ~ to school, ate properly, and stayed out of trouble. ~ we must take charge of our own lives. We are responsible for determining how we will use the resources we are given.

The master does not leave any specific instructions about what his servants are to do with these gifts. Again this seems unfair. Why doesn't he give his servants better direction? Surely he knew his lesser servant was not as skillful as the others. Why didn't the master pay special attention to him, give him a little more guidance?

This is, of course, what we all wish for in our weaker moments. Sometimes we feel abandoned and alone, unsure of how to go on with life. If only we had some wise teacher to direct us in making the best decisions and tell us how to live correctly.

But again Jesus is being a realist. We have been given the freedom to choose how to live, and often we must make important decisions in the face of uncertainty. We can always find someone willing to take the role of a parent and tell us what to do. But we do know that in the end we must take responsibility for our own decisions.

We like to think that we would conduct ourselves like the faithful and wise servants. But most of us know only too well that we would probably be more like the foolish servant. We each have our own allotment of skills and resources. But too few of us make the best of what we have. More likely, we feel sorry for ourselves, complaining about how little time, money or talent we have. We indulge in "if only" thinking. "If only I had more time . . . If only I had more money . . . If only I were better looking . . . If only I had better and wiser parents . . . If only I could find someone who really loves me."

One point of Jesus' parable is that we must give up

this "if only" thinking, for it is really just a way of hiding from the true cause of our wastefulness. Jesus tells us that the foolish servant does not develop his resources because he is afraid. Here, Jesus is asking us to look within ourselves for our true motives. We hide ourselves and fail to grow usually because we live in terror of failing, of being foolish, of not living up to the expectations of others.

Of course, we wish that the master in the parable were more compassionate. We want to see him soothe the fears of the foolish servant and excuse his error. After all, the world is, at times, terrifying. But Jesus is again being realistic. There is no excuse for not living life to the fullest on any grounds, not even fear. Once our opportunities have passed they are gone forever.

Jesus condemns a subtle but severe failing that afflicts us all now and then—living life incompletely. We are so addicted to security and so afraid to take risks that we fail to make our happiness and joy grow to its fullest potential. Jesus is so strong in his condemnation because he knows how widespread the condition is.

We *can* overcome it. The trick is to understand and recognize those times when we are acting like the frightened servant. We must banish any hint of "if only" thinking. And we must not allow our fear and insecurity to hinder us in the search for love and fulfillment. That is the path to further loss and deeper despair.

In the concluding paradox Jesus seems to be describing a world turned upside down. He tells us that a person who has much will be given more. But a person who has little will lose everything. If Jesus were talking only about the economic situation of the story, he would be describing a terrible injustice. But he is really laying out the realities of our spiritual life. The more willing we are to risk security by opening ourselves up to life, the more happiness and joy we can gain. The more love we give to each other, the more we receive in return.

We need to follow the lead of the faithful servants and search out the best life for ourselves no matter how meager our resources. We cannot afford to hide from life and waste our precious gifts.

You Can Become More Creative

In the beginning, God created the heavens and the earth. The earth was without form and void, and darkness was upon the face of the deep; and the Spirit of God was moving over the face of the waters.

And God said, "Let there be light"; and there was light. And God saw that the light was good; and God separated the light from the darkness. God called the light Day, and the darkness he called Night. And there was evening and there was morning, one day.

GEN. 1:1–5

God wants us to find joy and happiness in our lives. Sometimes it takes some real creativity to do as he asks. We know that creativity is not confined to painting a picture or composing an opera. In its true sense, creativity is our response to the continually changing world around us and within us. It means we adapt to life's experiences, both good and bad, and learn from them.

We can be as creative in giving loving support to friends and family in need, as any writer or painter in creating a masterpiece. Our life, taken as a whole, can be seen as a work of art, with each action a stroke in our masterpiece.

But now and then, the creative juices run dry. We fall into boring routines. We lose the energy it takes to see the world afresh. We watch with envy as others strike out on new paths or work to develop their gifts, while we feel stuck. We want to become more creative in our lives, to regain the productive energy we once felt. But where do we start?

Genesis holds a wealth of insight into the creative process, insights we can apply to our own life.

Genesis tells us that God created the universe from nothing at all, and on the seventh day, he rested. But as we read along we find a surprise. The narrator begins the story again.

This repetition is no mistake. The biblical author wanted to tell us that although God has finished the initial phase, the process of creation did not end on the sixth day. It is still going on all around us and within us. And we are part of the amazing creative process.

The feelings of dullness and boredom invade our lives when we fail to pay attention to the creation that is always present. We can see this watching children at play. They are an ever-renewing fountain of innovation. Their games and songs seem to arise from some infinite source of energy that we adults too often lose contact with. That same creativity is still with us as adults. We only need open ourselves to it.

Too often we think of creation as making something out of nothing, as if we are required to create from a complete vacuum. But this sort of creation is up to God alone. Our role is to stay in contact with the never-ending creative process that goes on in the universe. That is how we maintain intimate contact with the Divine Creator.

Artists tell us that they often see their painting, hear their music, or imagine their stories almost as if their creative works came from outside themselves. Like children, artists don't—really can't!—force themselves to make something out of nothing. Rather, they must get themselves—their fears and anxieties—out of the way so God can guide their creative powers. This is a clue to creativity for all of us.

Creativity lies in our willingness to be patient, to listen to and watch the grandeur of God's masterpiece unfold in every moment of our lives. Every day is full of new sights, sounds, and smells. Our thoughts and feelings of every moment give us new opportunities for self-understanding and self-expression. If we pause to observe life's intricate and ever-renewing patterns, we can break our boring routines simply by realizing how wonderfully new and different each moment can be.

God's creativity brings its own special form of energy—a flow of warmth and goodness that enlivens and energizes us. We feel it in every moment of happiness. God wants us to be open to his joy all the time, as part of his ongoing creation.

Conquering the Inertia
of Your Life

Now there was a man of the Pharisees, named Nicodemus, a ruler of the Jews. This man came to Jesus by night and said to him, "Rabbi, we know that you are a teacher come from God; for no one else can do these signs that you do, unless God is with him." Jesus answered him, "Truly, truly, I say to you, unless one is born anew, he cannot see the kingdom of God." Nicodemus said to him, "How can a man be born when he is old? Can he enter a second time into his mother's womb and be born?" Jesus answered, "Truly, truly, I say to you, unless one is born of water and the Spirit, he cannot enter the kingdom of God. That which is born of the flesh is flesh, and that which is born of the Spirit is spirit. Do not marvel that I said to you, 'You must be born anew.' The wind blows where it wills, and you hear the sound of it, but you do not know whence it comes or whither it goes; so it is with every one who is born of the Spirit." Nicodemus said to him, "How can this be?"

JOHN 3:1-9

Something about Nicodemus, the powerful ruler in John's Gospel, makes us want to shake him and scream, "*Wake up!*" He reminds me of my friend Benjamin, a successful businessman, recently divorced. I have known Benjamin for nearly a decade, and for all that time, he has been deeply dissatisfied with his life. Benjamin never misses an opportunity to tell friend or stranger about the profound misery he feels in his existence. He will ramble on for hours about his plans for change.

But in the same decade we've known each other, I've never seen him do a single thing to make his plans real or to change his life in any significant way.

Benjamin always has a good reason for not changing. He doesn't have enough time. He needs just a few thousand dollars more in his bank account; then he can quit his job and become a writer. But, of course, he has to make a few home improvements, and finish the mortgage payments before he leaves the company. And, perhaps he should take a course or two at the local college as a preparation for the new career. His list never ends, and Benjamin never changes anything.

Benjamin is an extreme case, but we all share his problem to some extent. Most of us are dissatisfied with some part of our lives, but we can't make the changes we know are necessary. We yearn to escape from our dull routines—if only we had the time, the energy, or the resources. If only we wouldn't have to take too many risks and could be sure of success.

Nicodemus symbolizes this tendency toward inertia. He is a powerful ruler who searches Jesus out "by night." He feels something wrong in his life, so he takes a tentative first step toward healing by meeting with a spiritual leader.

He wants something to change. But he doesn't want to commit himself by openly coming to the Master. So he sneaks in under the cover of night.

Nicodemus begins by flattering Jesus. Probably, a powerful ruler such as Nicodemus has been flattered most of his life. He hopes to manipulate Jesus the same way, so he tells him what he thinks Jesus wants to hear. Nicodemus expects something in return, naturally. This is how power works.

Jesus, of course, will have none of it. He cuts through the facade immediately and gets right to the point—the Kingdom of Heaven. Jesus knows what Nicodemus needs, better than Nicodemus himself. Jesus also knows that Nicodemus is not ready to take the action necessary to find it. Nicodemus wants an easy answer. He wants a way out of his inertia that doesn't cost too much. He wants assurances that he is doing the right thing, and that nothing will go wrong.

We can sympathize with Nicodemus to some extent. He is faced with a miserable dilemma. His life has satisfied at least some of his needs. He has power and prestige. We can presume that he is quite comfortable financially. But his satisfaction has come at great cost. In order to keep his position, he has given up the deep sense of fulfillment that comes only from a serious commitment to higher ideals.

Jesus' answer is designed to shock Nicodemus from his complacency. He wants to goad him from his inertia. When Jesus tells Nicodemus that he must be born anew to see the Kingdom, Jesus is offering sound therapeutic advice. Nicodemus needs a fundamental change in his outlook.

He needs to start again and rethink his life entirely. Piece-meal solutions will fail. If Nicodemus truly wants to escape from the snares of his seemingly successful lifestyle, he must commit himself to the full endeavor. Half-hearted tinkering with minor details will solve nothing.

Nicodemus, like Benjamin, refuses to acknowledge the seriousness of the task. He quibbles inanely with the literal words Jesus has spoken. Can an old man crawl back into his mother's womb? he asks.

Jesus is not willing to give up yet. He knows that Nicodemus, like most of us, wants the assurance that changing his life will be risk free. Nicodemus wants a rational plan. He wants to be sure that if things don't turn out, he can always return to his old ways. He wants to change his life without feeling the fear and discomfort that such change often implies.

Jesus patiently tells Nicodemus the truth. To be born of the spirit does not mean a secure and well-ordered life. The changes you make will be real. You will not know for sure how they will turn out. You must risk the comfort and security of your power and prestige, if you honestly want to begin again.

We do not know if Nicodemus ever accepted Jesus' message. However, we can use Jesus' wisdom in our own fight against inertia. Jesus teaches that we can overcome inertia by letting go of a bit of our security and comfort. Like Benjamin and Nicodemus, we endure unsatisfactory situations because some of our needs are satisfied there. Jesus is showing us that life has far more to offer. If we take the risk, we might find that the rewards of a new beginning exceed any of our expectations.

A Fresh Look
at Self-Assertion

🌿 But I say to you that hear, love your enemies, do good
to those who hate you, bless those who curse you,
pray for those who abuse you. To him who strikes
you on the cheek, offer the other also; and from him
who takes away your cloak do not withhold your
coat as well. Give to every one who begs from you;
and of him who takes away your goods do not ask
them again. And as you wish that men would do to
you, do so to them.

LUKE 6:27–31

Sylvia, a close friend of my family, spends much of her
spare time attending seminars and workshops in psychology.
She also attends church regularly and reads the Bible
avidly. One morning, recently, she called me for some
help in unraveling a tangle of confusion and conflict
between her courses and her Bible reading.

"In my seminar on assertiveness training, the group
leader told us that a healthy ego is a strong ego," she said,
"and we should have a clear sense of self-worth and pride.
He told us that we should express our wants and goals
clearly, and work to get what we want. We are supposed
to be persistent and forceful in the way we deal with other
people," she went on. "We are working for self-esteem
and personal power in taking control of our lives."

"Yes," I said, somewhat hesitantly, "so what is the problem?"

"The Bible tells us just the opposite." Sylvia replied. "It tells us we should be pliable and giving. We should turn the other cheek, and always love one another. You keep saying the Bible gives us the best psychological advice there is. Now I'm not so sure."

It would have been easy to be flippant. I could have reminded Sylvia that the Bible has been healing people for nearly two thousand years, while assertiveness training has been around for only a small fraction of that time. But that would not have resolved the deeper problem this passage of the Bible and others like it, pose for Sylvia and many others.

Jesus gives us advice here that looks completely unworkable these days. The world is tough and unfair. We can't allow people to take advantage. We need to be persistent and aggressive just to keep up with the pack. Jesus seems to be advocating a passive, pliant attitude. Not only should we compromise, we should give in to others' demands no matter how unreasonable or cruel they are. We should not even resist evil! At first glance, this seems a formula for abject personal misery.

But Jesus isn't counseling us to be weak. In fact, Jesus is showing us how to achieve the height of personal power through personal and spiritual development.

Jesus' advice to turn the other cheek makes no sense if we are inwardly furious and pretend to be loving and forgiving. Jesus wants us to have such strength and peace of mind that we are above being disturbed by an insult or injury. We will have such inner abundance that the loss of a few dollars will not matter at all. Most of all, Jesus wants our love for others and ourselves to be strong enough for us to see beyond the evil act. Instead of evil, we see a person who is in such pain that he can only relate to others harmfully.

The process of learning and growth that confers this degree of inner strength and this amount of inner wealth requires a lifetime. Part of this learning involves the ability to be assertive and express inner feelings. A person who never learns to do that will always be a child, forever dependent on others for help in fighting battles and making decisions.

Of course it's important for us to be strong and proud of who we are. But once we learn self-assertion it's important not to get stuck at this stage. It's easy to get so involved with the benefits of a strong ego that we become self-centered and uncompromising. We might become hostile to other people or disregard their feelings and needs. If we become insensitive to the pain and misfortune of others and unconcerned with their rights, we know we haven't learned the lesson yet. We must go further.

The Gospel of Luke shows what to strive for in the next stage. We want to become so strong inwardly that ego becomes a secondary concern. Then we no longer have to prove anything to ourselves or to anyone else. Our strength is so abundant that we can give to others even when they seem capable of relating to us only with hatred and conflict.

The Bible shows that a healthy ego and a strong sense of self provide an important foundation for emotional and spiritual life. But it also recognizes the necessity for growth beyond the self-assertive phase, to achieve a state of love and concern for others.

Love Yourself
by Choosing What You Love

🌿 If I speak in the tongues of men and of angels, but have not love, I am a noisy gong or a clanging cymbal. And if I have prophetic powers, and understand all mysteries and all knowledge, and if I have all faith, so as to remove mountains, but have not love, I am nothing. If I give away all I have, and if I deliver my body to be burned, but have not love, I gain nothing.

Love is patient and kind; love is not jealous or boastful; it is not arrogant or rude. Love does not insist on its own way; it is not irritable or resentful; it does not rejoice at wrong, but rejoices in the right. Love bears all things, believes all things, hopes all things, endures all things.

1 COR. 13:1–7

We can live our lives filled with the intensity of love. It is the goal of all spiritual existence. And it is the goal of psychological health as well.

Life with love is healthy and complete. Without love, life is misery. We could not sustain ourselves mentally without some love in our lives. Alienation and despair would overwhelm us.

Paul's verses on love are among the most inspiring ever written. His words can work miracles of healing for all of us.

Paul teaches that love is the fundamental gauge of the worth and value of whatever we do or say. No matter how impressive our projects appear, no matter how successful we have become on the job, unless we love what we do, we miss what is most essential in life.

Ask yourself, in all honesty, "Do I love what I am doing?" and "Is my life full of love?" The answer will be clear enough. Love is an intense emotion that is easily felt. And we can sense all too well when that intensity is missing.

Paul recognized our willingness to exchange love for cheaper substitutes, and to settle for bland imitations of love. It's easy to pretend to love. And we tend to do so. We know we should love each other. Too often we are afraid to admit that we do not.

Paul insists that we abandon any such pretense or facade. But what can we do when we lack the love Paul speaks of?

The answer lies in our willingness to follow love's lead. We cannot force love. And love will not force itself upon us. It is a path we ourselves must choose to follow. That is the secret.

How often have you made a choice because it was practical or safe? How often have you put aside your true desire in exchange for security? The way of love was there for you all the time. You could have followed it. It's there for you now.

Choosing the way of love fundamentally alters our life. When we act and work from a base of love, we uncover an intensity and energy in ourselves we may never have suspected. But when we act without love, the inner conflicts that arise drain our resources. The lack of meaning poisons our psyches.

Love brings an excitement to life; a joy in doing, a delight in being. It is, in the end, all we need.

TAKE ON
LIFE'S TRIALS

Overcome That "Overwhelmed" Feeling

🌿 I called to the Lord, out of my distress,
    and he answered me;
out of the belly of Sheol I cried,
    and thou didst hear my voice.
For thou didst cast me into the deep,
    into the heart of the seas,
      and the flood was round about me.

JONAH 2:2–3

We all know the feeling of hopelessness about all we have to do. We look at all the duties we are expected to perform and it seems impossible, overwhelming.

Usually the feeling disappears once we're on the job. Inertia itself is a major cause of feeling overwhelmed; we just hate to start new tasks. Some tasks can be put off for another day; some are not as vital as we first thought. Best of all, we get started by dealing with the most important matters. Once we're up and doing, these negative feelings usually disappear on their own.

What if the feelings persist? Suppose we feel continually overburdened and despair that we can ever get out from under? A career woman often feels this way. She is expected to be a loving mother, a sexual bombshell, a gourmet cook, a civic leader, and a success in business, all at the same time. Often she succeeds. But the cost is high. She has no time for herself. She resents one part of her life because it takes time away from another. She feels her life is falling apart, though everything seems fine to others. Psychologists call it the "super-woman syndrome." It can lead to a variety of stress-related problems including ulcers, high-blood pressure, depression, and anxiety.

The story of Jonah provides a therapeutic message for situations like this. God assigned Jonah a seemingly impossible task: Turn the whole city of Nineveh away from sin. Jonah knew he couldn't do it. This was no small town. It took three days just to walk through it! So many people lived there, how could one man convince all of them to change their ways? It was an unreasonable assignment. It seemed like a waste of time to even try!

Jonah did what all of us would like to do when we find ourselves faced with overwhelming tasks—he ran away. He took a cruise.

We all have our own ways to escape problems. Some of us watch television. Others simply procrastinate. For some, raiding the refrigerator does it. Others choose to keep busy with trivial tasks they pretend are important. Many run to a therapist or a clergyman and beg him to solve their problems. None of it really works.

Jonah's boat ran into rough sailing. Storms overwhelmed it. Jonah's companions became terrified. When Jonah honestly admitted that he thought his presence was responsible for the storm, they threw him overboard.

Running away from obligations and tasks is a sure road to disaster. It may seem to promise relief, but in truth, matters just get worse. This is the first therapeutic message of this story.

Most of us know we really can't run away. But staying around can drive us crazy. We are drowning in our despair. What can we do?

Here Jonah's story takes a strange turn, just the kind that often hold the healing magic of the Bible. God sends a "great fish" to swallow Jonah. Three days and three nights Jonah spends in this fish's belly. Of course, the thought of spending seventy-two hours in a fish's stomach is absolutely revolting. But consider the matter from a different perspective. For a person truly overwhelmed by life, spending time hidden away in the depths of the sea might be a perfect way to clarify concerns. To be in the fish's belly is to be safe in the depths of your inner soul. It means that we can find the courage to confront overwhelming tasks from our inner world.

Taking an inner voyage is quite different from running away from the problem, hoping that it will disappear if we ignore it. The inner voyage is time we spend gathering our spiritual wits about us so we can return to the world renewed and reenergized. These moments of quiet reflection allow us to gain a new perspective on our lives.

Of course we cannot arrange to have ourselves swallowed by a whale. (Not that we'd want to!) But we can spend some time alone, even if it is only a few moments. We can lie down on a bed, turn the lights low and allow ourselves to just "be" for a few moments. Perhaps a prayer will calm our mind. Perhaps we will simply listen to the torrent of thoughts and emotions that surround us, as Jonah must have listened to the sounds of the sea from inside his fish. During these moments we need not work on our problems. Our unconscious can sort them out for us. We need only give it a chance to work without our anxious interference.

When he was thrown up onto the shore, Jonah went straight to his most important task. By the time he had walked one-third of the way through the city proclaiming God's message, the people were convinced of the wisdom he offered. They repented and the city was saved. The task turned out to be far easier than Jonah expected. The days of quiet reflection had prepared Jonah by healing his anxiety and fear. Quiet moments of reflection can be just as therapeutic for all of us.

Find Significance in Inescapable Pain

 Then Jesus went with them to a place called Gethsemane, and he said to his disciples, "Sit here, while I go yonder and pray." And taking with him Peter and the two sons of Zebedee, he began to be sorrowful and troubled. Then he said to them, "My soul is very

> sorrowful, even to death; remain here, and watch
> with me." And going a little farther he fell on his face
> and prayed, "My Father, if it be possible, let this cup
> pass from me; nevertheless, not as I will, but as thou
> wilt." And he came to the disciples and found them
> sleeping; and he said to Peter, "So, could you not
> watch with me one hour? Watch and pray that you
> may not enter into temptation; the spirit indeed is
> willing, but the flesh is weak."
>
> MATT. 26:36–41

A major task of modern medicine is to relieve or prevent
pain. A primary goal of spiritual striving is a joyful,
fulfilled life. One issue both spiritual leaders and medical
practitioners must face in fulfilling their aims is the challenge of coping with inevitable suffering. Naturally, we
want to keep pain out of our lives and the lives of those we
love. But we all must face it at times. Life holds periods of
darkness for everybody.

Modern psychology tends to ignore this inevitability.
Better to work with issues that have a happier chance for
solution. The Bible, however, provides a model we can
use in accepting unavoidable suffering and in making that
suffering meaningful.

After the Passover meal on the night of his betrayal,
Jesus takes his disciples to the garden of Gethsemane. Jesus
knows he is about to be arrested and crucified. His disciples are forwarned. Judas, the betrayer, has been confronted.
Everything is settled.

As Matthew tells the story, Jesus could have escaped
from the authorities. The disciples must have wondered

why he did not grasp the opportunity. They could have smuggled him past the gates of the city, and back to Galilee. But Jesus knew his mission. He could not accomplish it without sacrifice. Either he had to abandon his task, or face crucifixion. Anyone who accepts a calling in life knows that crucifixion was the only choice Jesus could make.

Though we hope our path will be smooth, we must be willing to accept whatever pain and effort arise as we struggle to our goal. One of the greatest difficulties we face in our struggle is the loneliness we feel. We want someone to help us or to take away the burdens. We want a wise leader to show us what to do.

This is how the disciples felt in the garden. They had always depended on Jesus to help them through hard times. But in Gethsemane, the disciples saw a side of Jesus that dismayed them. Jesus was "sorrowful and troubled."

Jesus was always a source of strength and energy before. He always knew the answer. He could come up with a miracle to save the day. But on this evening, it was clear that there was no easy way out.

What could they do? Jesus told them to sit and wait; he must meet his fate alone and so must they. Now they must take responsibility for their own actions, without a teacher to show them the way. It was time to apply Jesus' teachings to their own lives.

In the midst of his crisis, Jesus tries to ready his disciples for what is about to happen. He tells his disciples three times to "watch and pray." Jesus even shows them how to do this. In the garden, Jesus prays for a clear vision of what is to come. This is not a prayer of weakness or cowardice, but one of resolve and hope. Jesus asks to avoid unnecessary pain, but he also shows his determination to do what must be done.

This is a valuable lesson. We are not required to suffer more than is absolutely necessary. There is no reason to seek out affliction. Some may see merit in taking on suffering to atone for some real or imagined guilt. But the Bible teaches that mercy toward ourselves and others is the foundation for all righteousness and love. Any unnecessary suffering only makes matters worse.

The disciples neither understood nor followed Jesus' lesson. Instead, they slept. They could not confront the crisis. They could not muster the faith and hope to go on so they retreated into unconsciousness.

Their sleep symbolizes not just a failure of courage, but a lost opportunity to make the inevitable pain meaningful. Jesus wanted to give the disciples a new mission: They would make his betrayal and crucifixion significant for all humanity by showing how brutality and injustice, represented by this crucifixion, could be eliminated from the world forever. Jesus' faith that such meaning could be found allowed him to meet his destiny in the garden with serenity. The lack of such faith led the disciples to fall asleep, and later, to run away, in the face of crisis.

Ultimately the disciples did accept their mission. Through the resurrection, their faith was restored. In later years, they too were able to face inescapable tragedy and pain with a Christlike calm.

The Bible shows us that suffering may be unavoidable at times. But if we find some significance in that suffering we make the pain worth something for ourselves and for others.

Learning to Deal with Betrayal

 While he was still speaking, there came a crowd, and the man called Judas, one of the twelve, was leading them. He drew near to Jesus to kiss him; but Jesus said to him, "Judas, would you betray the Son of man with a kiss?" And when those who were about him saw what would follow, they said, "Lord, shall we strike with the sword?" And one of them struck the slave of the high priest and cut off his right ear. But Jesus said, "No more of this!" And he touched his ear and healed him.

LUKE 22:47–51

Both modern psychology and the Scriptures agree on one matter completely. The way to healing and freedom from despair is through truth. " . . . And you will know the truth, and the truth will make you free." The truth we are urged to know is the truth about ourselves. That's why the Bible works so effectively as a healing tool—it reveals so much of who we are.

One element in the Bible's therapeutic power is that many of the characters contain some facet of our own psyche. Of course we like to think that we are mirrored only in the good characters and not the bad ones. But this is to miss the full value of the Scriptures. Uncomfortable as it may be, the evil characters can teach us some important truths about ourselves.

Judas, the very symbol of contempt, infamy, and dishonor, is a good example. Jesus' own disciple conspires with the authorities to deliver Jesus to them for thirty pieces of silver.

We all like to think we could never stoop so low. Yet the character of Judas demonstrates the darkness that can live within everyone. It teaches us how to recognize the suspicion and the sickness of betrayal that arises in so many relationships. Fortunately, the story of Judas also teaches us how to cope with and recover from the pain that betrayal can bring.

Actually we learn how to heal three different kinds of betrayal: the betrayal of ourselves by others; the betrayal of others by us; the worst of all, our own betrayal of ourselves.

When others betray us. We rarely consider Judas' motives for his horrible deed. But from the story it is clear that Judas turned against Jesus because he felt betrayed by him. Obviously, Jesus wasn't the Messiah the Scriptures prophesied. Where was the promised warrior who would scourge the legions of the Roman Empire and free God's people from the oppressive invaders?

Judas desperately wanted Jesus to live up to this picture. Instead, Jesus was preaching a far different kind of freedom and was establishing a spiritual kingdom that had little to do with conquering the Roman Empire.

When others fall short of our expectations, we often feel angry and hurt, too. We create an image of how another person should act and think. If we find that the image we built up is flawed, we hold the other responsible for betraying our hope. I have seen friendships, marriages, even business partnerships flounder because of this sense of betrayal.

If Judas had paid careful attention to what Jesus said and taught, he would have known the truth of Jesus' message from the beginning. It is important for us to see and hear each other honestly and objectively. When we feel betrayed, we must examine our expectations closely. Were they realistic and fair? Was the other person aware of them? Is it right for us to demand that someone live up to our image of them? Honest answers to these questions can eliminate any sense of betrayal before it damages a relationship.

When we betray others. Judas was so blinded by his hurt and disappointment that he struck out against the person he loved the most. We recognize this kind of pain. All of us have been so deeply wounded that we lash out to hurt or destroy what we love the most. It is as though some sinister force takes over to separate us from our best source of comfort and joy. Often the cause of our betraying others is a feeling that we've been cut off by them, when, in fact, it is we who run away! Our isolation is self-imposed. Jesus never excluded Judas from his love and caring, even when he knew Judas' darkest plans. Judas could have been healed if only he had allowed it.

But Judas had given up on the possibility of love. He didn't realize that even in our deepest despair, love is possible. We can fight the impulse to hurt those we love by persisting in the belief that love and caring exist for us.

Self-betrayal. Judas' betrayal was finally a betrayal of

himself. He let his despair and pain drive him to kill the thing most precious in his life. The real tragedy of Judas' act is its self-destructiveness.

Jesus' compassion in the moment of crisis shows the only rational answer to this and all other betrayals. As the soldiers begin their arrest, it spurs a violent response from a disciple who nearly kills the servant of the high priest, cutting off his ear. The disease threatens to become contagious, just as the sickness of betrayal will spread if we permit it to do so.

But Jesus does not allow it to go on. He cures the servant with a touch. Here lies the greatest cure for this disease. In touching others and allowing them to touch us we can stop the epidemic of pain and loneliness that can come with betrayal. It doesn't matter whether we betray or are the one betrayed. We can end the cycle simply by understanding and reaching out in love and compassion.

How to Learn from Times of Pain

Then he made the disciples get into the boat and go before him to the other side, while he dismissed the crowds. And after he had dismissed the crowds, he went up into the hills by himself to pray. When evening came he was there alone, but the boat by this time was many furlongs distant from the land, beaten by the waves; for the wind was against them. And in the fourth watch of the night he came to them, walking on the sea. But when the disciples saw him walking on the sea, they were terrified, saying "It is a ghost!" And they cried out for fear. But immediately he spoke to them, saying "Take heart, it is I; have no fear."

And Peter answered him, "Lord if it is you, bid me to come to you on the water." He said, "Come." So Peter got out of the boat and walked on the water and came to Jesus; but when he saw the wind, he was afraid, and beginning to sink he cried out, "Lord, save me." Jesus immediately reached out his hand and caught him, saying to him, "O man of little faith, why did you doubt?" And when they got into the boat the wind ceased.

MATT. 14:22–32

Rachel is a close friend who learned from the Bible to use a deep and painful emotional crisis as a basis for growth and learning. She had been suffering for months in a depression she could not shake. She was nearly thirty-five and her life so far was a disaster. She felt her decisions about career and marriage had been horrible mistakes. Her spiritual foundations were crumbling. Nothing was satisfying or pleasurable to her. She couldn't pull herself together. She was able to do her job. But she was in a constant state of deep emotional pain.

She had tried a number of psychotherapists. But she always felt worse after a session. Eventually she quit. That left her feeling even more desperate. She even considered suicide. Finally, she turned to the Bible and she was drawn to the story of the strange boat voyage of Jesus' disciples.

The story changed her life. She had read it before, of course. But in her emotional pain, it came to life with new meaning. It provided the courage she needed to endure the crisis. It gave her the faith that even the worst and most prolonged emotional suffering can be used to advantage.

"As I read this story, I imagined myself in the boat with the disciples," she said. "And I knew exactly how they felt. Jesus had sent them on alone. They were supposed to make the voyage on their own. They were supposed to be independent and strong. Then the storm came along. They were alone, afraid, unprepared, abandoned. The waves were rising around them. The wind was against them.

"The biblical description of that storm matched my depression precisely. I knew I was supposed to be a strong and independent career woman. But I felt nothing but terror most of the time. And worse, I felt completely alone."

Rachel saw herself in the disciples' reaction to Christ's appearance as he walked toward the disciples on the water. His arrival should have been soothing. Here was a man who knew how to weather the storm. In the middle of a crisis, Jesus was able to maintain his peaceful composure. He could walk unaffected in the stormiest seas. He could teach them how to manage this terrible situation.

But the disciples were nearly blinded by fear. Their terror kept them from seeing the rescue that was at their side. Rachel told me that her experience was similar. She knew there must be a way out of her emotional crisis, but she didn't recognize the solution when it came to her. Often, she rejected the help that would have lifted her from deep despair. Like the disciples, she felt the healing forces around her could not possibly be real.

It was Peter's response that touched Rachel deeply. Peter did recognize Jesus. He was not blinded by fear like the other disciples. He believed that Jesus had the answer. If he were to conquer his fear, Peter would have to learn the important lessons of faith. This was a risky matter.

"No matter how shaky and insecure the boat was," Rachel said, "imagine what it must have been like to step out onto that raging sea. That is exactly the step I needed to move toward others to find help and love. It was the one step I feared the most. Peter had the courage to take that step. When I read the story, I knew that I had to find that same courage."

Peter triumphed over his fear. But the task was not easy. As long as he kept his faith in Jesus' ability to see him through this ordeal, Peter persevered. But when Peter's resolve faltered, terror returned and he started to sink.

Jesus chastised Peter for having little faith. But, of course, Peter's faith was far greater than that of the disciples who stayed in the boat. His willingness to take the risk and venture out, even though he failed, was most important.

It was Peter whom Jesus chose as his successor. Peter's attempt, faulty and hesitant as it was, meant far more than the security of the reluctant disciples who stayed in the boat. Peter learned the measure of his own faith, the strength and power of what he could accomplish through it. He also learned about his own weakness and the ever-present possibility of failure.

Reading the story made Rachel realize she could learn from her own emotional crisis. She saw that, like Peter, she would have to take risks and that she might even fail sometimes. But now she also saw that there was always spiritual help to lift her from despair. She had only to recognize it and allow it to work for her.

Rachel had made it through the worst storm in her life, she told me. Now she had found the strength to rebuild her life on a new and stronger foundation.

The First Step in Recovering from a Tragedy

 Now Thomas, one of the twelve, called the Twin, was not with them when Jesus came. So the other disciples told him, "We have seen the Lord." But he said to them, "Unless I see in his hands the print of the nails, and place my finger in the mark of the nails, and place my hand in his side, I will not believe."

Eight days later, his disciples were again in the house, and Thomas was with them. The doors were shut, but Jesus came and stood among them, and said, "Peace be with you." Then he said to Thomas, "Put your finger here, and see my hands; and put out your hand, and place it in my side; do not be faithless, but

believing." Thomas answered him, "My Lord and my
God!" Jesus said to him, "Have you believed because
you have seen me? Blessed are those who have not
seen and yet believe."

JOHN 20:24–29

Kathleen was a lovely college sophomore, an outstanding
student, whose young mother died of cancer while Kathleen
was taking my course. Kathleen had been unusually close
to her mother, and, to the end, the mother had been
courageous and loving. The death was a profound loss for
the whole family. Unfortunately, Kathleen's father was
unable to cope with the loss of his wife, nor could he give
Kathleen the support she needed.

I was relieved when Kathleen asked to speak privately
with me a few weeks later. Her class participation had
been uncharacteristically meager and she was even late
with her last paper. She needed someone to talk to. In my
office, Kathleen shared her feelings of grief and loss. Then
she said, "The worst thing in all this is that I cannot
imagine feeling happy again. I don't think I will ever
enjoy my life. I miss my mother terribly. I worry about my
father. Life seems absolutely hopeless."

Grief is a natural and important part of the healing
process, especially after the loss of a parent. Despair is not.
Kathleen's hopelessness threatened her college career and
her long-term emotional well-being. The story of Thomas
after the resurrection of Christ teaches us how to deal with
tragedy and overcome the kind of pessimism that Kathleen
felt, the kind that often accompanies grief.

In the disciples' life, the crucifixion of Jesus was the

greatest tragedy they could have known. Their leader was dead. He had been taken away, killed as a common criminal. They were left alone and feeling despair. In the time after the crucifixion, the disciples must have felt the shock of tragedy that often leaves us numb and hopeless.

When some of the disciples came back to the group telling of the resurrection of Jesus, Thomas refused to accept the possibility that such a miracle could happen. At first, Thomas might strike us as a commonsense skeptic. To him, these resurrection stories were too good to be true. Thomas knew how fervent wishes and desires can distort our thinking and even our perceptions. Thomas needed proof. He wanted to see the wounds for himself. He would have to touch the flesh itself before he would believe crazy stories like this.

After some consideration, we realize that skepticism cannot fully explain Thomas' disbelief. Thomas had been a disciple of Christ. He had witnessed Christ performing miracles again and again. Why would Thomas choose this moment to become a skeptic? Why was his need for proof so overwhelming here?

The answer is that Thomas' skepticism was a disguise for despair. Thomas had lost faith in the possibility of ever finding the grace and joy he had known while Jesus was alive. He couldn't allow himself to believe that he could once more feel the energy and fullness he had known in Jesus' presence.

The despair lasted eight days. For Thomas, this must have been a period of deep suffering. Finally, Thomas was healed by Jesus' presence. But Jesus gives a message for those of us who cannot experience his historical presence.

He says we must learn to believe in the power of love and joy on our own.

Jesus knew that belief and faith themselves are healing. The first step in conquering despair and pessimism is to make a choice. The choice is to believe that we will finally overcome the suffering we feel. This is true "faith." As the story shows, we may have to choose without any solid evidence that the joy will return. There may be no visible reason to accept hope. But we must accept it anyway. The alternative is allowing ourselves to be convinced that we will never be healed. How can we ever progress from that?

The psychological message of the resurrection is that life conquers death. Joy and wonder can and will always return, even after tragedy, if we allow them to return. The story of Thomas shows that doubt can sometimes block this return. Only when we put aside our doubts, make the leap of faith, and believe in the chance for our renewed happiness can we begin to enjoy life again.

How to View Suffering as Part of God's Plan

"He has put my brethren far from me,
  and my acquaintances are wholly estranged from me.
My kinfolk and my close friends have failed me;
  the guests in my house have forgotten me;
my maidservants count me as a stranger;

I have become an alien in their eyes.
I call to my servant, but he gives me no answer;
   I must beseech him with my mouth.
I am repulsive to my wife,
   ~~loathsome to the sons of my own mother.~~
Even young children despise me;
   when I rise they talk against me.
All my intimate friends abhor me,
   and those whom I loved have turned against me.
My bones cleave to my skin and to my flesh,
   and I have escaped by the skin of my teeth.
Have pity on me, have pity on me, O you my friends,
   for the hand of God has touched me!
Why do you, like God, pursue me?

                                JOB 19:13–22

The book of Job has a special message for the victims of
senseless tragedy. Perhaps you have lost a child or other
loved one to disease or death. Perhaps you or someone
you care about deeply has suffered a physical disability or
an emotional setback. Perhaps a dear friend has found it
impossible to endure life, and has ended the pain of it in
suicide, leaving you with a sense of anger and guilt.
Perhaps you are the victim of continual emotional or
physical pain. Whatever your suffering, the story of Job
provides a special healing wisdom that can both comfort
and show the way to recovery.

   According to the Bible, Job is a blameless and upright
man. He provides for his family both materially and
spiritually. He worships God and teaches his children to

do the same. Yet Job becomes the victim of tragedy. His property is destroyed. His children are murdered. He falls prey to painful disease. Job becomes the symbol of suffering for all mankind.

Like Job, when we become the victim of tragedy we ask, "Why am I suffering? Why have I been given this burden? What wrong have I committed to deserve this pain? How can I find the strength to endure?" These are the same questions Job asks. These questions arise naturally as we struggle to adjust to the reality of our situation. They are part of the coping process. We need not feel guilt at our need to search for answers and understanding.

Victims also feel a wide range of emotional responses, some of which may seem irrational or irreverent. Some feel that they must have done something terribly wrong. It is difficult to accept that in a world governed by a loving and all-powerful creator, innocent people must suffer and die. It's logical to assume that those who suffer must be guilty of some transgression: "Since I am suffering immense pain, I must have done something wrong to deserve it."

We need only think of the needless suffering of thousands of innocent children, victims of poverty and starvation throughout the world, to realize that this proposition isn't true. We do not know the reason, but we live in a world in which innocent people do suffer. It is a difficult but unavoidable fact of life. At least we can take comfort in the fact that we need not add guilt to the pain we experience.

The agony we feel may be a necessary part of some

grand plan. But for us, we feel rage and resentment. It is only natural to be angry in the face of what seems to be meaningless suffering.

One comfort of Job's story is in knowing that at least one other has asked the same questions and experienced the same frustrations we feel. Another is that Job finds meaning in his suffering. The Bible tells us Job spoke with God and through this encounter discovered "things too wonderful for me, which I did not know."

According to Victor Frankl, a therapist imprisoned in a Nazi concentration camp who lost his family to the Holocaust, suffering can be tolerated only when we are able to find meaning in that suffering. Frankl believes this meaning comes through our decision to accept our role in life, whatever that might be. Suffering presents us with a challenge: to find goals and purpose in our lives that make even this situation worth living through. Once we find that life task, we can face our suffering with equanimity.

The story of Job teaches us that we can all discover our challenge in life. Our choice to answer that challenge can give meaning to the pain and agony we feel.

CONQUER
PERSONAL DEMONS

Free Yourself from Inner Demons

🌿 And he said, "What comes out of a man is what defiles a man. For from within, out of the heart of man, come evil thoughts, fornication, theft, murder, adultery, coveting, wickedness, deceit, licentiousness, envy, slander, pride, foolishness. All these evil things come from within, and they defile a man."

MARK 7:20–23

What is a truly religious person? One who follows specific ethical rules and attends church or synagogue? One who lives in peace with others? Both count, of course, but according to Jesus, commitment to the search for self-knowledge is indispensable to being a truly religious person.

Most therapists agree that the path to healing is an interior one. As we come to know ourselves more deeply, our wounds mend and we grow to our fullest potential.

But the journey along the inner path is not always pleasant. The Bible warns us about frightening moments, and promises the strength for us to endure them. It assures that the victory is more than worth the battle.

Recently Jane, a woman with a strong religious commitment, returned exhausted from a spiritual retreat she made with the women's group of her church.

"I was hoping for a vacation," she said. "This was not fun. I spent the first day in prayer, and, that evening, suddenly began to see my faults and shortcomings in a far clearer light than ever before. I was searching for the inner treasure the Scriptures promise. What I found was an inner conflict and confusion. Why do I have to face all this? Isn't there some way to avoid all this darkness?"

I told Jane that, unfortunately, I knew of no way to avoid the stage of growth she was experiencing. Even Jesus spent time in the desert confronting the temptations of evil. I also assured her that the trials of her search were worth enduring and that she could find help from the Bible.

In this passage from Mark, for example, Jesus tells his disciples where and how the work of the spirit needs to be done. We cannot blame anything in the world for "defiling" us. The problems come from within. Jesus shows how well he knows the human heart. He knows full well that when we see ourselves as we truly are, we confront much that is negative, even painful.

But the Bible assures us time and again that our own imperfections are no cause for despair. God sees the darkness inside us far more clearly than we do, and He loves us in spite of it. This awareness of God's infinite love is an inexhaustible source of strength, always there to draw upon.

The Scriptures provide even more hope. They promise that with God's help, we can change. We are not condemned to live with this darkness. Even the most horrible, most powerful inner shadow can be dispelled.

Self-searching makes this possible, since evil only holds its power over us if we hide it away and run from it.

The secret is to gather our courage, and squarely confront the "defilements" present inside. Once we acknowledge our faults to ourselves, we can accept the forgiveness of God that has been there for us all along.

In another part of the Bible, Jesus makes this promise of victory. " . . . and you will know the truth, and the truth will make you free." He assures us that we need only face our faults head-on, and their power over our lives will be broken. That means freedom from the inner demons that attack us all, occasionally, is within our grasp.

Jane faced her demons, the first step in conquering them. She was on her way to being a truly religious person.

Learning How to Cope with Our Fears

So have no fear of them; for nothing is covered that will not be revealed, or hidden that will not be known. What I tell you in the dark, utter in the light; and what you hear whispered, proclaim upon the housetops.

And do not fear those who kill the body but cannot kill the soul; rather fear him who can destroy both soul and body in hell. Are not two sparrows sold for a penny? And not one of them will fall to the ground without your Father's will. But even the hairs of your head are all numbered. Fear not, therefore; you are of more value than many sparrows.

MATT. 10:26–31

For some of us, fear is an ever-present emotion. At times, it makes us feel as if we live under a gray and forbidding shadow. And sometimes fear stabs us so sharply and painfully that we want to fight or run away.

When fear occurs in response to an obvious danger, it's a perfectly natural and healthy mechanism for survival. But when it lurks as a vague constant in the background of our emotional life, it can paralyze us, holding us back from taking the risks and making the changes that would improve our lives. Such fear can ruin our happiness and leave us spiritually and emotionally exhausted, unable to enjoy life.

Matthew describes a situation in which Jesus teaches his disciples a valuable lesson on how to cope with both healthy and unhealthy fear. It is, at once, practical and comforting.

Jesus is giving his disciples some advice on how to spread the gospel. These men must have been frightened at the prospect of preaching a new and different religious message to a people who had suffered years under the oppressive occupation of the Roman Army. The people were hungry for a king who would lead them into a battle to overthrow the military rule. The message the disciples had to bring—peace and love—was far different; one that their audience probably didn't want to hear.

We can imagine our own apprehension if we were in the disciples' place. We can relate to their fears from our own experience. We've all agreed, with some reluctance, to take on jobs that eventually led us into serious problems. And who hasn't felt fear at the prospect of facing specific conflicts and obstacles that are unavoidable? In these times we're tempted to let fear take over. We want to stay home, take the phone off the hook, and escape the scheduled pain and turmoil.

Jesus understands this reluctance. He realizes that the disciples' fears are legitimate. He even warns them that the going will not be easy, that they will face hostility from their audiences. They may even be subject to physical abuse and legal harassment. Though this assessment doesn't make the job any more attractive, Jesus wants the disciples to know that they have every reason to be scared, and that he understands their fear.

There are legitimate grounds for our own fears about living in the modern world as well. It is foolish to pretend that we needn't be concerned. Those who live in a city must deal with the real dangers of crime and violence every day. All of us may justifiably fear the effects of debilitating disease or economic ruin. It's easy to conjure up oceans of despair simply by reading a medical journal. If we think only for a moment about the prospect of nuclear disaster, we can plunge ourselves into terror.

There is no end to it. We can spend all our time generating scenarios of misery and withdraw into a life of self-imposed terror. We can focus on the negatives and paint a picture of existence that would frighten the most heroic soul. What a way to live!

The problem fear poses is: how to be realistic about the dangers of the world, and still let ourselves be free of the paralysis that fear can bring.

Jesus tells his disciples that what is hidden will be known and what is covered will be revealed. How or why can this revelation and knowledge help us cope with fear? What sort of things will be uncovered? What sort of knowledge will help us in this matter?

Therapists tell us that fear of the unknown is our deepest fear. We fear the future most when what will happen is least clear to us. It is often better emotionally to know the worst than to fantasize about what might happen. That's one message Jesus is giving his disciples. He is also telling them how to cope with this problem. Jesus assures them their fear of the unknown can be and will be conquered as they learn and grow. As they travel, encounter the world, and expand their experience and knowledge, the courage to face unusual situations and new dangers will develop within them.

This holds true for all of us. We are most fearful when we isolate ourselves from others, yet, ironically, it's often the first impulse we have when we are afraid. But we should fight it or such fear will only feed on itself. We can't conquer fear by hiding from the world and its problems; victory lies in our active efforts to confront what we fear.

Jesus knows this experience is not always pleasant. Knowledge and experience have a price. We cannot escape paying for wisdom and growth. At times confronting our fears will leave us battered and bruised. We are sure to suffer hardship in the pursuit of our goals. We may even fail. But our return for the pain and failure is strength and endurance. Our setbacks help us to grow and learn. They can give us enormous practical wisdom.

Jesus' message speaks to the inner dimension of our soul as well. When Jesus says that what is hidden will be revealed, he is not speaking only of the experience and knowledge we will gain about the world around us, but of what we will also learn about ourselves. We will uncover truths within us that are hidden and secret. This is frightening, too. One of the greatest fears we have is that self-revelation will show how shallow, mean, and unworthy we truly are. We fear that some unknown evil within will rise to the surface for all to see.

But Jesus helps us to put this fear aside. God has numbered every hair on our head. He has also taken notice of every thought and emotion that goes on underneath that hair. God knows the value of our inner soul, even if we do not. Jesus wants to show us that we can discover virtues within us we never knew existed. Once we face the world and begin to battle our fear, we will find unsuspected inner resources. We will amaze ourselves and others with our inner strength; we will find talents and skills we never realized we had for coping with situations.

Jesus is realistic. The world is full of danger. We are always susceptible to harm when we venture out. But obsession with security and safety only leads to isolation and stagnation. We have within us a wealth of resources. These can only be developed by confronting the world and facing the dangers there. This development will make us strong and courageous enough to overcome our fears.

How to Stop Being Stubborn

🌿 Then the Lord opened the mouth of the ass, and she said to Balaam, "What have I done to you, that you have struck me these three times?" And Balaam said to the ass, "Because you have made sport of me I wish I had a sword in my hand, for then I would kill you." And the ass said to Balaam, "Am I not your ass, upon which you have ridden all your life long to this day? Was I ever accustomed to do so to you?" And he said, "No."

Then the Lord opened the eyes of Balaam, and he saw the angel of the Lord standing in the way, with his drawn sword in his hand; and he bowed his head, and fell on his face.

NUM. 22:28–31

The story of Balaam's ass is one of my favorites in the Old Testament. This story about spiritual stubbornness always makes me wince when I read it. I know only too well how closely this story describes my own pigheadedness.

All great spiritual traditions teach us that we have a spiritual guide within us. We are well-advised to heed it. It tells us when we are about to embark on a course of action that may lead to trouble.

The traditions tell us, too, that we usually *don't* listen to this inner voice because of our stubbornness. The story of Balaam's ass teaches us a lesson and shows us how to overcome this fault.

Balaam was in a ticklish situation. A great king had called him to place a curse on the Israelite people as they made their way from bondage in Egypt to the Promised Land. Balaam knew the Israelites were under God's protection. But he found it difficult to resist the royal request. He set out on his faithful donkey, to do the king's bidding.

We've all been in Balaam's position: suspecting that we are heading down the path to disaster and feeling uncomfortable about it, somehow aware we are doing the wrong thing. But we put aside our best intuition and go ahead, hoping all will work out. We might even manage to convince ourselves we are doing right. Then we set our minds and refuse to listen to the voice within. In short, we become stubborn.

As Balaam traveled he ran into an unexpected difficulty. His donkey refused to move forward. Balaam tried to force the animal back to the path. It only ran against the roadside wall. Finally Balaam began to beat the animal with his staff. But no matter what Balaam did, the donkey refused to go on.

Balaam did not realize it, but the donkey had an excellent reason for not going on—an angel of God with a flaming sword was blocking the road! Though the donkey could see the angel quite clearly, Balaam was too stubbornly intent on reaching his destination to see the obstacle.

I cannot say how often I have been blinded by my own stubbornness just as Balaam was on that road. After getting myself deeply involved in a mistaken course of action, I reflect on how I managed to be so stupid. I see how many clues there were to tell me I was headed in the wrong direction. Angel after angel stood in my way. I was too arrogant to see. I was so sure I knew what was right.

One of the sure clues that something is amiss is a persistent inner reluctance to go on. I can nearly always recognize it within myself. Of course, I can ignore the message, but I've learned that it's wiser to pay close attention to it. The stronger and more persistent the hesitation, the more likely that something is wrong.

Balaam was saved from destruction because he finally listened to his donkey and recognized the danger of the path he was taking. Our inner voices can alert us to pitfalls we cannot consciously see. Watch for the signals. They are always there if we are willing to recognize them.

Eliminate Resentment from Your Life

× # 1 kólla
offende 4

🌿 **Now Abel was a keeper of sheep, and Cain a tiller of the ground. In the course of time Cain brought to the Lord an offering of the fruit of the ground, and Abel brought the firstlings of his flock and of their fat portions. And the Lord had regard for Abel and his offering, but for Cain and his offering he had no regard. So Cain was very angry, and his countenance** fell. The Lord said to Cain, "Why are you angry, and why has your countenance fallen? If you do well, will you not be accepted? And if you do not do well, sin is crouching at the door; its desire is for you, but you must master it.

GEN. 4:2–7

Resentment is one of the most destructive human emotions—and unfortunately, one of the most common. The poison of it can damage even the closest relationships. The story of Cain and Abel warns us of the dangers of resentment, and shows us how to prevent it. If resentment does enter our lives, we learn how to heal it before it permanently scars any of our relationships.

I recently watched as a friendship nearly fell apart because of resentment. Two close friends, Betty and Sheryl, had met in high school and maintained a supportive and loving relationship over the next decade. Sheryl found a job in a thriving advertising agency, and when the agency needed more help, she recommended Betty to her boss. Betty got the job and worked hard to be successful.

A year later, Betty and Sheryl were both nominated for promotion to the same administrative position. Betty got the offer.

Sheryl's resentment exploded a few days later as she spoke with me. "I suppose I'm not being fair," she said. "But I was the one who got Betty her job in the first place. I went out on a limb for her, and now look what she's done to me. I really wanted that promotion. I wish I didn't feel this way, but I do. I don't think I want to associate with her any longer."

I assured Sheryl that her resentment at being turned down for the promotion was understandable. However, I suggested that she consider the dangers inherent in the emotion she harbored toward Betty. The story of Cain and Abel is a dramatic case in point. In it we see the very origins of human violence, the full range of passion and misunderstanding. Look here to find hatred, arrogance, guilt, repentance, fear, and despair.

But above all, the story centers around the emotional sickness of resentment. God's choice of Abel's sacrifice so infuriates Cain that he murders his own brother in a jealous frenzy. Talk about a dangerous emotion! Resentment clouds our vision, so that we are blinded to our own value and sense of self-worth. It dims our rationality. Worst of all, resentment poisons our relationship with others and it encourages conflicts. It can even lead to murder.

Our resentment often grows from a misunderstanding about the sacrifices we make. Cain sacrificed the best of his crop to God. He had worked hard to bring in his harvest and he offered its abundance. But there was something wrong in Cain's attitude regarding his sacrifice. His reaction to God's choice showed that he expected something in return for his offering. He did not present his gift freely, with thankful joy for all he had received in life. Cain wasn't making a loving sacrifice, Cain was making a deal. He expected to win in what he saw as a competition for God's approval and love.

Often our resentment arises from our anger over failure of friends to keep a bargain they never made. Our sacrifice for them—perhaps a favor we did, or a bit of help we gave them—had hidden strings attached. When they failed to live up to this hidden expectation, we felt hurt and cheated.

To combat the resentment we must become aware of these secret bargains that are so unfair to our friends. We can *prevent* resentment in ourselves by examining our motives, making sure that we have no such deals in mind when we do a favor or give something of ourselves. We can *cure* our resentment, if it does arise, by mentally releasing our friends from these phantom bargains.

The Bible's message is clear: Sacrifice is meaningful only when it is given out of love. Real sacrifice requires nothing in return. It should not be the painful surrender of a precious possession, but the willing gift of it made from a sense of love and overflowing gratitude for God's goodness to us.

After discussing the story, Sheryl realized that she had expected Betty's eternal appreciation for the helping hand Sheryl had given her. She also expected Betty to always maintain the same level with her in the company—perhaps even a little behind. Sheryl realized that Betty was not aware of (and did not share) these expectations. Sheryl apologized for the misunderstanding bred of false expectations and the friendship was saved.

Never Be a Victim Again

Then the kingdom of heaven shall be compared to ten
maidens who took their lamps and went to meet the
bridegroom. Five of them were foolish, and five were
wise. For when the foolish took their lamps, they
took no oil with them; but the wise took flasks of oil
with their lamps. As the bridegroom was delayed,
they all slumbered and slept. But at midnight there
was a cry, "Behold, the bridegroom! Come out to
meet him." Then all those maidens rose and trimmed
their lamps. And the foolish said to the wise, "Give us
some of your oil, for our lamps are going out." But the
wise replied, "Perhaps there will not be enough for us
and for you; go rather to the dealers and buy for
yourselves." And while they went to buy, the bridegroom came, and those who were ready went in with
him to the marriage feast; and the door was shut.
Afterward, the other maidens came also, saying "Lord,
lord, open to us." But he replied, "Truly, I say to you,
I do not know you." Watch therefore, for you know
neither the day nor the hour.

MATT. 25:1–13

When we read Jesus' parables, it's tempting to side with
the winners and look down on the losers. But we can miss
the depth of Jesus' message when we think this way. We
need to realize that Jesus often speaks to the side of us that

secretly feels lost and dejected. He shows us how to conquer the character flaws that lead to unhappiness, how to heal life's hurts and suffering.

The parable of the wise and foolish maidens is a wonderful example of Jesus' system for healing. To understand his message we have to reverse our normal train of thought; to read, so to speak, in reverse.

Our first impulse is to see ourselves as one of the wise maidens, and feel superior to the foolish women. But try the opposite for a moment! Try thinking of yourself as one of the foolish maidens. You have been excluded from the marriage feast. Inside, joy and celebration; outside, disappointment and dejection. What a miserable feeling.

Is the feeling familiar? Most of us have to say yes. We have all envied other people's lives. Everyone else is happy and satisfied. Why not me? Why am I so unlucky? Why do I always miss the parade?

Some people feel this way most of their lives. Denise was one of these people. She was on her third husband. Each relationship was a disaster. Her first husband ran off with her best friend; the second was an alcoholic who refused treatment. Her current husband was chronically unemployed even though he was well trained in a technical field in high demand. She had decided to divorce him.

"Men are rotten," she said. "They're all babies, they just want a mommy to take care of them."

"Are all men as terrible as that?" I asked.

"All the available ones. The good ones get married off early. I seldom meet decent men. When I do, they don't want anything to do with me. Just my luck! I'm not the type the good ones like. They all want sweet young things with bank accounts. I'm too old. I'll just never have a happy relationship. I know it."

Jesus' parable shows us that Denise's foolish-maiden feeling of being left out stems from emotional immaturity. The lamps of the maidens in the parable symbolize the inner light and satisfaction in our lives. The parable shows us that maturity and wisdom means taking care of this inner light. No one else can do it for us.

Denise, for instance, never saw her own role in the failure of her relationships. She blamed her husbands or her age. She saw her situation as bad luck. But she never acknowledged that she chose the men she married, allowed herself to be manipulated. Denise had yet to realize that only she could change her life to bring satisfaction.

When their lamps run out of oil, the foolish maidens try to borrow more. They depend on others to provide for their joy and satisfaction, another sign of emotional immaturity. In Denise's case, she looked for fulfillment exclusively through her relationships with men. For Denise, happiness could only come from others. She was unaware that she could sustain happiness through her own resources.

Aren't the wise maidens selfish in this parable? Where's the generosity we expect with true wisdom? The parable answers with a deep message about helping others.

Of course we should be generous to those truly in need. But when we act as a crutch to those who must learn to walk on their own, we do more damage than good. Fostering dependency and self-pity only cripples the recipient more.

Denise needed to learn she could make her life meaningful and significant through her own resources. She did not need others for approval; she could make the right choices for her own happiness.

The lesson is clear. The wedding feast that celebrates life is open to all who learn the maturity of self-reliance demonstrated by the wise maidens. Apply their wisdom to your own life, and never be a self-pitying victim again.

How to Fight Temptation

 Then Jesus was led up by the Spirit into the wilderness to be tempted by the devil. And he fasted forty days and forty nights, and afterward he was hungry. And the tempter came and said to him, "If you are the Son of God, command these stones to become loaves of bread." But he answered, "It is written, 'Man shall not live by bread alone, but by every word that proceeds from the mouth of God.'"

MATT. 4:1–4

Temptation is universal. We all have felt the urge to do or say something we knew was wrong. No matter how strong we are, temptation seeks us out, invading our thoughts and feelings. Jesus felt temptation. He even included a plea concerning it in the prayer he taught his disciples: "Lead us not into temptation. . . ." Fortunately, we can learn from the Bible how to battle temptation. In fact, the Bible's advice on the subject might be more helpful than some modern therapeutic measures.

First, the Bible assures us that temptation is no sign of

101

moral failure. In this story from Matthew, we are told that the Spirit of God leads Jesus into the wilderness to be tested. In other words, temptation is unavoidable. Don't feel you've done something wrong because you've been tempted. You haven't. You are only experiencing a normal part of being human.

Second, we are warned to watch out for those temptations that are truly insidious. The devil asks Jesus to perform a miracle that on the face of it seems rather mild: turn a few stones into bread. Why not? Who would be hurt? Jesus is hungry. A small, insignificant miracle like this should be simple for him to do, and it would solve a problem effectively. But Jesus realizes that this temptation involves more than the moment, more than this one request.

All of us are tempted to do little things we know we shouldn't do—overeat, overdrink, lie a little, sneak a cigarette when we've promised to quit, or cheat on our income tax. These "little" temptations are difficult enough to resist. This seems to be the sort of temptation Jesus faced.

In fact, the temptation holds far more danger. The devil has a sinister desire. He wants Jesus to abandon his ideals by choosing the easier path in life. The devil wants to distract Jesus from his true goal and purpose. He wants to convince him to quit the struggle for justice and peace. The temptation to perform the simple miracle of turning stone into bread is really a temptation to exchange the highest aspirations for a bit of comfort and security.

This kind of temptation can damage us most when we give in. When we compromise to avoid a bit of conflict, temptation has won a real victory. When we ignore the pain and suffering around us so we can enjoy our good fortune, free from concern about our fellow man, temptation has succeeded. The Bible says these kinds of temptation are the most insidious, the ones to guard against most carefully.

Now let's turn to the practical side. What can we do to fight temptation? What are the best strategies for fighting these urges?

Jesus used two powerful weapons. The first was a clear sense of values. He knew what he wanted to accomplish. He was wary of anything that might deter him from his ultimate goal: to serve as an example of the qualities we all aspire to.

You can use this same single-mindedness in battling your own temptations. Know clearly what you value. Concentrate on the ideals you cherish. When you are tempted, consider how destructive giving in could be to you and those you love. Think how little the momentary pleasure might be, and how much you might sacrifice for it. Such thoughts can help keep you strong and safe.

Second, Jesus battles temptation with something most modern therapists ignore: old-fashioned willpower. Modern psychologists have pretty much abandoned the notion of the will. People, they say, are driven by instinctual forces from the conscious, forces that are beyond our control.

But we do have a will and we can make it more powerful by using it every day. Willpower grows in strength the more we bring it into play. Like physical exercise, start slowly and practice everyday. Set modest goals at first to have early success and give yourself rewards when you accomplish these goals.

For example, maybe you can't quit smoking altogether. But you can will yourself to stop smoking when the children are present. Perhaps, you can't go on the strict diet you should adopt, but you can give up fattening desserts at lunch. These seem like small matters, it's true. But with each success, you gain a clearer sense of what your will can do and learn how it feels when it is working. You will be surprised at how quickly your sense of self-control will grow.

A clear sense of values and a strong will can strengthen our resistance to even the strongest temptations. Unfortunately, they cannot eliminate the temptations themselves. But high ideals and self-control can help us to handle whatever comes along.

How Labels Can Destroy Self-Esteem

 Then they said, "Come let us build ourselves a city, and a tower with its top in the heavens, and let us make a name for ourselves, lest we be scattered abroad upon the face of the whole earth." And the Lord came down to see the city and the tower, which the sons of men had built. And the Lord said, "Behold, they are one people, and they have all one language; and this is only the beginning of what they will do; and nothing that they propose to do will now be impossible for them. Come, let us go down, and there confuse their language,

**that they may not understand one another's speech."
So the Lord scattered them abroad from there over
the face of all the earth, and they left off building the
city. Therefore its name was called Babel, because
there the Lord confused the language of all the earth.**

GEN. 11:4–9

Children taunt each other with the sing-song, "Sticks and
stones will break my bones but words will never hurt me."
The ancient biblical writers knew the falsity of this idea as
well as the modern therapist does. The power of language
is a central theme of the story of Babel. Language can heal
us or make us sick. The ancient story reveals the power of
language and shows us the importance of using it carefully.

Emotions and behaviors accompany the words we
use to describe ourselves and to communicate with others.
Therapists believe that many forms of depression have
their roots in the words we speak to ourselves and the
names we give to our experiences. Chronically depressed
people repeatedly use negative words to describe themselves and the events around them.

Ken was a successful college professor whose thinking fit this pattern. Ken found himself unable to continue
with his classes one semester because of a severe depression.
He later told me that during this time he found himself
repeating over and over again, in his mind, the words,
"I'm such a failure. I'll never amount to anything."

Ken was convinced that his outward success was a
clever deception he carried on throughout his life. He was
sure he was incompetent and stupid. He honestly believed

he had been fooling everyone around him for more than twenty years.

Ken managed to find negative labels to turn every successful experience into a disaster. If a colleague complimented his work, or a student praised his teaching, he "heard" a touch of sarcasm in their voice. They had really meant to show him they were aware of his defects and incompetence, and he worried for days about it. If he thought the compliment was sincere, he told himself he had them fooled temporarily. He lived in fear that they would eventually discover his deception and expose him to the world.

Ken's depression hinged on one word, "failure." The word dominated his life because he believed it named him in some absolute way. His repetition of this word in his mind led to emotional pain and intellectual confusion. He had created his own Tower of Babel and could not escape.

Ken's sense of failure began to affect his work. Because he expected to be rejected by others for his imagined failure, he believed he actually was rejected. This only increased his sense of failure. Worse, because he felt that failure was inevitable, he stopped serious work on his projects or full preparation for his classes. Eventually he found it necessary to take a leave of absence.

The story of the Tower of Babel emphasizes the danger of misusing language. The people became caught up in the "name" they wanted to make for themselves. They built a tower based on false assumptions and unrealistic thinking. The result was utter confusion.

The story teaches us to take great care in the labels and names we use for ourselves and others. We can avoid building towers of self-deception and pain by watching over our patterns of inner thinking. We have the capability to interrupt these patterns. The labels we use have such power only when we convince ourselves that they can't be changed.

The biblical message shows us how to escape the confusion. We can substitute healthier labels for ourselves and our experiences. Once we recognize the power of language, we can select words and phrases to describe accurately who we are and what we do.

We also need to be careful of the labels and words we use to describe other people. This is especially true of children. As children learn to use language, one of their most important tasks is to find the labels that will form their identity. The labels they choose will influence their perceptions of themselves, their attitudes toward others, and the paths their lives will take. No child should ever be labeled in a negative way. Even a joking remark with a sting in it can have strong defeating influence. Instead, children need the encouragement that positive labels provide.

Ken learned through months of intensive therapy that he had been labeled a "failure" by a thoughtless adult when Ken was very young. He did not have the understanding to fight the power of the label at that age, but now he was able to see how inaccurate the word was. With this realization, he soon freed himself from its effects forever. We can prevent this type of illness in our own lives and in those we care about by remembering the confusion of Babel. It teaches us to take steps toward responsible and healthy communication inwardly and with others.

Fighting the Fear of Death

🌿 Now as they were eating, Jesus took bread, and blessed, and broke it, and gave it to the disciples and said, "Take, eat; this is my body." And he took a cup, and when he had given thanks he gave it to them, saying, "Drink of it, all of you; for this is my blood of the covenant, which is poured out for many for the forgiveness of sins. I tell you I shall not drink again of this fruit of the vine until that day when I drink it new with you in my Father's kingdom."

MATT. 26:26–29

We may have great faith. We may be courageous. We may think we're strong. But, when we come right down to it, we all have a basic fear of dying.

The fear of death is natural. Our bodies are programmed to avoid danger instinctively. Because of fear we make the strenuous effort to protect ourselves and others from harm.

In some cases, however, this healthy fear of death is exaggerated to a sickness. It becomes obsessive, intruding on our thoughts and poisoning our emotional life. Then it prevents us from finding the happiness in life.

Evan was a young college student whose best friend died in a boating accident. Evan experienced grief and anger at the death of his friend. After three months, his emotional life was still so troubled he could hardly leave his room. His grades suffered. He avoided parties—even one-on-one conversations. Evan was a virtual recluse.

"Part of it is guilt," he told me. "I keep wondering why Chuck is dead and not me. I was fishing with him on that same boat two weeks before the accident. Why didn't I die?

"But the problem goes deeper," said Evan. "I can't find any reason to do things. Life seems so ridiculously fragile. I could die at any moment—so could any of my friends! It terrifies me. If we can die just like that, what's the use of going on? I feel sick to my stomach all the time."

Matthew's description of the Last Supper offers invaluable help for dealing with the fear of death.

At the time of Passover, Jesus knew his own death was imminent. He was aware of the plot to have him arrested and executed. He told his disciples clearly this was their last meal together on earth.

Jesus was not immune from the fear of death. His prayer in the garden of Gethsemane was filled with human sorrow and anxiety. Yet, Jesus did not allow his fear of death to overwhelm him. Instead, he gave his disciples a therapeutic gift to help them cope with their own anxiety.

This is the gift of communion that is central to Christian ceremony. But behind the ceremonial observance lies a powerful message.

Jesus knows that death is so fearful because it separates us from people we love, from this joy and wonder life holds. But the *fear* of death can also keep us from our friends, and smother our happiness in the world. If we allow this to happen, death wins over life.

Jesus shows his disciples that the way to deal with the

fear of death is to celebrate life with those we love. And the celebration should infuse all we do and feel every day.

The celebration isn't intended to deny fears. Rather it acknowledges them and finds joy in spite of them. We can celebrate life in a thousand different ways aside from religious services. Compliment a friend or do someone a favor. Help a child to achieve a goal, or share a new and wonderful recipe with a neighbor. Just have fun with others. This is a kind of communion that enhances our life and helps us triumph in the battle against fear.

CONTROL
YOUR EMOTIONS

Finding the Calm to Face a Crisis

 And behold, one of those who were with Jesus stretched out his hand and drew his sword, and struck the slave of the high priest, and cut off his ear. Then Jesus said to him, "Put your sword back into its place; for all who take the sword will perish by the sword. Do you think that I cannot appeal to my Father, and he will at once send me more than twelve legions of angels? But how then should the Scriptures be fulfilled, that it must be so?"

MATT. 26:51–54

The inner peace so many saw in Jesus and later in the disciples was no accident. Jesus knew the healing power of calm inner assurance and he was able to give this calm to his followers. This same gift is available to all of us as a weapon against the conflicts we face every day.

Our conflicts are rarely as violent as the fight that broke out between Peter and the soldier. But they can still leave us frazzled and drained, just as if we had been in physical combat. Driving a car has become a matter of needless competition and hostility. Arguments over defective appliances, utility bills, or bank statement errors are commonplace. Domestic quarrels, even between loving and understanding couples, are inevitable.

How can we find the inner calm to cope with conflicts and not come out of them an emotional wreck? Where is the inner peace we need when our temper is about to flare? Counting to ten may work sometimes, but we need a firmer base for our emotional stability.

When he is taken away by the Roman soldiers, Jesus demonstrates his principles for dealing with violent conflict. When Jesus' companion (we learn in the Gospel of John that it was Peter) attacks the slave of the high priest, we understand; we can see ourselves reacting with anger, even violence, when something or someone we value is threatened. The act is futile. The slave is not responsible for Jesus being apprehended. Peter's attack is little more than an empty gesture that only does harm.

This is nearly always the case when we strike out in senseless rage, even for a good cause. We only make the situation worse. Even in his moment of crisis, Jesus teaches us that irrational explosions are as damaging to us as to those on the receiving end of our anger.

When we are about to strike out emotionally toward another, we must ask ourselves whether the outburst will really help anyone. If the answer is no, then we must restrain our actions.

The incident also reveals a tactic that can calm inflammatory situations. Don't escalate! Jesus was about to become the victim of violence. The situation was tense. Had

POWER

behind you.

To look ahead of you is as great as the

he allowed Peter's attack to go unchecked, he would have risked not only his own life, but also the lives of his followers. Conflict, unchecked, always seeks higher levels of expression that end only with devastation.

This is true in domestic arguments, too. Try to identify the points at which you are tempted to raise the level of conflict another step. Guard against moments where the argument would shift from the problem at hand to emotionally charged, personal issues. Observe those moments, and then refuse to make the shift. Hold yourself back. If the argument stays focused on one issue, the emotions will play themselves out and calm will return.

The third point of the story is that Jesus knows the pain and suffering he is about to encounter is part of a higher plan or goal. He could not fulfill this plan without being taken by the soldiers. That knowledge allows him to meet this crisis with calm assurance. Peter attacks the slave because he did not have Jesus' sense of purpose and meaning. Had Peter known the necessity of what was about to happen, he would never have struck out.

It is a lesson we must all learn in our search for the depth of inner peace that will allow us to cope with crisis effectively. We can't reach this level of assurance until we come to know the values and goals that guide our life. We can deal with frustrations and setbacks without emotional distress if we see them as part of the price for achieving what we really want.

If we can learn to avoid useless conflicts, to prevent escalations, and to maintain a true sense of direction in life, we can hold fast to inner peace. Not only will the calm we feel help us to cope, it may also soothe the tempers of others and lead to a resolution of the problem at hand.

Rid Yourself
of Anxiety Forever

 And he said to his disciples, "Therefore I tell you, do not be anxious about your life, what you shall eat, nor about your body, what you shall put on. For life is more than food, and the body more than clothing. Consider the ravens: they neither sow nor reap, they have neither storehouse nor barn, and yet God feeds them. Of how much more value are you than birds! And which of you by being anxious can add a cubit to his span of life? If then you are not able to do as small a thing as that, why are you anxious about the rest?"

LUKE 12:22–26

Anxiety—the most common psychological problem in the modern world. Nearly everyone feels it. We are anxious about our job, the way we look, and the impression we make. We are anxious about our home, our relationships, and our health. More than anything else we worry about money.

Anxiety can show up as a sharp and nagging pain, a knot in the stomach, or a headache that goes on for days. Sometimes anxiety lurks just beneath the surface of consciousness as a vague sense of unhappiness and fear. Many turn to drugs or alcohol for relief; others use exercise or work as an escape. For everyone, anxiety threatens to

114

block the pleasure and happiness of life and interfere with productive, creative work.

Jesus saw this kind of distress in his disciples who were anxious about their own place in the Kingdom of Heaven. He was aware of their fears concerning the future, their worries about family and friends.

Jesus was not on earth to eliminate the turmoil and trouble of life that come with being human. But he did have a healing prescription for the anxiety they can generate in us. And it applies as effectively today as it did in biblical times.

Jesus' program to eliminate anxiety from our lives has two phases. First, he wants us to understand that anxiety will not add one cubit to our span of life. In other words, anxiety is simply useless. No matter what the problem, anxiety won't solve it.

Think, for a moment, about problems you've encountered. Perhaps a friend or relative was seriously ill. Certainly, you were anxious about it, but did the anxiety cure the disease? Of course not! We've all known the anxious feeling overdue bills can cause. Unfortunately that anxiety never raised the balance in our bank account one penny. Anxiety won't fix the car if it breaks down, and it won't get us to work any faster when we're caught in traffic.

Anxiety *never* solves problems. Just the opposite, anxiety strangles effective action. It clouds our thinking and interferes with our ability to make choices. It exaggerates our problems and leads us to imagine difficulties we don't really have.

The realization that anxiety is a useless emotion pre-

pares us for the second phase—the action phase—of Jesus'
anti-anxiety program.

When he says, "For life is more than food, and the
body more than clothing," Jesus presents us with a strategy for dealing with anxiety. If we would only set our
sights on matters of real concern, most of our anxieties
could be eliminated forever. Anxiety often comes when
the unimportant and mundane tasks cloud the larger picture of how we want our life to be.

No matter how hard working and successful we are,
unless we pursue what really matters, we will feel we are
failing. In a sense we will be right. We are only accomplishing
meaningless and unimportant goals, and leaving unat-
tended what really matters.

In other words, Jesus is telling us to work on real and
present problems, and to get rid of our "what-ifs." What if
the boss doesn't like my presentation? What if we're robbed
during our vacation trip to Mexico? What if my party
flops? These imaginary problems can have no solution
because they are not real.

Jesus urges us to stop wasting time with problems
that don't exist. Of course, he doesn't mean we should
stop preparing for the future. He was a practical man. But
preparing for the future is quite different from fretting
over nonexistent calamities. We need to focus on what we
are trying to achieve here and now, to plan ahead for
realistic possibilities, not dwell on troubles that only exist
in our heads. If we do that, anxiety will drain away. We
can become alive to the present and work to achieve our
full potential.

How to Express Anger without Hurting Others

 And they came to Jerusalem. And he entered the temple and began to drive out those who sold and those who bought in the temple, and he overturned the tables of the money changers and the seats of those who sold pigeons; and he would not allow any one to carry anything through the temple. And he taught, and said to them, "Is it not written, 'My house shall be called a house of prayer for all the nations'? But you have made it a den of robbers." And the chief priests and the scribes heard it and sought a way to destroy him; for they feared him, because all the multitude was astonished at his teaching. And when evening came they went out of the city.

As they passed by in the morning, they saw the fig tree withered away to its roots. And Peter remembered and said to him, "Master, look! The fig tree which you cursed has withered." And Jesus answered them, "Have faith in God. Truly, I say to you, whoever says to this mountain, 'Be taken up and cast into the sea,' and does not doubt in his heart, but believes that what he says will come to pass, it will be done for him. Therefore I tell you, whatever you ask in prayer, believe that you receive it, and you will. And whenever you stand praying, forgive, if you have anything

against anyone; so that your Father also who is in heaven may forgive you your trespasses.

MARK 11:15–26

Usually dinner at the Albertson's was a pleasant affair. Tonight was different. John's five-year-old daughter, Victoria, accidentally knocked her plate onto the carpet and John went into a rage. Then his younger son, Benji, started to cry, and John sent both children to bed. John's wife became upset. Dinner that evening was definitely *not* pleasant. I took John for a walk to sort things out. "It's not the kids," he said. "It's my job. I should have gotten a promotion. I worked hard for it. They gave it to someone with half my experience. This has been eating away at me all week. But I can't go and scream at my boss. Besides it's too late now. The final decision was made last week. So I come home and take my frustration and anger out on Sharon and the children. I hate myself for it, but what can I do?"

Everyone experiences anger. Yet we all seem to have trouble learning how to handle it well. Anger expressed is painful, difficult to live with, and often destructive. Holding anger in is often worse. Anger can make our life miserable. We might seethe repeatedly over a painful incident that occurred years ago. Unresolved anger can destroy friendships and even a good marriage.

How can we deal with this emotion in a positive way? When you think of anger in terms of the Bible the story that comes to mind is the one of an enraged Jesus turning out the money changers in the temple of Jerusalem.

On a visit to the temple, Jesus finds merchants making a substantial personal profit selling sacrificial animals and changing foreign currency, both common practices of the time, sanctioned by the temple priests. Nevertheless, Jesus becomes enraged at what he perceives as a violation of the spirit of worship and sanctity. He charges at the businessmen, whipping them and driving them out of the building, upsetting the tables of coins and cages of birds and animals. His anger is righteous and corrective.

"Well, I certainly know how he felt," John said, as we discussed the story. "But you're not suggesting I tear up my office to express my anger, are you?" I assured him that such extreme action wasn't necessary. But the story does provide some useful guidance.

First, we learn that expressing anger is perfectly proper in certain situations. Jesus would not have made his point so effectively if he had stayed calm. While it's true that situations do call for restraint, and that inappropriate anger can generate conflicts and hurt people unfairly, at times anger is necessary and right. The trick is in knowing when and how to express anger.

Jesus provides some guidelines. He tells his disciples that anger must be used in combination with two other spiritual elements: faith and forgiveness.

Anger expressed in faith has a constructive purpose. Ask yourself, "If I get angry, will it help someone? Is this anger a healing anger?" If you can honestly answer, "Yes," have faith that your anger is good. To be constructive we must have faith in the purpose of our anger. We must trust our inner voice crying out against injustice and wrongdoing. Faith combined with anger can truly "move mountains."

Jesus also teaches that forgiveness is a necessary partner to anger. Without forgiveness anger is always destructive. We can forgive once we acknowledge our anger, express it, and use it constructively.

Finally, we learn that faith and forgiveness also provide the key to controlling anger. True control means finding effective ways to express our emotions, ways rich in healing and forgiveness. Emotions don't disappear. They always manage to surface. Control means making our anger work to the benefit of everyone.

John wrote a memo to his boss, pointing out unfair practices and other problems in the personnel department. He stated forcefully how angry he felt and noted that he was not alone. Bad morale was having a negative effect on productivity throughout the company. Though his boss was resistant at first, he finally saw the wisdom of John's approach. John was put in charge of reorganizing the whole department.

Anger can be healthy and productive when properly used. You can combine anger, faith and forgiveness into a powerful force to make yourself happy and well at any time. Be enraged at depression. Get furious at fear. Have faith that you can be joyful. Forgive yourself, your faults and failures. Anger can be the source of a wonderful energy you can put to work in changing yourself and your world for the better.

CALL ON
YOUR INNER RESOURCES

Seeing Integrity
as a Source of Strength

 And the scribes who came down from Jerusalem said, "He is possessed by Beelzebul, and by the prince of demons he casts out the demons." And he called them to him, and said to them in parables, "How can Satan cast out Satan? If a kingdom is divided against itself, that kingdom cannot stand. And if a house is divided against itself, that house will not be able to stand. And if Satan has risen up against himself and is divided, he cannot stand, but is coming to an end. But no one can enter a strong man's house and plunder his goods, unless he first binds the strong man; then indeed he may plunder his house."

MARK 3:22–27

Recently a young woman came to me in an emotional state she herself described as one of utter disgust and frustration. She had just been fired from her job because she had defended another employee against charges of mismanagement. The real culprit was the owner's nephew. Unfortunately, as a reward for her courage and honesty in standing up for the truth, the woman and her co-worker lost their jobs.

"Why should I keep my integrity?" she challenged. "What good is it?"

I believe integrity is a character trait far more common in today's world than we know. We hear so often of dishonesty, philandering, cheating, and lying in all our modern institutions, including, unhappily, the church. It's understandable if we think that integrity is going the way of the buggy whip. But I keep seeing people like this young woman who do the right thing without regard for her own well-being.

Nevertheless, the question she asks is important. Is there a reason to be true to our ideals and moral beliefs even when our actions might get us in trouble? The Bible provides us with a clear and practical answer: Integrity is a source of immense spiritual and emotional strength. It can be a powerful healing force in our lives, even if it causes us inconvenience for a time. To give up our integrity is to risk our spiritual and psychological lives.

The Bible gives us example after example of men and women who are able to achieve seemingly impossible goals because of their integrity. The lives of heroic biblical figures such as Abraham, Moses, David, and the prophets attest to this. So do the lives of the disciples in their efforts to spread the gospel after Jesus' death. The story of Jesus, taken as a whole, shows the strength our integrity can give even against death.

The response Jesus gives to the scribes who accuse

him of healing through evil makes the point explicitly. The scribes' attack implies that Jesus lacks integrity in the most fundamental sense. They accuse him of drawing his healing power from sinister and corrupt sources. They accuse him of pretending to be from God, when in fact, they say, he is possessed by demons.

Jesus' response teaches both the scribes and his disciples a fundamental truth about human existence. He asks them to consider, in their own experience, what happens when a nation of people fall prey to internal conflict. The nation becomes weak and hardly capable of functioning. We can think of the turmoil in this country during the Vietnam War as an example. Similarly, consider what happens to a house when the structural support of the building leans in two opposite directions. The house falls. It does not have the power to stand up.

The same is true of human consciousness. When we violate our integrity, we become internally divided. We say one thing but do another. We believe one thing, but act against our own belief. We claim to have one set of values, but in fact hold another. We generate conflicts within ourselves that pull us first one way and then another. Inward disintegration is bound to take place. We become weak and dysfunctional. We trap ourselves with our lies and deceptions until our resources are plundered. As Jesus points out, losing our integrity is like being robbed by thieves, making us helpless and unable to resist their entry into our life. In this case we are responsible for our own inability to act.

Jesus' message to the scribes is that it would be impossible to heal without a firm inner power. Such power only comes from living honestly. Without this inner integrity, Jesus would have been totally ineffective.

I suggested that the young woman test the truth of this precept in her own situation. I asked her to imagine what her life would have been like had she not spoken the truth. How would she have felt if she had remained silent, or lied to keep her job. She thought a moment, and smiled. She knew she would have been miserable and tormented. "I would have left anyway," she told me. "And I would never have been able to live with myself."

Because of her integrity, she was able to face the hardship of temporary unemployment. Ultimately she was strengthened by her ordeal. She knew that she was capable of maintaining an inner unity of spirit and action that would sustain her in any circumstance.

This is the strength our integrity gives us. Often it is inconvenient. At times it is painful, especially when, like Jesus, we find ourselves challenged by others who mean to hurt or destroy us. We may not be able to see our way through at first. But ultimately, if we respond honestly and directly, our inner unity will nourish us.

The Key to Increased Energy

Being asked by the Pharisees when the kingdom of God was coming, he answered them, "The kingdom of God is not coming with signs to be observed; nor will they say, 'Lo, here it is!' or 'There!' for behold the kingdom of Heaven is in the midst of you."

LUKE 17:20–21

Daily living drains us—physically, emotionally, *and* spiritually. When evening finally comes we can't wash another dish, face another crisis, speak another kind word. Then we think of those hardy characters in the Bible who kept functioning at full throttle in spite of age, workload, and overwhelming obstacles. How can we tap into their energy sources?

We all have our own quick fixes for a daily or hourly energy rush. We drink a cup of coffee; we take a few vitamins; we raid the refrigerator.

When the going really gets rough some turn to heavier, more harmful "helpers," such as alcohol or drugs. Others choose danger and excitement—a secret affair, driving at breakneck speeds, big-time gambling. We seek thrills to charge up the adrenaline system for those few blessed moments that mimic the spiritual and emotional energy we all crave.

Modern psychology directs us to a different source: energy that comes from within from our unconscious. It is what Freudian psychologists call libido; basically, sexual energy. The Freudians claim we feel run down because we stifle our sexual energy and don't give rein to the instinctual satisfaction we crave.

Of course, uninhibited satisfaction of sexual desires is dangerous, not to say immoral. But the real problem with the Freudian position is that it doesn't work. If the Freudians are right, then the more sexual experience we have the more of that sought-after energy we should find. The truth is that no such thing happens. We are no more energized through the satisfaction of our sexual needs than we are by any other physical exercise.

There must be a different source of spiritual energy.

But what is it? The Bible tells us that the true source of all energy is our Creator. This is true of the physical energy that fuels the material aspects of the world, as well as the spiritual and emotional energy that fuels our thoughts and feelings. God has endowed each of us with a conduit for his love and power. This vast reservoir is always ready for us to use.

The question is, how can we make use of it? How can we learn to release the energy within us and use it practically in daily life?

This inward search is not nearly as mysterious or complicated as it seems. It takes no special training. There's no need to pay for instruction in a special technique. It is merely a matter of what some traditions call "inner silent prayer," simply a quiet request for knowledge, understanding, and insight. Then a calm period of waiting silently for an answer from our own depths. That's all there is to it. The answer will come. You need only be patient.

But the answer, whatever it is, will assuredly give you not only information and insight, it will also free the spiritual energy within. I cannot tell you why such release occurs. I only know that it does, and it will happen as long as you trust in the spiritual power of the Creator to move within you as well as in the world.

You need only try "inner silent prayer" for yourself to be convinced of its benefits. The energy you find there will be far superior to anything that might come from any outward stimulus. It is a never-ending supply of a mysterious joy that will always be with you if you only allow it to be.

The Healing Power
of Your Imagination

🌿 Then God said, "Let us make man in our image, after
our likeness; and let them have dominion over the
fish of the sea, and over the birds of the air, and over
the cattle, and over all the earth, and over every
creeping thing that creeps upon the earth."

So God created man in his own image, in the
image of God he created him; male and female he
created them.

GEN. 1:26–27

We are products of God's imagination. This is one way of
understanding the ancient story of the creation of the
human species. We have our form and nature because of
God's ability to image us like him.

As beings made in God's image, we have a creative
imagination, too. Its power is far less than God's, of course.
Still, it has a hidden force to shape and change our experience,
and we use it all too seldom.

Medical men make effective use of the healing power
of our imagination in their therapeutic efforts. Most of us
know about the "placebo" effect: The doctor gives a
patient a sugar pill, but pretends to the patient it is an
effective pain killer. In nearly every case, if the patient
believes the doctor's story, the patient finds some relief

from pain. The effect is so powerful that all scientific experiments to test the power of a real drug must be designed to take the placebo effect into account.

Doctors also use the imagination more directly in other healing methods—to help us to relax and relieve stress, to lower our blood pressure, to raise energy levels. Many therapists believe imagination can bolster our immune system and prevent disease.

We don't need to consult a psychologist to tap the healing power of imagination. Nor do we need a physician to suggest images. The Bible can supply them. The force of our imagination and the wisdom of the Bible as a guide give us a supercharged combination for healing energy.

Let me show you one method I have found very useful. Find a quiet spot in your home, where you can spend an hour or so undisturbed. Be sure there is a chair, a bed, or place on the floor where you can sit or lie comfortably. Have a pencil and paper in case you want to write down any thoughts to remember later on. And, of course, have your Bible.

Next, prepare yourself for an adventure in your imagination. Breathe deeply and regularly for a few minutes and allow your mind to become as peaceful and as empty as possible. Relax your body and mind with any prayerful meditation you find useful.

Next, focus on your general state of emotional and spiritual health. Decide your goals for this adventure. What questions do you want answered? What problem would you like to work on?

Then decide which biblical figure would best help

you to reach these goals. Who could give you the most help? You may want to open your Bible at this point and read a few verses about this person. Now begin your adventure. Imagine as clearly as possible the surroundings and the circumstances where you would like to meet your biblical advisor—a modern setting or in ancient Israel? Would you meet in the wilderness or in a town? Picture in your mind how he or she would be dressed, how you would meet, the tone of voice, the gestures and movements you would see.

In all this, let yourself be guided by your own sense of rightness. If one image seems uncomfortable, let it pass and wait patiently for another. If no images come, allow yourself to experience the *feelings* of the scene as you describe it to yourself in words.

After a few moments, you will begin to feel a presence, a sense of being with someone else. Then you can begin an imaginary conversation. You can ask anything you would like to know. No need to fear revealing secrets; no need to be ashamed of what concerns you. Your biblical advisor is confidential, discreet and understanding.

After you ask your questions, wait patiently for an answer. I cannot tell you how the answer will come. In my own experience, I tend to feel the answer, rather than hear it. I find something in myself shifting, almost as if an emotional weight has been lifted.

I am constantly surprised by the answers my inner advisors give. They are usually unexpected and seem novel, at least to my understanding.

As you receive more advice, you may want to write down words or phrases that will help you remember. My memory alone is rather unreliable, as it is in remembering dreams, unless I write them down as soon as I wake up in the morning.

When you finish, you may want to offer a brief prayer before you return to the everyday world.

I find the advice I receive from meditations like these to be extraordinarily helpful in my own life. But I never hesitate to put the answers to the test of reason and practical wisdom. They must make sense, not merely reflect some projected desires or secret wishes. And they usually do!

Try this exercise and you will find that your imagination is a powerful and effective force in bringing a healing wisdom into your life for positive and practical changes.

Overcoming
Those "Impossible" Obstacles

 And David said, "The Lord who delivered me from the paw of the lion and from the paw of the bear, will deliver me from the hand of this Philistine." And Saul said to David, "Go, and the Lord be with you!" Then Saul clothed David with his armor; he put a helmet of bronze on his head, and clothed him with a coat of mail. And David girded his sword over his armor, and he tried in vain to go, for he was not used to them. Then David said to Saul, "I cannot go with these; for I am not used to them." And David put them off. Then he took his staff in his hand, and chose five smooth

**stones from the brook, and put them in his shepherd's
bag or wallet; his sling was in his hand, and he drew
near to the Philistine.**

1 SAM. 17:37–40

Sometimes we face an obstacle in life that seems absolutely
overpowering. Something blocks us from happiness and
success and we feel we can't break through the barrier.
The Bible has a solution. It teaches us how to conquer
these obstacles and reach our goals. Here is one example.

Sophy was a 55-year-old woman wrestling with the
"empty-nest syndrome." She felt the sense of isolation and
emptiness many older couples experience when their children leave home to follow careers and/or marry. Sophy's
husband still worked at his profession. But Sophy's whole
life had been spent working to make her home as supportive and comfortable as possible for her family. Now, with
her children gone, Sophy felt useless and miserable.

"I can't face another day of watching television and
cleaning the house," she said. "I have nothing left to do. It
will be another ten years, at least, until Jack retires. I don't
want to waste ten years of my life just waiting for that,
doing nothing."

When I suggested a few alternatives, Sophy quickly
rejected them. I sensed a need or desire hidden beneath the
surface of Sophy's mind. I asked her one of my favorite
questions: Suppose you could do anything at all, what
would it be?

Sophy immediately answered, "Oh that's easy. I would
go back to college and get my degree. But that's impossible for me."

"Why?" I asked.

"Well, of course, I'm too old. I can't even remember where I put my keys in the morning. How could I possibly compete with those bright young kids? I would feel ridiculous walking into a classroom where the instructor would be younger than I. Really, I don't have the time. Why, I would be nearly sixty by graduation time, even if I did make it through."

I knew I would not be able to convince Sophy to go to school by telling her that age makes no difference and that we learn throughout life. She already knew that. She had built a roadblock in her life. My advice alone would not break it down. This required a more potent remedy.

I asked her to remember the story of David and Goliath. We all heard and loved that story as children. It holds a powerful and healing wisdom for adults as well. Sophy remembered, of course, and said, "That just shows what I am talking about. I am certainly no young David."

"No," I said, "But you are acting just like the Israelite Army."

The Israelite Army was far more powerful than the Philistines. But the Philistine giant, Goliath, had terrified the Israelite men. They simply assumed that he was unbeatable. Goliath had them convinced that they were powerless against him.

Like many people, Sophy had an inner Goliath. She had convinced herself that she was fighting against an unconquerable enemy, her age. This imagined inner enemy was as oppressive to Sophy as Goliath was to the Israelite army. Sophy was blocked, unable to get on with her life. She was prevented by her fears from attaining her goals.

Her happiness and growth were threatened. The story of David shows us how to overcome our personal Goliaths.

David bravely offers to fight Goliath. Saul, the leader of the Israelite army, convinces David to wear the traditional armor of a warrior. But the armor doesn't fit. David is unable to move in this kind of gear. It doesn't protect, it hampers.

David is wise enough to see that he must trust in his own methods and go his own way if he is to conquer the enemy. Borrowed weapons and techniques will just get in his way, and worse, might lead to failure.

This was exactly the lesson that Sophy needed to learn. It wasn't David's youth that made him successful. David conquered the seemingly invincible foe because he believed in himself and trusted in his own vision. We often try to fit ourselves into other people's image of what we should be or how we should act. These images, like an ill-fitting suit of armor, can hamper our progress or stop us completely. We need to get rid of them and foster a belief in our own ideals, trust our own insights. Then we can conquer any obstacle that stands in our way.

A year later Sophy visited me with her first report card in hand. She had made the dean's list.

"Another giant bites the dust," she said proudly.

Preparing
for Emotional Crises

 The flood continued forty days upon the earth; and
the waters increased, and bore up the Ark, and it rose
high above the earth. The waters prevailed and
increased greatly upon the earth; and the Ark floated
on the face of the waters. And the waters prevailed so
mightily upon the earth that all the high mountains
under the whole heaven were covered.

GEN. 7:17–19

The story of a catastrophic flood resonates deeply within
the human psyche. Nearly every religious tradition contains a narrative of calamity parallel to the one about
Noah in Genesis. It is an ancient and universal tale that is
repeated generation after generation because it affects us
so deeply.

The story of Noah shows us how to prepare for times
of emotional and spiritual crisis. It also wisely advises us to
anticipate those periods in our life that might be sad or
unfulfilling. The Bible shows us how to prepare for such
emotional "floods" and thereby avoid catastrophe.

The Ark symbolizes psychological preparation. It
represents the tools we need to face times of turmoil and
transition: in other words, a support system for our personal program of mental health and well-being. We save
money to be ready in case of an economic crunch; we

weatherproof our house against a storm. Shouldn't we insure ourselves against emotional ruin as well?

This support system must be set up *before* a crisis comes into our life—before we can be overwhelmed by an emotional flood. In the stress of hard times, it's difficult to make prudent decisions. God got Noah started on the Ark long before the rains began. The time to build our support system is when things are good and we have the advantages of energy and wisdom at hand.

What shall we put in this emotional "ark"? What resources do we need to cope well with hard times? What preparations can we make against psychological storms?

Follow Noah's lead. First, he brings his family on board the Ark. In times of crisis the family can sustain in ways that no one else can, but don't wait for crises to emerge before you assess the strength of family ties. Do it now. If there are weaknesses in your family relationships, work to strengthen them.

Noah also brings on board the Ark all the food and provisions he will need for his long voyage. Symbolically, this points to the necessity for a cache of spiritual nourishment to use in times of crisis. It can take many forms. Many find strength and guidance from a community beyond the family: friends or associates, church or synagogue, a support group consisting of those who have similar problems. Some keep a list of Bible passages and other inspirational readings to sustain them. Others find music uplifting and helpful. It's a good idea to prepare a list of things to celebrate, places to visit, or cheering activities. Ask others where they look for fortification and strength.

Another component of our emotional support system is responsibility and obligation. This may sound a bit strange because we tend to think of responsibilities and obligations as burdens rather than comforts. In reality, the opposite is true.

God entrusted Noah with the chore of taking care of all the animals on the Ark. This formidable task was probably a blessing for Noah, who surely felt despair at times, as he watched the storm destroy the world. He must have wondered what sense there was in going on. The mission of keeping God's animals gave him a purpose. They were necessary for the future of the world and mankind. It was his duty to preserve them. The responsibility kept him going.

Even in times of emotional distress, we must find the strength to protect and preserve what we care about. Some responsibilities—our family and friends—cannot be ignored no matter what the circumstances. It's part of our spiritual support to be aware of and satisfy these obligations. They give us a center, a focus.

Building an ark for ourselves that includes our family, provisions for spiritual nourishment, and a clear sense of our responsibilities can help us ride out nearly any emotional or psychological storm. And, like Noah, when the storm has passed, we can return to life, renewed.

BECOME
A BETTER PERSON

How to Be Truly Generous

 And he sat down opposite the treasury, and watched the multitude putting money into the treasury. Many rich people put in large sums. And a poor widow came, and put in two copper coins, which make a penny. And he called his disciples to him, and said to them, "Truly, I say to you, this poor widow has put in more than all those who are contributing to the treasury. For they all contributed out of their abundance; but she out of her poverty has put in everything she had, her whole living."

MARK 12:41–44

We tend to think of generosity in economic terms. We give to charity. We put our offering in the plate the church stewards pass through the congregation, confident that the money will be used to help the poor and hungry. This giving is important and necessary.

But there is also a deeper and more spiritual meaning to generosity. We can be stingy with our soul and with our emotions just as we can with our money. Inner generosity

137

is as important to our spiritual health and well-being as economic generosity is to the world around us. But what is true inner generosity? How can we learn to give of ourselves in this way? The story Mark tells can help us.

Jesus is sitting near the treasury at the temple watching the powerful and rich come to make contributions. Then a widow, bent with age, shyly steps up to the offering plate and puts in two coins of the lowest value.

Jesus knows the sacrifice this woman has made. She could, of course, have contributed only one coin and saved the other for herself. We know she needed that money. We can imagine what she must have felt as she watched others put in far greater offerings than she could ever hope to afford.

Jesus immediately calls his disciples. Jesus tells them a striking truth. The widow is truly generous because she gives all that she has.

In hearing this lesson, most of us wonder how it is possible for us to be truly generous. Is Jesus saying we should empty our bank accounts? Must we live in absolute poverty in order to make the contribution that really counts? Is Jesus' advice so impractical that we could never follow it, even in our best moments?

It's true that many of us are so caught up in living the good life that sacrificing our creature comforts and our social status is almost unthinkable. And we know that Jesus, in his teaching, reminds us again and again that we cannot find true happiness or inner healing in material goods and possessions.

Still, it would be bad therapy to ask any of us to do what is impossible. How could we possibly give up all that we have?

Sure, we'd all like to make larger charitable contributions. But we have obligations for our children's education and current bills to pay. There is much need in the world and so many causes we would like to support. But we can't possibly give to all of them.

There are also times when we feel unable to give emotionally and spiritually to others. We feel as if we cannot give of our time or our store of consolation. We are simply out of strength. We have become poor inside. So how can we be truly generous?

Note that what is profoundly important to Jesus about the widow's true generosity is that it arises not from her riches but from her poverty. This is a paradox. What can it mean? Clearly, he is saying that the amount of money we are able to give is not at all the measure of our virtue. True generosity has nothing to do with outward show or economic well-being. It is an inward willingness to give from the depths of our soul.

Once we get this message we can begin to distinguish times when those around us have been generous beyond measure. So often we are aware of people who give comfort to others even though they feel no comfort themselves. We see people give love to others though they have none themselves. We see people give love to others even though they feel no love in return. Some give others wisdom and guidance, even though they feel their own lives are lost in darkness and misery.

We see true generosity whenever people give all they have. It is there when a mother gives all her love to her children and family, and when an artist gives all his talent and genius to create his masterpiece. True generosity is present when we make the full use of our resources and skills to do our job, and create something valuable for others. We see true generosity in the sportsman who gives everything he has for his teammate or his game. We see it in the student who does his best on a paper without regard for the eventual grade. All of these are examples of giving out of poverty, of giving all that we have. But this kind of generosity is also a prescription for a healthy life. It is the life in which we do not hold back; where we give everything we have to living fully and completely.

Such generosity is miraculous. It is in those moments that we give from our deepest resources and feel we have nothing left to give, that our giving rewards us in unexpected ways. The gift of true generosity heals and enriches the giver as much as one who receives. It shows that the resources within us are far beyond any expectations we might have had. Through true generosity we can find within ourselves an inexhaustible source of love and reward beyond any pleasure we might derive from material goods.

Sticking to Your Best Resolutions

 Now Jericho was shut up from within and from without because of the people of Israel; none went out, and none came in. And the Lord said to Joshua, "See, I have given into your hand Jericho, with its king and mighty men of valor. You shall march around the city, all the men of war going around the city once. Thus shall you do for six days. And seven priests shall

**bear seven trumpets of rams' horns before the ark;
and on the seventh day you shall march around the
city seven times, the priests blowing the trumpets.
And when they make a long blast with the ram's
horn, as soon as you hear the sound of the trumpet,
then all the people shall shout with a great shout; and
the wall of the city will fall down flat, and the people
shall go up every man straight before him."**

JOSH. 6:1–5

If we could only stick to our best resolutions longer than
the few weeks after New Year's Day! We honestly intend
to work harder, get slimmer, be kinder, think deeper—
and, once and for all, quit smoking. But somehow, when
our moment of decision passes into memory, our good
intentions go with it. We slip a little here, cheat a little
there, and soon the only reminder we have of our original
plan is an occasional twinge of guilt. And it is *so* easy to
ignore that guilt as time passes.

Although we laugh at our small failures, we're not
proud of our weakness in giving up on our resolutions.
The ability to hold to decisions has much to do with
success in life. It builds character. Who doesn't admire a
person who chooses goals and then works hard to achieve
them? The story of Joshua and the battle of Jericho is a
perfect model of persistence.

The walled city of Jericho was well fortified, and
protected by a strong army. The weary Israelites could just
as well have passed by this city, daunted by the prospect of
an extended siege. If they chose to attack, they would
have a long, persistent wait until the inhabitants gave up.

Our resolutions tend to cool as we consider the effort,

perhaps even the pain, in trying to keep them. A resolution to quit smoking is one thing. Resisting the temptation to pull out a cigarette after a good meal is quite another. Our own urges tempt us to trivialize our decision. "Just one cigarette won't hurt." "I can have a bite of cake this once." Even our best resolutions seem to whither and die.

If you want to keep your resolutions active and alive, follow the plan that God gave Joshua!

First, God told Joshua that he had already won the battle. He planted the image of success in Joshua's mind. This is a never-fail psychological strategy: tell him he's a success—and he's a success!

So the first thing to do is to see yourself as already successful in carrying out your resolution. Imagine as vividly as possible how clear your lungs feel without that tobacco, or how svelte you are without those midmorning snacks. Reactivate the image every day. Keep it, and any other supportive ideas, strongly in your mind.

Second, block out images of yourself that run counter to your resolution. Don't let yourself imagine how nice just one more cigarette might be, or how satisfied you could feel while eating a dish of ice cream. These seem like positive images because they promise pleasure. In fact, they are negative and you know it. When these negative images come into your mind, block them with the positive thoughts immediately. Don't let them take root. They can easily break your resolve and wash away all the progress you've made.

Third, use every possible resource to hold on to your resolution. God tells Joshua to bring the soldiers, the priests and finally all the people of Israel to join the battle.

Do the same. Bring in your family, and friends, your church and your associates at work. Join a support group or a club that works toward the same goals you have.

Fourth, get excited about your new life. God tells Joshua to blow the ram's horn, march around the city and shout. Follow suit. Use your emotions to conquer apathy or forgetfulness. Celebrate every success. Promise yourself wonderful rewards when you reach important milestones. Tell your friends how important and exciting your new life is and get them to appreciate your success.

See yourself as successful, eliminate negative thoughts, gather your helpful resources and shout for joy when you succeed. Then watch the barriers in your path to fulfillment crumble like the walls of Jericho.

Learning to Be More Flexible

 You shall not make for yourself a graven image, or any likeness of any thing that is in heaven above, or that is on the earth beneath, or that is in the water under the earth; you shall not bow down to them or serve them; for I the Lord your God am a jealous God, visiting the iniquity of the fathers upon the children to the third and fourth generation of those who hate me, but showing steadfast love to thousands of those who love me and keep my commandments.

DEUT. 5:8–10

Vincent, a young painter and sculptor, was in my psychology and religion classes. He was good-natured, and full of energy and rebellion. He loved to challenge and sometimes shock his teachers and his classmates with irreverent questions. He sparked wonderful conversations and debates in and out of the classroom.

One morning he arrived in class carrying his Bible. "I want to read you the second commandment," he said, and proceeded to read the verses from Deuteronomy.

Then he continued, "And what does that mean? It means God hates art. No wonder artists and church people don't get along. If I followed this commandment, I could never be an artist. To make matters worse, God is irrational and unfair. He, himself, tells us he is jealous. Why should God be jealous? He has all the power. He says he is the only god there is. Why should he worry about our worshipping other gods? And why does he threaten to punish children for what their parents or grandparents have done? This simply does not make sense."

Vincent's tirade opened a heated debate. A number of students agreed about the conflict between art and religion, mentioning the long history of clashes between the church and the arts. Other students countered that much of the most beautiful music, sculpture, painting and architecture is focused on religious subjects and found in places of worship. Nearly everyone was baffled about the jealous notion and the threat to visit the iniquity of the fathers onto the children.

"On that point, I think you're missing the inner message of this commandment," I told them. "This commandment is a warning against the damaging effects of psychological rigidity. It is really a therapeutic principle."

Vincent was curious. "Show me," he said.

I explained that the second commandment was based on a sophisticated understanding of how the mind works. When we try to understand God, life, the universe, or even ourselves, we use concepts, ideas and images that are always incomplete. Our thoughts and images are finite. They must be limited to be understandable. When the mind tries to comprehend anything infinite, it grinds to a befuddled halt. It just cannot grasp the infinite complexity of existence.

The problem comes when we begin, as the Bible says, to "worship" these "images," or ideas and concepts, as if they encompassed the infinity they point to. It is like taking a photograph of your boyfriend or girlfriend, and then falling deeply in love with the picture and ignoring the person.

"So that's why God is 'jealous,' " Vincent said.

"Yes, you could see it that way," I replied. "But the matter is much more serious."

Think how prone we are to allow our images and concepts of God to influence how we see ourselves and how we act toward others. Once we become convinced that our picture or concept is the right one, and everyone else's is wrong, we are bound to create conflict. Even worse, as long as we are convinced we have the full picture of reality, we are not likely to change or revise that picture. We become rigid and inflexible. We tend to resist any kind of change, even when that change is necessary if we are to adapt to new experiences and points of view.

"But why would God punish the sons and grandsons of people with this kind of rigid thinking?" another student asked. "It seems so unfair."

The language is harsh, I admitted to my students. But I think it is so severe because the ancient sages were anxious to impress us with how far-reaching the effects of our inflexibility can be. The attitudes we adopt for ourselves are sure to be imitated by our children. If we are narrow and close-minded, our children learn that style of thinking from us and pass it along to their children. God is not unjustly punishing children for crimes committed by their parents. Rather, he is warning us to be careful in how we train our children to think.

The antidote to this rigidity is understanding that no picture of God, life, even of our own psyche is ever complete. We need to form images and concepts in order to talk and think about religious and spiritual matters. We can find beauty and wonder in the way others express their love and reverence for the Divine. We can appreciate that many of the different concepts and pictures say something new and important. There is always something to learn about ourselves and our relationship to the cosmos.

The Gift of Accepting Others

 Then the King will say to those at his right hand, "Come, O blessed of my Father, inherit the Kingdom prepared for you from the foundation of the world; for I was hungry and you gave me food, I was thirsty and you gave me drink, I was a stranger and you welcomed me, I was naked and you clothed me, I was sick and you visited me, I was in prison and you came to me.' Then the righteous will answer him, "Lord, when did we see thee hungry and feed thee, or thirsty and give thee drink? And when did we see thee a stranger and welcome thee, or naked and clothe thee? And when did we see thee sick or in prison and visit thee?" And the King will answer them, "Truly, I say to you, as you did it to one of the least of these my brethren, you did it to me."

MATT. 25:34–40

Laura was a young woman who attended a nontraditional and morally rigid church. The religious community there had served her needs well. She felt comfortable and at home with the church people for some time. Recently, however, her life had filled with deep conflict. She explained her problem to me one evening after dinner.

"You know my father died suddenly two years ago. My mother was emotionally devastated and her finances were a shambles. I really couldn't help much and neither could my brother. Luckily, my Dad's business partner, Abe, stepped in. Well at least I thought it was lucky then. He put Mom's finances in order. He took care of all the legal matters involved in transferring Dad's share of the business over to Mom. I have to admit, he was really wonderful and completely honest. I don't know what we would have done without him."

"You seem to have changed your mind about Abe now. What made you switch?" I asked.

"Three weeks ago Mother announced she and Abe are going to be married."

"And you disapprove?"

"Don't you see? Abe is Jewish. My church says this marriage is wrong. They tell me I should cut off all contact with my mother unless Abe joins the church or the marriage is called off. I don't know what to do. I can't say I approve of the marriage. But I don't want to abandon my mother forever."

The problem Laura faces is complex. Her conflict reflects the dilemmas we all face more and more often in a world filled with diversity and difference. Her difficulty has historical, ethical, and theological aspects that have been debated for ages.

The problem also has a psychological dimension. We live with others whose religious and ethical beliefs differ from ours. In order to live and grow happily with these people, we need mutual understanding and respect.

Without that, hostility and hatred flourish. This sickness can destroy us all.

This Gospel about the day of judgment can help us combat this sickness and deal compassionately with problems like Laura's. But the story, like so many others that Jesus tells, has a strange twist.

Jesus tells us that on the day of judgment, the King of Heaven will reward the righteous. His reward will be given for only one kind of merit. The righteous are rewarded for the care and concern they have shown to the King.

Then comes the twist. The righteous are surprised. They have no knowledge of helping the King. They did, of course, remember helping their fellow human beings who were in pain and need. But they had no idea they were helping anyone special. These were just ordinary people in trouble. The righteous did not know the sick, thirsty, hungry, or imprisoned people were God's brethren. Evidently they did not even ask. They simply gave of themselves and their time without reserve or condition.

Jesus teaches us an important lesson here. In his story of the final judgment, no one is labeled. The King does not care at all whether the righteous person is a Christian, Jew, Moslem, Hindu or Buddhist or even atheist. The righteous do not belong to a particular denomination. They do not have the one correct set of beliefs.

In exactly the same way, the righteous do not care whether people they are helping have the right lifestyle, or go to the right church. Jesus is telling his disciples that the Kingdom of God will come to us when we are able to put aside all the labels that separate us from each other. True righteousness comes for all of us when we can show compassion to all of humanity.

After reading and discussing the passage, I asked Laura to use her imagination. I told her to think of herself on that final day of judgment. If she had to judge whether or not Abe's life and his actions fit the Gospel's description of the righteous, what would she answer? Then I asked her to think of the course of action she was contemplating. Would breaking off ties with her family fit in with that same description?

Laura quickly saw that her anger would only hurt everyone. She still did not agree that the marriage was a good idea. But now she was willing to listen and discuss her concerns with her mother and Abe. She found a new determination to help her mother find happiness in whatever choice she made.

Service—The Cure for Self-Centeredness

 Jesus, knowing that the Father had given all things into his hands, and that he had come from God and was going to God, rose from supper, laid aside his garments, and girded himself with a towel. Then he poured water into a basin, and began to wash the disciples' feet and to wipe them with the towel with which he was girded. He came to Simon Peter; and Peter said to him, "Lord, do you wash my feet?" Jesus answered him, "What I am doing you do not know now, but afterward you will understand." Peter said to him, "You shall never wash my feet." Jesus answered him, "If I do not wash you, you have no part in me." Simon Peter said to him, "Lord, not my feet only but also my hands and my head!" Jesus said to him, "He who has bathed does not need to wash, except for his feet, but he is clean all over; and you are clean, but not all of you." For he knew who was to betray him; that was why he said, "You are not all clean."

When he had washed their feet, and taken his garments, and resumed his place, he said to them, "Do you know what I have done to you? You call me Teacher and Lord; and you are right, for so I am. If I then, your Lord and Teacher, have washed your feet, you also ought to wash one another's feet. For I have

given you an example, that you also should do as I
have done to you. Truly, truly, I say to you, a servant
is not greater than his master; nor is he who is sent
greater than he who sent him. If you know these
things, blessed are you if you do them."

JOHN 13:3–17

It is a disease that threatens to overtake each of us at one
time or another. Tom Wolfe, the great satirist and critic of
modern culture, showed how widespread it has become
when he coined the phrase that describes so well the
current decade—the "me-generation." Clinical psychotherapists have a technical name for this disease—narcissism.

Jesus showed his disciples and us how to cure narcissism and combat its widespread effects. He taught that the
cure lies in the healing power of service to others. It is a
lesson we must all write in our hearts.

The word "narcissism" comes from a Greek myth.
Narcissis was a young man who fell in love with his own
reflection in a pool of water. He finally wasted away and
died, hypnotized by his own image.

Jesus probably did not know this strange story. He
did recognize, however, the symptoms of the dangerous
disease. We suffer from narcissism when we allow our
anxieties, fears, and pain to hypnotize us. We pay attention only to ourselves. We withdraw into a shell of self-
pity and self-indulgence that excludes anyone else.

Narcissism is insidious. We drift into the condition
without knowing it. We become so concerned with ourselves that we hardly notice our distance from our friends
and loved ones. We become isolated and protective.

Eventually, we begin to see even those who are closest to us as enemies.

At its worst this disease can affect whole communities. People stop caring for each other. They only look out for themselves. They come to believe that only their own interests matter. When too many people act out such a cutthroat attitude, the community is already ailing. Unfortunately, this way of living is all too common in today's world.

How can we fight this disease in ourselves? How can we prevent it from taking over our community? The Bible shows us the best technique.

Jesus realized that his disciples might suffer from narcissism in the face of the pain and terror of the crucifixion of their Teacher and Lord. We naturally tend to withdraw into ourselves when the world around us is too painful to face. But when this becomes a permanent attitude, we are in great danger. Jesus wanted to make sure his disciples knew how to fight this tendency in themselves.

As he did so many times before, Jesus used a kind of shock therapy with his followers. It was Passover, one of the most solemn and holy days of the Jewish calendar. Suddenly, before their eyes, Jesus took a towel and began to perform a task usually performed by the lowest servant— washing the dirty feet of travelers who had entered the household.

Jesus is teaching his disciples a lesson they must absorb before he is taken from them. They must learn that each of them can fulfill his life and find wholeness and peace through service. The lowest and most menial task, when done for another, is healing.

Peter is astonished. He fails to understand the lesson. Why is Jesus acting so crazy? Is this a test of some kind? Or a joke? Why would such a great man stoop so low?

Peter, like most of us, does not see his own condition. Peter would never wash someone's feet if he were a great man. He would be above that kind of service. He has not yet caught on to the fact that Jesus' whole life is a life of service to others. Peter still thinks in terms of status, privilege, and upward mobility.

Peter desperately rejects the service Jesus offers and his teaching as well. "You shall never wash my feet." He wants to remain isolated and untouched. Peter knows that once he allows Jesus to break through the shell of self-indulgence and pride, his life will change.

Jesus responds that Peter must come to understand the healing power of service. It is healing for the person who serves as well as the person who receives the service. "If I do not wash you, you will have no part in me."

Peter responds with the same bombastic pride. "Lord, not my feet only but also my hands and head!" Again the narcissism crops up. Peter wants to be made pure. He wants Jesus to affirm his dedication and faith. He still wants to be the center of attention. He has not yet understood Jesus' message.

Finally, Jesus explains his actions straightforwardly. Peter is not impure. His concern for himself is not unusual or bad. But it will never bring him the happiness or fulfillment he seeks. Paradoxically, only when we forget ourselves and seek to serve others, as Jesus served his disciples and his people throughout his life, can we find satisfaction and healing.

Jesus' teaching is especially relevant for our modern world. So many people are unhappy and directionless. They attempt to fill the emptiness and loneliness in their lives with hollow entertainment or anxious striving for success. When this fails, they turn in their misery to the therapist. Unfortunately, some therapists promote the same self-indulgence and narcissism that gave rise to the problem in the first place.

Jesus shows us that service to others is the best cure for narcissism. When we serve others, we allow ourselves to forget our own petty aches and pains. We see the courage of others in facing the tragedies of life. We become part of a community that cares for and supports its members through hard times and celebrates the good. Such caring is as crucial today as it was for the time of Christ and his disciples.

SAVOR
YOUR GOOD SENSE

Solomon's Technique
for Making Wise Decisions

 Then two harlots came to the king and stood before him. The one woman said, "Oh my lord, this woman and I dwell in the same house; and I gave birth to a child while she was in the house. Then on the third day after I was delivered, this woman also gave birth; and we were alone; there was no one else with us in the house, only we two were in the house. And this woman's son died in the night, because she lay on it. And she arose at midnight, and took my son from beside me, while your maidservant slept, and laid it in her bosom, and laid her dead son in my bosom. When I rose in the morning to nurse my child, behold, it was dead; but when I looked at it closely in the morning, behold it was not the child that I had borne." But the other woman said, "No, the living child is mine, and the dead child is yours." The first said, "No, the dead child is yours, and the living child is mine." Thus they spoke before the king.

Then the king said, "The one says, 'This is my son that is alive, and your son is dead'; and the other says, 'No but your son is dead, and my son is the living one.' " And the king said, "Bring me a sword." So a sword was brought before him the king. And the king said, "Divide the living child in two, and give half to the one, and half to the other." Then the woman whose son was alive said to the king, because her heart yearned for her son, "Oh, my lord, give her the living child, and by no means slay it." But the other said, "It shall be neither mine nor yours; divide it." Then the king answered and said, "Give the living child to the first woman, and by no means slay it; she is its mother."

1 KINGS 3:16–27

Few of us make the kinds of life-altering judgments for others that Solomon handed down in his royal court. But we have inward conflicts that affect our lives deeply, and we must make Solomon-like decisions to resolve them. This story about the custody of a baby shows us a technique we can use to cut through our own confusion to find the wisest course of action.

As king, Solomon was responsible for settling disputes among his subjects, and for providing a good example as well. He needed to teach them the value of justice and fairness in their own relationships. In this famous case, the two women presented the king with a seemingly impossible custody case, and conflicting stories that appeared impossible to resolve. Solomon's celebrated decision verified his wisdom and certified his worthiness to be the leader of his people.

We need Solomon's kind of wisdom on a personal level when we try to sort out contradictory emotions, attitudes and impulses that pull us in opposite directions. How do we judge what is the best course of action, the wisest decision when several legitimate alternatives present themselves?

Consider the inward conflict my friend Sarah faced. She had worked for years in a voluntary agency teaching adults to read and write. She was a talented instructor, and had enriched countless lives through her efforts. When the director of the agency retired, Sarah was asked to take the position. For Sarah, the choice was not easy.

"I want to take the job," she told me, "but maybe for the wrong reasons. It is quite an honor to be asked. That's part of the problem. Am I accepting this job for all the praise and recognition it gives me? Could I do more good as a teacher than an administrator? How can I make the decision that's right for the students I want to help, and right for myself, for my needs?"

The story of Solomon provides some clues on how to proceed in a situation such as Sarah faced.

The spiritual meaning of this story becomes clear when we recognize that each woman in the story represents a different side of our own inner self. One side is the part of ourselves whose inner promptings lead to growth and honesty. This is the part of ourselves we hope to encourage and to trust. This is the voice we want to follow.

But there is another part that is afraid and guilty. It reflects the pain and apprehension built up from our past. Often it is selfish, destructive or mistrustful. Its voice can confuse us and lead us astray. But how can we decide which voice is speaking? Which voice is truly motivating our actions?

Solomon's answer is to put each voice to the test. Though his threat to kill the child is not real, his harsh pretense shocks both women into revealing the truth about their deepest desires.

We can use the same technique to test our own motives. We don't have to threaten ourselves, of course. But we can imagine how we would feel after following each course of action. We can ask ourselves tough questions about what we stand to lose and what we might gain as the result of each decision. What is the possible cost of making the wrong decision? How would we deal with possible failure?

For example, Sarah needed to see that if she became the director she might lose the one-to-one contact with many of her students that made her teaching so rewarding. She needed to face the fact that this contact provided her with personal satisfaction that might be lost if she were busy administering the program. On the other hand, to remain as a teacher meant she would lose the opportunity to shape the program to better serve the community.

As Sarah inwardly considered and tested each option, sifting through her emotional responses to the possible effect of her choice, a renewed sense of her own commitment and direction developed. Slowly her confusion lifted, and she saw more clearly where she could best use her talents. She was an effective, compassionate teacher. It made her happy to see firsthand the valuable results of her work. To her, administration was a function others could handle as well, or better than she. As a teacher, she was unique, so Sarah chose to continue in that rewarding role.

Solomon's wisdom is based on faith that the right direction will emerge for each of us. We need only the sincere resolve to find the right path and the courage to test each alternative.

Learn to Conquer "False Prophets"

 Beware of false prophets, who come to you in sheep's clothing but inwardly are ravenous wolves. You will know them by their fruits. Are grapes gathered from thorns, or figs from thistles? So, every sound tree bears good fruit, but the bad tree bears evil fruit. A sound tree cannot bear evil fruit, nor can a bad tree bear good fruit.

MATT. 7:15–18

When Jesus tells us to beware of false prophets he is speaking on at least two different levels. On the one hand, he is certainly speaking of religious charlatans and liars. There are plenty of these fellows around in modern times. Jesus gives us sage advice about spotting them. We should listen to what they say, but also carefully watch what they do in life. No matter how well any of these slippery preachers speak, if their life is a cheat on the public, they are riffraff.

On another level, Jesus is also speaking of the false prophets we carry around inside us. These are harder to spot than the external misfits. But they do far more damage in the long run.

Psychologists tell us that we spend much of our inner life talking to ourselves. We carry on inner conversations, usually rather dull affairs, in which we repeat phrases and slogans to ourselves.

These slogans usually arise from fear and insecurity:

"Don't try that. You'll only get hurt."

"Be careful what you say. Don't be too honest. Someone will use it against you."

"You're too fat," or "You're too skinny."

"No one will like you the way you are."

"You don't have time to do what you want."

Psychologists believe that these slogans we repeat to ourselves, these mental false prophets, are the cause of tremendous unhappiness. We often gauge ourselves by what they say. Our lives are hampered by a set of false and unconscious beliefs we picked up somewhere along the way.

Jesus' rule for telling false prophets from true prophets applies to this inner realm just as it helps us evaluate religious crooks and liars.

The first therapeutic message from Jesus in this passage is that we must "beware" of the inner slogans. This means that we should "be aware" of their presence. Often we repeat these slogans and stories to ourselves without really noticing. They become what psychologists call subliminal voices. We hear them without really paying attention. Nevertheless, they deeply affect the way we think and feel.

It takes a little effort. But we can learn to observe our thoughts. We can catch ourselves listening to these false prophets and stop ourselves from following their lead. It's just a matter of watching our emotions. Check during those times when you feel a sudden sense of inner fear and pain. Try to bring back the message you gave to yourself right before you felt that twinge. Soon you will begin to recognize patterns of negative thinking repeating themselves every so often. These are the false prophets.

Once we become aware of them, we can use Jesus' fruits criterion to overcome the false prophets within us. Jesus tells us to consider the fruits of what the inner voices are saying. We don't need an advanced degree in psychology to see what they do to us. We can tell quickly that they are frightful and damaging. Our simple common sense tells us that what they say is not only wrong, but potentially damaging if we accept it as true.

For example, a common inner false prophet is the prophet of doom and failure. We may hear an inner voice saying something like, "Don't bother aiming for that goal. You'll never succeed. You always mess your life up somehow. No one will ever respond to your idea. You know everyone is against you. Just give up."

First, become aware of this voice and recognize how often it crops up. You will probably notice that it usually speaks up just when you want to try something that can be new and wonderful in your life.

Once you become aware of this pessimistic voice,

you can fight it. Ask yourself, "What are the fruits of following its advice? How would my life be if I trusted this voice? How would it affect the way I feel about myself and others?"

We need to recognize that the voice is misleading us. It tells us that we have never done anything right. We know that's not true; if we had failed at everything, we would not be alive to hear the voice. The voice also tells us everyone is against us, that we have no friends. We know that's false too. We all can have a circle of people who care about us, if only in our church or synagogue.

But the voice is not only misleading us, it is giving seriously damaging advice. Think of it! If we were to believe this voice, we would sit in our room afraid to go anywhere or try anything. We could never trust others to be helpful and loving. The voice presents us with an unlivable world.

The trick in dealing with these false prophets is to unmask them as the silly and ridiculous things they are. As Jesus suggests, they have power only when disguised.

Make it a habit to expose your inner false prophets as often as possible. Listen carefully to the inner voices. Catch any false and pessimistic ideas before they affect your emotions. You will be amazed at how quickly and easily your spirits will lift and your life will improve.

Escaping No-Win Situations

And they sent to him some of the Pharisees and some of the Herodians, to entrap him in his talk. And they came and said to him, "Teacher, we know that you are true, and care for no man; for you do not regard the position of men but truly teach the way of God. Is it lawful to pay taxes to Caesar, or not? Should we pay them, or should we not?" But knowing their hypocrisy, he said to them, "Why put me to the test? Bring me a coin, and let me look at it." And they brought one. And he said to them, "Whose likeness and inscription is this?" They said to him, "Caesar's." Jesus said to them, "Render unto Caesar the things that are Caesar's, and to God the things that are God's." And they were amazed at him.

MARK 12:13–17

"We know the biological clock is ticking away. If we want to have a child, it needs to be soon. But we can't afford for Mary to quit her job," Dan told me, as he and his wife, Mary, sat across from me in my office. "We are really in a spot," he went on. "If we have the child, we will end up in debt. If we put it off much longer we face a risky pregnancy. Either alternative presents serious problems. What should we do?"

The couple had put themselves in a double bind—a damned-if-you-do and damned-if-you-don't situation.

Certainly, it was not for me to tell them whether or not to have children. They would need to decide something so intensely personal for themselves. But I could, with the help of the gospel, show them the way to clear up their thinking on the issue.

Double-bind thinking is a very effective way to confuse yourself and other people, and to invite unhappiness. And everybody has been exposed to these double messages. Bosses tell employees, "Hurry up!" and "Be careful! Don't make mistakes!" Mothers counsel their daughters, "Never be dependent on a man," and "Find a rich husband." Even our everyday axioms contradict each other: we should "Look before we leap," but "Grab opportunity! It only knocks once."

The consequences of double-bind thinking often go deeper than mere confusion. Many people find themselves double-binded in virtually every decision they face. They see adverse consequences in every alternative. And they are paralyzed by the sense that there is no clear road to happiness or success. To them, every path is dangerous or impassable.

It was just this kind of trap the Pharisees and Herodians tried to set for Jesus in this Gospel. Jesus' enemies knew he would be in danger no matter how he answered their question. If he said to pay the tax he would lose the support of many of his followers, for he would be admitting to the legitimacy of the oppressive Roman government. On the other hand, if Jesus advised against paying the tax, he could be arrested by the Romans for treason and insurrection.

It's interesting to note that the Pharisees and Herodians must have faced the question themselves and found no real answer. They had used it to trap Jesus, but they too were trapped and they knew it.

Jesus resolves the problem with a deft stroke of genius. His answer, "Render unto Caesar the things that are Caesar's, and to God the things that are God's," shows all of us how to escape the traps of double-bind thinking.

Jesus makes it clear that this kind of entrapment comes not from the reality of the situation, but from limitations of vision. Victims of this thinking see the world as black or white, yes or no. They can only imagine the answer in terms of paying or not paying the tax.

Jesus cuts through such yes-or-no limitations. He reveals that the issue of taxes and political action can only be decided in the light of the larger and more important question of our relationship to God. Now the question of paying taxes rests on a more fundamental consideration: How can we decide between our obligations to the state and our obligations to God? Though this does not solve the problem for the Jews in Mark's Gospel, it does draw them to a higher level of thought.

By widening the range of options and considerations, Jesus shows the way out of the trap of double-bind thinking.

Life's opportunities are fuller and richer than either-or solutions would suggest. Don't be seduced into thinking that you must choose only from the possibilities offered; you can create or discover new ones! Step back a bit from the situation and try to look at it with a fresh point of view.

When Dan and Mary recognized the limitations in their own thinking they began to think of ways out of their own double bind. For one thing, they might adopt a child if they decided to wait. They could look into alternative sources of income, maybe a part-time job for Mary would do, or perhaps, they could live more cheaply, if they chose to have a child now. It wasn't an either-or situation anymore. There were lots of possibilities!

By widening our point of view and searching for creative ways to solve problems and reach goals, we too can put the limitations of double-bind thinking behind us forever.

How to Make the Right Decisions

 And Jacob was left alone; and a man wrestled with him until the breaking of the day. When the man saw that he did not prevail against Jacob, he touched the hollow of his thigh; and Jacob's thigh was put out of joint as he wrestled with him. Then he said, "Let me go, for the day is breaking." But Jacob said, "I will not let you go, unless you bless me." And he said to him, "What is your name?" And he said, "Jacob." Then he said, "Your name shall no more be called Jacob, but Israel, for you have striven with God and with men, and have prevailed." Then Jacob asked him, "Tell me, I pray, your name." But he said, "Why is it that you ask my name?" And there he blessed him. So Jacob called the name of the place Peniel, saying, "For I have seen God face to face, and yet my life is preserved."

GEN. 32:24–30

It must have been a terrifying experience for Jacob, the grandson of Abraham and one of the greatest patriarchs of the nation of Israel. He was traveling alone in a strange land and had stopped for the night to sleep. Suddenly, he woke up to find himself wrestling with a powerful adversary.

All too often, like Jacob, we find ourselves struggling in the dark with a problem, not knowing right from wrong and nearly exhausted from our efforts. We must make a decision, but we just don't know which choice is best. We don't know where the truth lies. We are not sure what is most valuable or important for us. The battle goes on inside for days or even weeks as we try to decide. The story of Jacob wrestling with the angel gives us wonderful insight in how to handle situations like this.

My friend Michael is an example of a man in a struggle. He is a brilliant scholar and also the young minister of a small church. Michael was caught between his love for books and scholarly debate, and his desire to help and minister to others. For some time he was able to handle both interests, preaching part time and attending school whenever he found the chance. But eventually, he came to a point in his life where the two paths diverged. He had to make a choice.

"I can't even sleep at night," he said. "All I can do is lie awake trying to figure out which direction God wants me to go. I know that this is a choice that only I can make. Whichever I choose, I will be leaving behind something I love and want."

"Sounds like you are wrestling with an angel," I said. Michael smiled and said, "Yes, and I am beginning to understand how Jacob felt."

Michael was right when he recognized that no one could tell him which path to follow. I knew he would be successful in whatever he chose to do. But no amount of advice or research could give him the insight he needed into his own soul. Michael struggled for a long time before he felt sure of the best thing to do. At times, he told me, he wanted to just give up. But he simply could not. He knew he had to make the choice.

Jacob's story shows us how to handle situations like this. Jacob wrestled with the angel all night. He did not give up. He felt pain. He was even wounded. He might have taken the easy way out. He might have run away. But he recognized that there was something sacred and wonderful in the struggle.

In the morning Jacob clings to the angel tenaciously, demanding a blessing. Jacob is not being irreverent. He knows full well that in spite of the pain and exhaustion from the struggle, there is a potential here for growth and joy. He also knows that potential can only be achieved if he is willing to hold on and not give up until he finds what he is seeking.

As I watched Michael struggle with his decision, I knew there was nothing I could do to make it easier for him. He needed to fight the battle within himself alone. Like Jacob, I knew that Michael was strong enough to persist until he received the blessing of new self-knowledge and new inner understanding.

The story of Jacob teaches us to see times of struggle through to their end, even though we may be left limp from exhaustion. There are periods of conflict and turmoil we must go through in order to find out who we are and what our place is in the world.

Jacob receives two rewards for his persistence; a blessing and a new name. The blessings we receive make these struggles worthwhile. We find ourselves with a new sense of strength and resolve. We go on with our life with a confidence that the choice we have made is right for us, and not the result of blindly following someone else's plan or living up to another's image of who or what we should be.

Jacob also receives a new name. The new name is a symbol of a new life for Jacob, a new resolve, a new goal, a new vocation. He knows now that it is his place to lead the nation of Israel in the moral path. Michael, too, emerged from his struggle more sure than ever of his ministry and his place in life. While it was painful and difficult, the struggle was worthwhile.

Escape the Comparison Trap

 And an argument arose among them as to which of them was the greatest. But when Jesus perceived the thought of their hearts, he took a child and put him by his side, and said to them, "Whoever receives this child in my name receives me, and whoever receives me receives him who sent me; for he who is least among you all is the one who is great."

LUKE 9:46–48

The comparison trap: It's a deadly prescription for unhappiness and conflict. It's a sure road to misery. Jesus' disciples were about to fall into this trap and his teaching showed them how to escape. His wisdom can help us as well.

Luke tells us that the disciples argued with each other about who was the greatest. Jesus immediately recognized the "thought of their hearts." Each disciple wanted to be number one. Each wanted to be on top. They were imagining their positions in the heavenly hierarchy, feeling important because of their supposed superiority.

We may not like to admit it, but most of us are caught in this trap as much as the disciples. We all want success. This is only natural. But we often mistakenly judge success by comparing ourselves with others. We want to know who works in the most prestigious job; who dresses the best; who lives in the fanciest neighborhood and drives the most luxurious car; who is the most attractive.

If we don't win in these imaginary contests, we believe we have somehow failed. What's worse, we judge others with the same yardstick. We form opinions about people based on their position on the success ladder. If they've not climbed high enough, we don't want to consider them as equals.

Modern society promotes this competition. We praise ambition. We teach our children that we live in a world whose rule is the survival of the fittest. In business, this means that success is a constant struggle to get to the top of our field. We teach our children that this struggle arises from realistic evaluation of what life requires of us. In truth, this competitive ambition can make us severely ill. ✳

Jesus knew how insidious the comparison trap can

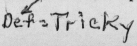
Def = Tricky

be. He knew that the disciples were in danger of thinking their self-worth lay in some special status or title. This is true of many today. They spend their lives frantically searching for competitors, anxiously comparing themselves to their neighbors, friends, or co-workers.

Be careful not to get caught in this trap. Such a tormented search can damage your self-image and block your emotional satisfaction with life. You put yourself in danger of living in a constant struggle to outdo others, losing any sense of real love or concern.

Jesus has a message for us, but one that is paradoxical and surprising. Jesus brings a child to the disciples' attention. The road to salvation and health lies in the childlike aspect of human consciousness. We need to receive the child; not only the children around us, but also the child that's within all of us. The child is full of wonder and awe and innocent surprise. The child doesn't judge by station or wealth. The child senses the goodness and evil in others directly, not by comparing them with the neighbors.

The paradox Jesus teaches is, "The least among you all is the one who is great." Jesus here is giving his disciples a healing message. He urges them not to fall into the comparison trap. He suggests they accept themselves as "the least." The prospect may seem frightening. What might happen if we stop the comparison? What if someone else should win? But Jesus knows the conditions for real greatness have nothing to do with outward trappings of success and achievement. Accepting ourselves as the least means giving up the stress and anxiety that comes from the chase. It means a blessed escape from the constant fear that we will be outdone or bested by someone else.

Once freed from the comparison trap, we will regain the sense of elation we had in childhood.

We can grasp Jesus' therapeutic advice here by recognizing that in our own life, the truly wonderful moments appear insignificant when judged by standards of status or prestige. Our joy in the beauty of the stars, our love for another person, our delight in springtime's first flowers, cannot be won in competition. Joy and fellowship work best when shared by all.

Once we understand that being the "least" allows us to feel great, we need never fear the comparison trap again.

But it is scarry. After all what will other people think of us or the neighbors what will they think.
That is God's business! what they think!
It's o.k. to be a nobody sometimes and in some circumstances.

THE JOY OF LIVING

Why Optimism Makes Sense

🌿 And Jesus answered them, "Truly, I say to you, if you
have faith and never doubt, you will not only do
what has been done to the fig tree, but even if you say
to this mountain, 'Be taken up and cast into the sea,' it
will be done. And whatever you ask in prayer, you
will receive, if you have faith." *not necessarily*
good feelings at all. MATT. 21:21–22 *Just Faith!!*

There are some whose religious faith seems fixed on a
gloomy and pessimistic view of the world. They think
mostly about destruction, guilt, and sin. They worry
profoundly about the power of evil, the weakness of
man's soul, and the horror of judgment.

Personally, I'm inclined to a more lively and optimis-
tic religious outlook. I sincerely believe that the Bible
shows how it is possible to face the evil of the world and
the pain that life may bring, yet possess a healthy optimism that leads to joy and fulfillment.

My students often ask me what reason there could
possibly be for optimism at this point in human history.
They point out, quite accurately, the full menu of evils we

face in our lives personally and as a human community. War and discord burn throughout the world. The history of man's inhumanity to man in this last century alone is more than enough to cause despair. Our own existence is threatened by pollution and nuclear war. Many of us—most tragically, many young people—believe we are helpless in the face of the massive forces that move our lives.

On top of it all, add the full weight of failure and unhappiness that falls upon every life. It's easy to understand those who listen to a voice within that says, "Optimism is stupid blindness to the facts. Better to face the painful truth than live an illusion."

This is the voice of a gloomy religious view. The Bible tells us God created the world and pronounced it "good." The Christian Gospel takes us a step further. God loves this world, and was willing to make the ultimate sacrifice to redeem it. Both images express the fundamental goodness of creation, not just at its beginning, but throughout time.

Even a quick reading of the Bible shows that this goodness is hardly undiluted. In it we get a realistic portrayal of the meanness of existence and the sorrow and heartache life can bring. The Bible does not sugarcoat reality. Yet God found the world good in spite of all this. He loved it anyway. Who are we to feel otherwise?

Just as important, the Bible shows us that this faith in the fundamental goodness of creation is the healthiest and most productive outlook to choose. Without it none of the heroic accomplishments described in biblical stories would have been possible. Abraham, Isaac, Jacob, Moses,

David would all have failed had they not trusted that their sacrifice and effort would help to shape the world to the good. The disciples could never have built and spread the gospel of the early church in spite of the persecution and oppression without their faith in the ultimate victory of love over death.

The Bible shows that optimism is not just a way of seeing the world. It is a force within us that leads us to act, often in spite of seeming hopelessness. Through our actions we shape the world, and bring God's plan into being. Without faith, our actions and those of millions before and after us would never take place. The optimism itself brings forth results that would not have been possible otherwise.

Pessimism tells us to give up and quit the task. No good will come of it. Ironically, this is a self-fulfilling prophecy. We make no effort, nothing changes.

But the same is true of optimism. It also comprises a self-fulfilling force. Faith assures us our contribution to the cosmic plan does make a difference. It gives us the courage and energy to persist in spite of temporary setbacks or failure. It shines through the gloomy viewpoint that sees only what is, and not what could and will be, in God's good world.

How to Put New Joy into Life

🌿 Jesus said to them, "Fill the jars with water." And they filled them up to the brim. He said to them, "Now draw some out, and take it to the steward of the feast." So they took it. When the steward of the feast tasted the water now become wine, and did not know where it came from (though the servants who had drawn the water knew), the steward of the feast called the bridegroom and said to him, "Every man serves the good wine first; and when men have drunk freely, then the poor wine; but you have kept the good wine until now."

JOHN 2:7–10

A middle-aged man attending one of my workshops confided that he felt strangely unhappy. He suffered no physical or mental disease. He was doing well in his job. His marriage was fine. But life, he said, had become bland. The colors were no longer bright for him, the music no longer moving. He didn't even enjoy his food very much. He functioned normally, all right. He just didn't feel alive. It troubled him deeply. Therapists observe such feelings as a common part of so-called "mid-life crisis." This period of natural transition comes to most people around the ages of forty to fifty. But the "blues" can hit any of us no matter how old or young we are. They are an undercurrent in many lives that appear full and meaningful on the surface.

What can we do when the joy and excitement of life seem to disappear? Many people try to recreate the excitement of their youth. They buy a sports car, quit their job, or take long vacations. Sometimes they carry these childish antics to an extreme and hurt themselves and their family in the process. Others follow a different path. They simply accept the dullness and lead what Thoreau called a "life of quiet desperation."

The story of Jesus at the Wedding Feast of Cana suggests still another way of dealing with life's periods of dullness, a way that is truly healing.

The events are familiar. Jesus and his disciples attend a wedding, and during the celebration, the wine runs out. We know that in most of the gospel stories, a wedding is a symbol for life. By implication, then, life, like a wedding, should be a celebration of happiness and love. Wine, in these stories, symbolizes that spiritual stirring within us that generates this happiness. We can call it "youthful well-being," "grace," "faith," or "inner harmony."

So how does the wedding story speak to our problem of what to do when life's excitement seems to be used up? Jesus' answer is profound. He turns ordinary water into wine! Of course, we could debate for hours the scientific possibilities of such an event, but that would be to miss the point. Jesus is teaching a therapeutic lesson: Recognize excitement and wonder in everyday events. Take tasteless, bland experiences and make them vibrant and electric. Learn to perform this miracle and you will never be bored again.

How can you miraculously transform ordinary living into a celebration? All you need is a bit of creative thought. Here are a few suggestions to get you started:

Prerecord your favorite music and enjoy an early morning concert while you dress or drive to work. Better still, get up early and watch the sunrise with music playing.

Make something you need instead of buying it. Choose something easy at first, perhaps a set of curtains or message board for the telephone. Try to get the whole family involved. You will be surprised how exciting it is to work together on a project.

Turn off the television and have a reading night. Let each person in the family select a favorite story or passage to share. Then discuss what you read. What does it mean? Why is it important?

Take a few moments to review your own achievements and talents. Recognize how wonderful you are. We often forget the best parts of ourselves. Do the same for everybody in your family. Your spouse and children have been able to accomplish extraordinary goals. Just recalling these accomplishments can regenerate enthusiasm and excitement.

Once you perform these miracles, you will think of thousands more. Dullness will be gone from your life forever.

Jesus teaches that real happiness does not arise from exotic adventure or extraordinary occurrences like winning the lottery. Real happiness lies in the taken-for-granted world—if we can learn not to take it for granted.

Realize the Fantasy
of Living the Good Life

And as he was setting out on his journey, a man ran up and knelt before him, and asked him, "Good teacher, what must I do to inherit eternal life?" And Jesus said to him, "Why do you call me good? No one is good but God alone. You know the commandments: 'Do not kill, Do not commit adultery, Do not steal, Do not bear false witness, Do not defraud, Honor your father and mother.' " And he said to him, "Teacher, all these I have observed from my youth." And Jesus looking upon him loved him, and said to him, "You lack one thing; go sell what you have, and give to the poor, and you will have treasure in heaven; and come, follow me." At that saying his countenance fell, and he went away sorrowful; for he had great possessions.

And Jesus looked around and said to his disciples, "How hard it will be for those who have riches to enter the kingdom of God!" And the disciples were amazed at his words. But Jesus said to them again, "Children, how hard it is to enter the kingdom of God! It is easier for a camel to go through the eye of a needle than for a rich man to enter the kingdom of God." And they were exceedingly astonished, and said to him, "Then who can be saved?" Jesus looked at

them and said, "With men it is impossible, but not with God; for all things are possible with God."

MARK 10:17–27

Oh, to live the "good life"! It's fun to fantasize about life with plenty of money and plenty of time to enjoy it. We'd spend our days as the rich and famous do, cruising on the Caribbean, exploring exotic lands, soaking up luxury, and buying expensive baubles.

But consider the question seriously for a moment. We know that traveling becomes tedious after awhile. Too much fancy food and drink soon takes its toll in the way we feel. In fact, most of our fantasies pale when they become too real. What can life offer that isn't doomed to fade with familiarity?

This is involved in the question of "eternal life" the rich man asks Jesus. At first we think the man is worried about death; that he wants to learn from the teacher how to become immortal. But that is far off the mark.

Jesus knew the more immediate issues this man needed to confront. His wealth must have been apparent. His well-tailored clothes, his educated speech, his bearing, all indicated his financial worth. Here was a man who could have most, if not all, the material goods he wanted. Yet somehow, this was not enough. Some part of his soul was not satisfied.

When he raised the question of eternal life the man was saying, "I have what all others think they want. I can tell you, it isn't satisfying. There is something wrong. What's missing?"

Jesus immediately sees the conflict in this man's life.

His first comment aims at the heart of the matter. "Why do you call me good?" Jesus is challenging his new student. What are your values? What do you think "good" means? You call me good because you believe I have a position of respect and regard. You search for the good life in your wealth, your culture, and your education. None of it works. You need to reconsider values in your life. You need to find a new way to make judgments.

Jesus follows his challenge with a succinct, but puzzling, solution to the problem. "No one is good but God alone."

Real value has nothing to do with material possessions, Jesus is saying. True goodness, the goodness that is eternal and does not diminish, has nothing to do with the traditional notion of the good life as this man lives it. He searches in the wrong places. He needs to set his sights on the kind of good that is at once deeper and higher.

As an abstract ideal, Jesus' advice sounds wonderful. But try to apply this advice in a practical way. Exactly how am I supposed to search and find the good life in Jesus' sense? Where can I learn to recognize ultimate good? Jesus presents the first level of teaching here. The good life is the moral life. The goodness that exceeds all outward appearances is the goodness of living in harmony with others—of fulfilling obligations, caring for others.

The rich man's answer to Jesus' teaching shows how deeply he searched before he came for help. It is this depth of searching that leads Jesus to love him so much.

"I have *done* all that," the rich man says, "and it is not enough. I still I feel the need for something more."

Jesus has now prepared the man for the message he

needs to hear. He has drawn the rich man to the point of realizing how serious his commitment must be if he is to realize his aspirations.

With total love and compassion, Jesus discloses the next step. The man must begin a new life. He must abandon the false support of his prestige and wealth. He must even surrender the benefits he has won through his moral strength and righteousness. He must commit himself entirely to finding the truly *good* life—a life based solely on the ultimate goodness of God.

This is a message for everybody. Like the rich man, we all seek eternal life. But we must be prepared to recognize that the riches we now possess are a poor substitute for it. To achieve the higher good we must be willing to abandon these substitutes.

It's easy to see why the rich man found this choice so difficult to make. Few of us have the strength or courage to give up our old comfortable ways.

Yet neither we nor the rich man need despair. Jesus tells his disciples, through the following passage, that "With men it is impossible, but not with God; for all things are possible with God."

Getting Ready for Happiness

 And when the Sabbath was past, Mary Magdalene, and Mary the mother of James, and Salome bought spices so that they might go and anoint him. And very early on the first day of the week they went to the tomb when the sun had risen. And they were saying to one another, "Who will roll away the stone for us from the door of the tomb?" And looking up, they saw that the stone was rolled back; for it was very large. And entering the tomb, they saw a young man sitting on the right side, dressed in a white robe; and they were amazed. And he said to them, "Do not be amazed; you seek Jesus of Nazareth who was crucified. He has risen, he is not here; see the place where they laid him. But go, tell his disciples and Peter that he is going before you to Galilee; there you will see him, as he has told you." And they went out and fled from the tomb; for trembling and astonishment had come upon them; and they said nothing to anyone, for they were afraid.

MARK 16:1–8

Every semester I ask students to tell me what happiness means to them. Then, I ask them to describe their happiest moment, the one occasion where they felt extraordinary joy.

Some students will describe a moment when they first fell in love, achieved a goal, or triumphed over some obstacle. But often their stories are quite different. Many students describe occasions where they suddenly found themselves in a state of extraordinary peace for no explicable reason. One young woman, Helena, described her experience like this:

"It was a few months after my father's death, in the late afternoon. I was at home standing on our back porch. Snow was falling and there was a cold wind. The chimes hanging from the porch roof were ringing softly. I paused for a second to look at the snow falling on the trees in the neighbors' backyards. Suddenly, for no reason, I felt a sense of wondrous peace and joy. It was as if I had entered a new world, a world full of beauty and music. I knew, somehow, this was the way the world really was. I had missed it, blocked it out in my daily life. But the reality of absolute peace and beauty was always there. The feeling stayed for a minute, maybe two at the most. Then, as quickly as it came, it left me. I was back to 'normal.' "

Helena's description resonated with a number of other students' experiences. During the following discussion, one question they all asked was, Why do these experiences leave us? Why don't we feel this way all the time?

I have pondered this question myself many times. These times of quiet joy and peace are, I believe, examples of the highest spiritual, psychological and emotional health. Many people experience them for brief moments. But rarely do we find ourselves able to sustain them for long. Why?

The story of Resurrection morning shows us one answer.

As the three women climbed the path to Jesus' grave, they were still in pain and despair from the traumatic events of the past few days. The conflicts of life had taken their toll on them all. They had few expectations and little hope. The best they could want from life right now was a bit of help rolling away the stone from the tomb. It was heavy. They were tired.

Their state of mind is familiar. We live most of our lives this way. We expect, really, very little in the way of joy and happiness. We are satisfied with a bit of help to get us through our daily tasks.

But on this morning, the world is changed. At first, the women do not comprehend what has happened. The stone is away from the door. A stranger is sitting inside. He announces a new cosmos to them all: "He is risen."

The transition is completely unexpected. The movement from ordinary life and normal expectations to a world of beauty and joy is so abrupt it is beyond comprehension. Suddenly these women are faced with a truth so wonderful, they are unable to cope with it.

Their reaction is typical of us all. They run away. They flee from the tomb. The experience is so different from their ordinary expectations, it terrifies them.

We all react this way, I believe. Our sudden experience of joy and beauty so surprises and shocks us, we cannot assimilate its meaning. We are so taken aback by the abrupt release from pain and the sudden realization of the possibilities of life, that we push aside the experience and scurry back to the world of everyday emotions.

Like the women on that Sunday morning, we are unprepared for joy. Of course, like them, we have been warned to expect it. Jesus had spoken plainly of his resurrection to those in his inner circle. The man in white reminded them of Jesus' teaching. But they had ignored the message.

We too have been told that life holds possibilities beyond our greatest expectations. This is the fundamental message of the Scriptures. Like the women at the tomb, few of us pay much attention. We certainly do little to prepare in any practical way.

We are concerned with making sure we have the right job skills, or enough money in our bank account for a rainy day. We try to protect ourselves against tragedy and disaster with insurance policies. We take vitamins to prevent disease. There is nothing wrong with all this. But when happiness comes, we have little idea what to do with it. So we run and hide.

The sudden moments of healing and beauty such as Helena experienced are premonitions of the wonder and love that are to come. We can learn so much from them, even though we flee from them so quickly. Most of all, we learn that these experiences of ecstasy do exist. Healing and joy are possible for us.

The Resurrection holds a wealth of symbolic meaning. It represents hope fulfilled and death conquered. It promises the possibility of revitalization, new life, and inner transformation. We can prepare ourselves for the lessons the resurrection teaches. Such moments are foretastes of what life can be. We now have good reason to learn how to handle such joy in our lives. Like the women, we can run to tell others about the possibilities of new life, and work with them to find and explore the new cosmos.

How to Regain the Playful Joy of Childhood

And they were bringing children to him, that he might touch them; and the disciples rebuked them.

But when Jesus saw it he was indignant, and said to them, "Let the children come to me, do not hinder them; for to such belongs the kingdom of God. Truly, I say to you, whoever does not receive the kingdom of God like a child shall not enter it." And he took them in his arms and blessed them, laying his hands upon them.

MARK 10:13–16

Mary Ellen was one of the most successful people I knew. By working night and day she built a failing employment agency into a leading competitor in the field. Her husband had a job he liked that allowed him to care for their pre-school-age son at home. It seemed that life was going well. Then Mary Ellen's husband suggested they have a second child. She exploded. "I don't have time to spend with my family as it is," she said. "What makes things worse is I'm not sure anymore why I work so hard. I loved this business when I started. Now it's got me tense all the time. I've forgotten how to relax, how to have fun. I can't slow down because too many people depend on this firm for their livelihood. I'm trapped by my own success."

When Mary Ellen talked to me about her problem, we searched the Bible for ideas on how to handle it. The story of Jesus and the children caught her attention.

It was a hard day in the biblical Holy Land. The disciples were all business. Jesus had serious work to do. He was an important man—healer, theologian, politician, teacher. He was teaching about the law, divorce, and life after death. The local authorities were looking for an excuse to arrest him.

The kids must have been getting in the way—probably horsing around, laughing and teasing each other. Their mothers wanted them to see this great man. The disciples, trying to maintain order, shooed them away. Jesus quickly corrected his followers. The Kingdom of Heaven, he told them, belongs to the children. He said that unless we receive the Kingdom like a child, we cannot enter it.

The story touched Mary Ellen. But she wasn't sure she understood its full meaning.

"How can I become like a child again. That doesn't make sense. I have adult responsibilities. I can't just run off and leave."

I asked Mary Ellen to think for a bit about her own son, and describe him to me.

"He is so trusting and loving," she said, "so spontaneous and free. He gets into things constantly, but really he is just exploring the world. Everything is full of wonder for him. Everything is a surprise and a mystery."

I told Mary Ellen about one of the discoveries of psychotherapy: each person has an "inner child" within. This allows us to experience the world with the same trust and wonder her son shows. This inner child is always there. As adults we often deny it. We don't allow ourselves to be children again, even for a moment.

Jesus points out the dangers of denying the child in us. The physical, mental, and spiritual costs of too much seriousness can be high. Tension and stress can produce life-threatening physical symptoms. Emotionally we are drained of energy and hope. Therapists also know that childlike play is excellent preventive medicine. It reduces tension and stress. It refreshes and builds energy and enthusiasm. Play is essential in a good marriage and in all healthy human relationships. Couples who forget how to play together often forget about their love and caring. People even work better after a period of play. Those lucky enough to find playful elements in their job are the most productive and creative workers of all. The healing effects of play and laughter reach into every part of our lives.

Jesus was making this same point: To be emotionally healthy we need to touch that inner child, to reclaim the joys and wonders we once felt. This does not mean regressing to a childlike state indefinitely. Sometimes it's important to react and think as an adult. But play and fun are important, too.

Mary Ellen remembered that childhood feeling. "It's been so long since I felt that way. How can I get back in touch with my inner child?"

Together we came up with a number of practical ideas. First, Mary Ellen decided she and her family needed that vacation she had been putting off for two years. She was able to see that the business would survive a few weeks without her. She might even return refreshed and invigorated, full of new ideas and with a better attitude that would improve the business.

She also determined to find time in her busy schedule for outings with family and friends on a regular basis. She and her husband even decided to learn to ski and to take a class in Chinese cooking.

Some months later I saw Mary Ellen again. She was full of energy. She had learned the secret of the inner child. Mary Ellen took the time to feel the wonder and mystery of life around her. Success in her business was not the only thing that mattered, and it certainly wasn't the thing that mattered most in her life.

The Secret of Inner Happiness

🌿 "Do not lay up for yourselves treasures on earth, where moth and rust consume and where thieves break in and steal, but lay up for yourselves treasures in heaven, where neither moth nor rust consumes and where thieves do not break in and steal. For where your treasure is, there will your heart be also."

MATT. 6:19–21

It would be wonderfully convenient if the U.S. government or the Harvard University Psychology Department could publish a formula for happiness. It could tell us what income we should have to be happy, the ideal number of children, what neighborhood to live in, and how much education to get. It would be nice to know what books to read for happiness, and what music to listen to. Of course, we'd have to be healthy and professionally successful. (It's hard to imagine being happy if one were sick or a complete failure in life.) But what else do we need?

Unfortunately, nearly everyone makes the same mistake in searching for happiness. We all believe that the right external circumstances will add up to a sense of well-being. If misery comes along, we blame it on the fact that we don't have something we want. We fantasize about winning the lottery or finding the right man or woman to fall in love with. We *know* the right job or the right car would make us happy.

It's surprising to learn that psychologists find almost no relationship between external circumstances and happiness. Surveys asking people to describe their general state of mind and their lifestyle, reveal that there are happy people in nearly every conceivable physical, social, and economic situation. Poor people are about as unhappy or happy as wealthy people. On average, uneducated people are just as happy as people with Ph.D.'s. Older people are as happy as young people (though young people expect to be miserable when they become senior citizens). Even people who are blind or paralyzed are happy to the same degree as those who have no physical handicaps.

Of course, the Bible made this point 2,000 years ago. Jesus repeatedly tells his disciples and followers that the happiness and peace they seek doesn't lie in worldly success.

So what does make people happy? Jesus tells his disciples to lay up for themselves treasures in heaven. He warns them that treasures on earth are vulnerable to moths and rust. What exactly does he mean? For one thing, satisfaction comes from a sense of peace and well-being in the heart. Focus on the spiritual quality of life and external circumstances fade in importance.

The inward treasures Jesus speaks about are not difficult to find once we begin the search for them. We discover them through quiet prayer or meditation. That's the time to ask deeply what will make us happy. The answer always comes if we are patient and sincere. I believe we all have an interior radar that will lead us to the heavenly treasures if only we follow it.

The moths and rust that Jesus speaks of are really symbols of how easily the situation around us can lead to disappointment. If you can be happy only in the presence of success or prosperity, you are bound to be unhappy often in life.

Psychologists find that people are most unhappy when life fails to live up to their expectations or desires. We form an idea of what life should be, and are disappointed and miserable when life doesn't measure up.

It's so much better to avoid these false expectations of the world. Happiness is there for everyone, no matter who you are or what you do. Just look into your heart to find it.

Joy Is God's Antidote for Sorrow

Truly, truly I say to you, you will weep and lament, but the world will rejoice; you will be sorrowful, but your sorrow will turn into joy. When a woman is in travail she has sorrow, because her hour has come; but when she is delivered of the child, she no longer remembers the anguish, for joy that a child is born into the world. So you have sorrow now, but I will see you again and your hearts will rejoice, and no one will take your joy from you.

JOHN 16:20–22

The Bible is a book of joy. Even more important, it is a book that shows us how to have joy after sorrow. Usually, we rejoice when something wonderful happens; we save our rejoicing for a time of good fortune.

But the Bible teaches us that rejoicing has another function—it's also a cure for sorrow. Rejoicing is a way to reinvigorate our spirits and conquer the "blues," to find new sources of cheer when old sources dry up.

There is a difference between sadness and the clinical condition called "depression." To conquer depression, we have to search out its cause, confront the problem, and act to alter the situation. The cure for depression is action.

We usually know the cause of sadness or sorrow right from the start: an unfortunate occurrence; a disappointment or failure in the wings; a lost opportunity for love; the death of someone we love.

Such events bring an inner pain, but the matter is settled. No action on our part will change it. No remedy is possible. We are locked into a passive role.

In this Gospel of John, Jesus teaches us how to deal with sorrow and sadness, and how to find the energy to go on.

Jesus is aware that his disciples will soon face sad and sorrowful events that threaten to overwhelm them. Jesus will be arrested and executed, and nothing the disciples can do will avert this tragedy.

These events could lead the disciples into a state of despair. They might conclude that their lives will be joyless forever, that the forces of death have won over life. They might decide that continuing the search for happiness would be inappropriate.

Jesus uses a wonderful metaphor to intercept any such emotional slide. He tells his disciples that sadness and sorrow are like the pain of childbirth. This symbolic picture holds a wealth of therapeutic advice.

Let's explore the implications.

First, Jesus teaches us that pain and sorrow are necessary to life, indeed, part of giving life. It is impossible to be happy and cheerful all the time. Feeling low once in a while is natural. So we need not hide our unhappy feelings from everyone; that can make matters worse.

Second, Jesus shows us that sorrow will disappear naturally if we will let it go. Like a woman who forgets the pain of childbirth and feels only love for her new baby, the progression from sorrow to joy is natural.

Too often we cling to sorrow through a misplaced sense of guilt that we didn't do something to prevent what happened, even though we couldn't have helped. Jesus absolves us of this guilt. We cannot change what has occurred by suppressing the positive feelings that will come in their own time.

Third, Jesus shows us that we can help give birth to new joy and happiness, just as a woman does in giving birth to her child. We must express our feelings, make an effort to touch other people and allow them to touch us. New joy needs space in our hearts, so we must let the old sorrow out to make room for joy.

Finally, Jesus teaches us that the overwhelming grief and sadness of today will be forgotten in new joy. The natural course of events includes forgetting pain as an essential part of rejoicing.

You can find joy wherever you are. A walk in the woods, a bouquet of fresh flowers, a baby's smile, an oceanside picnic, or quiet meditation in the local park, all these can lift our spirits. Take joy at every opportunity. Make it a habit! Sorrow will disappear and new life will be yours.

Dance Is Prayer

🌿 And it was told King David, "The Lord has blessed the household of Obededom and all that belongs to him, because of the ark of God." So David went and brought up the ark of God from the house of Obededom to the city of David with rejoicing; and when those who bore the ark of the Lord had gone six paces, he sacrificed an ox and a fatling. And David danced before the Lord with all his might . . . .

2 SAM. 6:12–14

David's dancing before the ark is a marvelous image of the power and beauty of this ancient king's love of God. Of course it caused a scandal. Saul's daughter, Michal, thought the new King's behavior was shameless and told him so. But Michal did not understand the lesson the young king was teaching. Dancing is one of the best forms of mental and spiritual therapy. It is a way of expressing our closeness with the Divine.

I know what you are thinking right now. I am too old to dance, or too out of shape, or too fat, or too weak, or too embarrassed. For some people dancing seems to be the farthest thing from being religious or spiritual.

When I speak of dancing, I do not mean only dancing on a stage or at a party. Dancing need not involve great physical exertion or long training in a studio.

We can dance in spirit. We can move gracefully in all

that we do. Our eyes and lips can dance when we meet an old friend. Our hearts and minds can dance when we see the joy of a new birth. Our souls can dance when we encounter justice and compassion, or mercy and healing in the world. We can move through our work and relationships with grace and charm.

Religious faith is always a kind of dancing. You may have heard the phrase, "leap of faith." Kierkegaard, the great Danish theologian, first used that phrase. He believed that all religious faith requires a leap. Some people understand this leap as jumping over a cliff or falling into an abyss. They imagine it as a death-defying dive into the irrational.

But Kierkegaard really meant that religion was a dance, a leap of celebration and joy. Faith is the human striving to come close to God. It is making the impossible leap to heaven in spite of the weight of sin and sadness that so often envelopes our lives.

Dancing in some form or another should be as natural to the process of religious and spiritual growth as prayer. For King David, dancing *was* a kind of prayer. It was his way of communicating to God and his friends his feelings and emotions. Keeping our emotions hidden and repressed is a sure path to loneliness and isolation. The Bible teaches that dancing our faith means expressing our inner life outwardly and sharing it with those we love. With this expression we can find the healing community that shared faith can build.

Dancing our faith heals us in another way. It gets us moving. Being static and lifeless in our mental and emotional life can make us sick. Once we stop moving, we are reluctant to get started again. We seem to run out of energy. Like the athlete who neglects his practice, when we stop trying to attain higher goals, we lose that healthy tone in our spirit.

Dancing our faith creates energy. In fact, when we begin to dance, we can find energy that we never thought possible. To dance our faith is to celebrate life, to celebrate in spite of the aches and pains of living. Once we join the celebratory dance, our wounds and stiffness will disappear. Dancing our faith is a way to keep mentally and spiritually alive and alert. It is a spiritual exercise we all need to practice.

Spiritual dancers are "grace-full." Their inner goodness sparkles throughout their daily life. Dancing our faith means a commitment to finding grace and beauty in all we do. Preparing a meal, writing a letter, cleaning a room, or repairing an appliance—all can become an expression of how much we cherish the time God has given us in this world. The most insignificant or tedious task takes on a radiance when we make that task a prayerful work of art.

Dancing our faith has an even more important function. When we find ourselves stuck in life and our imagination fails to show us the right direction we can dance our dreams. To dance our faith is to move beyond the world as it is to the world as it could be, beyond complacency, beyond the status quo. It is to leap toward a world where beauty and love abound.

Finally, dancing our faith is a way to bring magic into our lives. It means reaching outward and upward beyond what we believe possible. There are times in our lives when we lose all hope. All the doors have closed in front of us. We feel lost and alone. We want nothing more than to crawl into our bed and pull the covers over us. The Bible tells us to do just the opposite. Instead of cowering in fear, we must hold ourselves with pride and grace. We must dance, like David, "with all our might."

When we learn to dance like David, we discover that all movement is a kind of dancing. Dance is motion through space and time. To dance our faith is to move in harmony and rhythm with the creative power of the Divine. When we learn to dance as David danced, not only do we express our own inner feelings but we are expressing the power of life itself.

What True Happiness Is

The kingdom of heaven is like treasure hidden in a field, which a man found and covered up; then in his joy he goes and sells all that he has and buys that field.

Again, the kingdom of heaven is like a merchant in search of fine pearls, who, on finding one pearl of great value, went and sold all that he had and bought it.

MATT. 13:44–46

In my course in religion and psychology, I always reserve one or two classes for a discussion of happiness. It is a glaring deficiency in modern psychology that there is no clear picture of what happiness is. It's disappointing that scientists who can diagnose mental disease with confidence become tentative when it comes to assessing the positive side of mental health.

Once the classroom discussion gets started, my students are always amazed at how varied their images of happiness are. For some, happiness means achieving a financial goal. For others, it means marriage and a home. Some expect to find happiness in adventure. Others see adherence to traditional values as the path to happiness.

When we consult the Bible on the subject of happiness, Jesus' parables about the Kingdom of Heaven are particularly helpful. I am convinced that he is talking as much about life on earth as he is about life after death. Jesus is teaching us about the kingdom that is "within us." Translate this into modern psychological jargon, and you realize he is teaching us what it means to be mentally healthy and, more important, how to be inwardly happy. In the passage quoted above, Jesus uses two analogies for the Kingdom of Heaven. In one he compares it to a treasure hidden in a field. Then he tells us that the Kingdom of Heaven is also like a merchant in search of a treasure. We must read these analogies carefully, understand what he wants to teach us here. Though they seem similar, they are really two sides of a coin, two snapshots of happiness from different angles.

The first point Jesus makes is that happiness is like a hidden treasure that must be searched for and discovered. Many of my students find this a lesson that's hard to take. They think happiness should come spontaneously. They feel they deserve it. However, those of us who have experienced a few of life's disappointments know that Jesus is being realistic. Happiness does not come easily for most of us. It can elude us even when we struggle and strain for it.

Jesus' second point is more subtle. He wants us to reflect on how we pursue happiness. Are we searching for it seriously? Or are we just making do with life? These questions come to mind as we wonder about the fellow who owned the field with the treasure. Perhaps he did not know what was hidden there. Maybe he knew, but didn't realize what it was worth. How surprised he must have been when a stranger offered him a small fortune for this land. Perhaps he thought the fellow was crazy. Here was a man who had sold everything he owned for the money to buy a piece of land. He probably thought he was pulling a fast one on the buyer.

But the buyer knew what he was doing. He took an enormous risk. In fact, he risked everything for this treasure. He knew he had found something more valuable than anything else in the world.

Ask yourself who you resemble in this story—the first owner of the field who has no idea of its true value, or the man who uncovers the treasure?

Most of us are like the original owner. Happiness may lie in our own backyard. But we never think to search for it there. In fact, few ever bother to search for the treasure of happiness at all. Instead, we complain about our lot in life and convince ourselves that we will never be truly happy. So why try?

Jesus' second story answers that question masterfully. He tells us that the Kingdom of Heaven is a merchant in search of a treasure, not just the treasure itself. In other words, we who search for happiness and spiritual truth, make up the Kingdom of Heaven.

Happiness comes to those who actively reach for what they love and want. It does not come to those who merely brood about their misery. Those of us who are unhappy are that way because we have stopped searching for happiness. We have accepted the blandness of our lives. We no longer strive to uncover the treasure of love and excitement we yearn for.

Jesus assures us that the treasure is there for us if only we will take a few risks. In both stories, the person who discovers the treasure is willing to trade everything for it, because he knows in his heart that nothing is more precious.

The Bible reminds us that the search for happiness has its own rewards. It is never futile. It's in this search that we acquire the fullness of life's treasures.

Beating the Doubts
That Surround a New Beginning

 Now the birth of Jesus Christ took place in this way. When his mother Mary had been betrothed to Joseph, before they came together she was found to be with child of the Holy Spirit; and her husband Joseph, being a just man and unwilling to put her to shame, resolved to divorce her quietly. But as he considered this, behold, an angel of the Lord appeared to him in a dream, saying, "Joseph, son of David, do not fear to take Mary your wife, for that which is conceived in her is of the Holy Spirit; she will bear a son, and you shall call his name Jesus, for he will save his people from their sins."

MATT. 1:18–21

It was not an auspicious beginning—a question of the child's legitimacy; Joseph's plans for a quiet divorce to avoid scandal. Yet to come were an arduous trip to Bethlehem late in the pregnancy; a perilous birth in a stable; the flight to Egypt to escape a slaughter of innocent children.

This story behind the birth of Jesus, the birth of a healer and the beginning of healing for all mankind, is marked by confusion and turmoil. But isn't the healing process a hopeful one? Isn't the healer a source of goodness and energy? Why is there so much violence and anguish in this story?

In fact, the story represents the ambivalence that characterizes every new beginning. Getting married, having a child, starting a new career—all bring a mixture of hope and dread. We dream about the possibilities; we worry about what might go wrong.

In many ways, Joseph represents the feelings of most of us when we start on the path to a new life. Imagine Joseph's reaction when he learned that his new wife was pregnant with a child that he knew was not his! We learn much about the man by his handling of the situation— neither vindictive nor abusive; simply a realization that the beginning was over. He would quietly divorce Mary and go his way.

Each beginning carries with it a point when expectations and reality clash. Then we must decide whether to go on or not.

Something kept Joseph and Mary together, in spite of Joseph's resolve to leave. We know of Joseph's dream, but like all dreams, it says much and still leaves us mystified. What does "conceived . . . of the Holy Spirit" mean? What sort of child will this be? How does one raise a healer and savior? This was not what Joseph expected of marriage and a family.

For Joseph it was a time of decision. Should he open himself to the unexpected possibilities of a new kind of life? Or should he insist on having the life he planned before all this happened? He decided to risk it.

Again we resonate to the mystery. New ventures have us tingling with anticipation. Somewhere within us is the desire for a bit of chance, something beyond our limited expectations. We hope for a direction we could not have foreseen. We surrender the plans we made and welcome a strange new dream, trusting that life will not betray us.

Was the dream alone enough to turn Joseph around? I suspect there was more. He must have loved Mary. He must have had the faith that with her he could find the strength and support necessary to nurture this new birth. Even a healer and savior would need two parents to cherish and support him. Even a man destined to free the race from sin and to battle the forces of evil would need loving care in the first years of life.

All new beginnings need love and support at first. Early weakness is no sign of failure.

Eventually, Joseph would see Jesus grow to manhood and accept the responsibilities of life. As children mature, parents become more the observers than the central players in the drama.

As our own new beginnings become stronger and more independent, we too must be willing to let them take their own direction. And we must wholeheartedly commit to the new possibilities. There is no turning back to old ways.

All births have a bitter-sweet quality. Eventually the young mature, and that maturity implies separation and loss—a break with the past. But we blow out the candles on the cake and clap our hands in an expression of hope for the future. Like Joseph, we embrace the new adventure. We have made the decision to go on with it. We *will* make this new part of our lives a success!

Finding Time for the Important Things in Your Life

 For everything there is a season and a time for every matter under heaven:

    a time to be born, and a time to die;
    a time to plant, and a time to pluck up what
        is planted;
    a time to kill, and a time to heal;
    a time to break down, and a time to build up;
    a time to weep, and a time to laugh;
    a time to mourn, and a time to dance;
    a time to cast away stones, and a time to gather
        stones together;
    a time to embrace, and a time to refrain from
        embracing;
    a time to seek, and a time to lose;

a time to keep, and a time to cast away;
a time to rend, and a time to sew;
a time to keep silence, and a time to speak;
a time to love and a time to hate;
a time for war and a time for peace.

ECCLES. 3:1–8

My friend Joan recently learned a difficult lesson about time. She thought of herself as well organized and efficient. And, indeed, she seemed to be all of that. Joan worked as a leader in a national church organization and lectured to religious and to civic groups. She also pursued a full social calendar. Even though Joan constantly rushed from one appointment to another, she managed to fit it all in.

But suddenly Joan's world fell apart. Her daughter attempted suicide. Luckily, the girl did not injure herself seriously. This was not a true attempt of self-destruction so much as a cry for attention. Joan had nearly lost what was most precious to her. In her rush toward efficiency, she had forgotten to allow time for a major element in her life. Joan's problem with time is familiar to many of us. Who isn't short of time?

We have hundreds of time-saving devices—washing machines, microwave ovens, electric can openers. Still, every one of us would welcome another day or two in the week. Why is it so hard to fit in all we want to do?

For some of us, concern about time causes stress and anxiety. We worry about being late, for a date or a deadline. We rush everywhere, often ignoring friends and relatives. We never have the time to visit, or even to renew ties. There isn't even time for love and friendship.

The beautiful passage from Ecclesiastes quoted above carries a healing message about the meaning of time for us.

It reminds us, first, that God provides time for everything of real importance. No need to worry about scheduling what is essential in our lives. Our inner impulses will direct us to what is timely and important for the present, but we must listen for these inner promptings. Often our artificial lifestyle and exhausting schedule lead us to ignore what we truly need and want. We permit them to shape our lives into a routine that leaves us exhausted and empty.

Next, the Bible tells us that everything has its own season. This is an important lesson in looking at time in a special way. We learn that each vital aspect of our lives has a proper and sufficient moment of its own. Just as there is a proper way to dress at certain seasons of the year, so there is a proper time for each of life's essential experiences.

As soon as we begin to think of time in terms of seasons, we are open to a new and healthy sense of the right and wrong way to use the time God has given us. This world of artificial light and heat, in the confines of the city far away from nature, encourages us to forget that there are seasons at all. We take charge of the seasons; we bend them to our schedules. In the process, we have lost the rhythm of the seasons, the sense that there is an order which exists apart from our personal plans.

But deep inside we know some things cannot be rushed. Some things cannot be made to happen on our schedules.

The Bible suggests that we pause and ask ourselves: "What season is this for me right now? What is the most appropriate thing for me to be doing in this season of my life?" These questions are different from, "Am I on schedule?"

If each fundamental part of life has its own season, we need to recognize what season we are in. We need to learn what is most important for us to be doing now. Unless we know that, we might be wasting our time no matter how important our activities might appear to be.

Joan learned this when confronted with the near tragedy of her daughter's death. It was a season for mother and daughter to reestablish ties of love and concern. It was a season for Joan to become closer to her family and de-emphasize her career. Discover the season of your life and the mode of life appropriate for that season. You will know that you have all the time you need to do what's important.

Break the Bonds of an Unhappy Past

Now there was no water for the congregation; and they assembled themselves together against Moses and against Aaron. And the people contended with Moses, and said, "Would that we had died when our brethren died before the Lord! Why have you brought the assembly of the Lord into this wilderness, that we should die here, both we and our cattle? And why have you made us come out of Egypt, to bring us to this evil place? It is no place for grain, or figs, or

vines, or pomegranates; and there is no water to drink."
Then Moses and Aaron went from the presence of the
assembly to the door of the tent of meeting, and fell
on their faces. And the glory of the Lord appeared to
them, and the Lord said to Moses, "Take the rod, and
assemble the congregation, you and Aaron your
brother, and tell the rock before their eyes to yield its
water; so you shall bring water out of the rock for
them; so you shall give drink to the congregation,
and their cattle."

NUM. 20:2–8

The story of the Israelites' escape from Egypt holds immense
historical, political, and religious significance for Jewish
and Christian people today. It is symbolic of the search for
social, political, and economic freedom by oppressed peo-
ples all over the world.

It also teaches valuable lessons about the journey of
the human spirit. It shows us how to cope with the obstacles that block the way to freedom from the inner captiv-
ity of emotional and spiritual unhappiness. If we read the
story as a source of solutions to problems in our own
healing and growth, it is clear why it has been preserved
and retold for thousands of years.

For example, we all have these basic questions: Why
are we unhappy? What holds us in bondage to self-destructive
patterns of behavior and emotion? How can we break free
of these patterns?

Psychologists know it is easy to recognize how other
people are sabotaging their own lives as they speak to us of
their problems. However, it is another matter to have them

acknowledge the self-destruction or show them how to change. It is even more challenging to see self-destructive behavior in ourselves, even when others point it out.

Why are we unhappy? The passage from the Book of Numbers shows one important cause. The people of Israel escape from Egypt's bondage, but their troubles don't disappear. In the wilderness their lives are in danger. They run out of water, and without water for their livestock, their livelihood is gone. Were they better off as slaves?

We often face problems in breaking free from spiritual and emotional unhappiness. The way we think and act makes us miserable so we resolve to change. We take the first tentative steps, then we meet an unforeseen obstacle.

Like the Israelites, our impulse is to return to our old ways of coping with frustration and difficulty. We forget how damaging they were. We blind ourselves to the importance of change. We may even remember our old life as far better than it was.

If we give in to this temptation we are worse off than before, stuck deeper in the mud of old habits, discouraged and disheartened. This sort of failure makes us feel that change is impossible.

To avoid downward spiral, tap the solution the story holds. Here's how. Picture in your mind what you might say to the Israelites if they had asked you for advice. You would probably have said, "Have you forgotten how bad your life in Egypt was? If you stayed there, Pharaoh would have worked you to death. You can't go back there. Trust in your vision! You have come so far. Don't give up hope! Your destiny lies before you!"

Wonderful advice! Now, apply it to your own life! With the help of this biblical story, you have become your own therapist. The advice you gave to the people of Israel can heal you just as it would have healed them.

Healing is often blocked by fear of the unknown. We retreat to old patterns when our new choice presents a problem because the old ways are easy and comfortable.

Overcome this temptation by reminding yourself of the importance of the journey. Think back to how damaging the old ways were to you and to others. Then renew your resolve to press forward to a better life.

How to Handle Your Later Years

 The Lord said, "I will surely return to you in the spring, and Sarah your wife shall have a son." And Sarah was listening at the tent door behind him. Now Abraham and Sarah were old, advanced in age; it had ceased to be with Sarah after the manner of women. So Sarah laughed to herself saying, "After I have grown old, and my husband is old, shall I have pleasure?" The Lord said to Abraham, "Why did Sarah laugh, and say, 'Shall I indeed bear a child, now that I am old?' Is anything too hard for the Lord? At the

appointed time I will return to you, in the spring, and Sarah shall have a son." But Sarah denied, saying, "I did not laugh"; for she was afraid. He said, "No, but you did laugh."

GEN. 18:10–15

Happily we have come a long way in recognizing the many misconceptions and falsehoods about aging. But the writers of the Bible beat us by three thousand years!

Sarah is nearly ninety, well past menopause, when God announces she is to bear a child. Overhearing God's promise, Sarah laughs in disbelief. God playfully teases her when she denies it.

Sarah does give birth to Isaac in the next spring. Of course, physically giving birth in old age is a biblical miracle that only happens once. Still, Isaac's birth symbolizes the miracle of joy and happiness that can come to all of us at any age.

The point of the story is that old age need not and should not be a time of barrenness and decline. Rather, it should be a time in which we give birth to projects, ideas, schemes and adventures. We become idle and nonproductive only when we let ourselves believe that we can no longer contribute to the family, the community, and the world.

Idleness in our later years is dangerous. This is just the time when we need to plan a full schedule of creative ventures. The world is waiting for us. We can travel and explore the physical world. Or we can explore the world of ideas and thoughts—poetry, art, literature, theology, philosophy, music. The young don't have exclusive rights to the realms of the spirit.

Older people have much to teach us.

We have no better resource for understanding the past than those among us who have lived through and formed this history. We can only understand who we are when we know what we have been. We need to listen as our elders tell their story.

God challenges Abraham and Sarah to remain active and creative, to begin a new phase in their lives, a phase that is the most important and fruitful of all in establishing God's kingdom. Ask yourself as you plan for the coming years, "What 'children' will I have when I am older? What creative offspring will I produce after I have raised my family?"

FAMILY TIES

How to Honor Your Parents

🌿 Honor your father and your mother, as the Lord your
God commanded you, that your days may be
prolonged, and that it may go well with you, in the
land which the Lord your God gives you.

DEUT. 5:16

Most college students go through a stage of rebellion
against the religious, moral, and social ideals of their
parents. Their rejection is usually dramatic and angry. The
parents are hurt and resentful. They sacrifice and support
their children only to find them turning against everything the family believes in and reveres.

When concerned parents talk to me about this issue, I
advise them that their child's rebellion is a natural part of
becoming an adult. A young man or woman needs to
establish a sense of independence. In college they have the
freedom to experiment with ideas and explore different
points of view. Usually, in a few years, they find a secure
footing in their religious and moral lives that is very much
like that of their parents.

Often in these discussions, the commandment to hon-
or our father and mother comes up. Is the rebellion of

the college student a sinful refusal to obey this part of God's law?

My answer is no. I remind the parent that the commandment is not that we should obey our father and mother, or imitate them. It says that we should "honor" them, and this is quite a different matter. Furthermore, the commandment is more practical than it is moral. It tells us that honor will "prolong our days" and make things "go well." In other words, honoring our father and mother has a deeply therapeutic effect.

What is it to "honor" our parents? How does such honoring heal us?

The law is more than an obligation to the man and woman who have sacrificed so much to raise and educate us. It is also an affirmation of the whole family of man. The Bible asks us to celebrate our history, our culture, our system of values and our religious tradition.

This celebration and honoring recognizes the magnificent gifts passed to us from the previous generation. Our parents, the generation before us, were given the responsibility of caring for these gifts and increasing them. This responsibility was given to them by their parents of the generation before.

To honor our parents is to recognize that they have fulfilled that responsibility as best they could. They have made the necessary sacrifices. They have preserved and improved life where they were able.

Of course, they made mistakes. So did their parents, and the generation that preceded them. So will the generation that follows. We can recognize these mistakes. There is no aim at dishonor in the new generation's striving to be better than the preceding one. But each generation must also be aware of the debt it owes and the foundation that was laid for the children to build a better life.

To honor our parents, then, means that we foster a deep recognition of how fortunate we are. Those who have gone before us have given so much. Through them we received the gifts that were showered on all mankind. In honoring our parents we show our gratitude for all creation.

Parents are asked, in return, to live in a way that encourages children to accord them honor. We pay our debt to those who have preceded us by sharing in the continuing creation of a world of peace and harmony for our children.

To honor and be honored are two of life's greatest joys. The reverence and esteem we give and receive nourish and heal us.

The world offers lots of phony substitutes for honor: flattery, prestige, fame, popularity. We don't need to settle for poor imitations. We can give and receive honor in all that we do and say. True honor comes to us through our work as stewards of the earth, caring for our world and passing its beauty and riches to all those who follow.

Strengthening a Marriage

 And she said to him, "How can you say 'I love you,' when your heart is not with me? You have mocked me these three times, and you have not told me wherein your great strength lies." And when she pressed him

hard with her words day after day, and urged him, his soul was vexed to death. And he told her all his mind, and said to her, "A razor has never come upon my head; for I have been a Nazirite to God from my mother's womb. If I be shaved, then my strength will leave me, and I shall become weak like any other man."

JUDG. 16:15–17

Marriage should be a source of love and support for each partner. In a strong marriage both members grow and attain goals that would be impossible if each were alone. When a marriage is ailing, however, it can become a battleground, a struggle for domination. These struggles often disguise a deep-seated weakness both partners fear to acknowledge. The story of Samson and Delilah is a warning against the destructive consequences of such power struggles. We can learn from it how to find the real strength that marriage can offer.

One couple I know well learned this lesson the hard way.

Anthony and Diane had been married for nearly twenty-eight years. Anthony behaved badly during those years. He had cheated on his wife, gambled heavily, and spent much of what might have been their savings to pay his debts. Anthony thought of himself as a "man's man." He often spent evenings playing cards with friends and drinking. He imagined that his behavior convinced others that he was tough and strong.

Anthony had many admirable qualities. He loved and provided for his two children. Underneath all his bravado, it was easy to see that he adored his wife and wanted to do the right thing. However, in many ways, Anthony had never grown up. He was too self-centered and irresponsible.

In spite of it all, Diane stayed with the marriage. She knew that she and the children were the center of Anthony's life, even though he seldom showed how deeply he cared. But a crisis suddenly threatened to destroy the family entirely.

Anthony accumulated insurmountable gambling debts. Secretly, he took out a second mortgage on the house, and hid the papers. Diane discovered them one day while cleaning out a closet. She exploded in fury. It was too much. She had overlooked many things in their relationship, but this was beyond her patience or endurance.

Diane came to me for advice. "Should I divorce him?" she asked. "I know I could take him to the cleaners. I could make sure he would never see the children again. My lawyer tells me I could easily win damages and get support for as long as Anthony lives. I wish all this had never happened. But now that it has, I want to make him pay."

I reminded Diane of the biblical story of Samson and Delilah and suggested that she reread it for its wisdom. The story shows us that the problem of power is one of the greatest threats to human relationships.

Samson was one of the most powerful men who ever lived. He could conquer any opponent in a fight. Delilah had the power of beauty and charm. She could seduce even a great warrior like Samson. Yet Samson and Delilah were unable to have a healthy relationship together. Both were locked in a power struggle that blocked out true love.

In the end both abused the power they had. Samson's life was consecrated to the Lord. It was he whom God chose to help free the Israelites from the oppression of the Philistines. Instead, he became involved in sordid affairs and rough exploits that fed his vanity.

Delilah also abused her power. She could have found a deep love with Samson. Instead she chose to betray him for eleven hundred pieces of silver. She used her sexual power to ruin a man she might have loved.

Neither of these unfortunate characters used their power responsibly. Both were so caught up in the struggle to dominate and weaken the other that they destroyed their chance for happiness.

Power badly used can destroy a human relationship. When one person needs to control another, catastrophe and failure are inevitable.

The story also leads us to ask an important question: "What does it mean to be strong in a relationship?" The Bible teaches that true strength arises from our ability to communicate honestly and lovingly with others, especially people we care for. We have to understand and forgive the faults of our spouses to prevent the catastrophes that can happen so easily in modern marriage.

Diane saved her marriage. She realized that Anthony's problem with gambling required professional help. She made him see that his behavior was evidence of a serious psychological illness, not merely weakness. She made him aware of how harmful his behavior had been, and how hopeless their future would be if he continued as he was.

Anthony became convinced of his abusive and self-destructive behavior. Fortunately, he also recognized how

important his marriage and family were to him. He saw
how powerless he was against his addiction to gambling,
so he agreed to seek professional help. Through the strength
of love and understanding, this marriage survived the
destructive effects of weakness masquerading as power.

You Can Draw Your Family Closer

 And the son said to him, "Father I have sinned against
heaven and before you; I am no longer worthy to be
called your son." But the father said to his servants,
"Bring quickly the best robe, and put it on him; and
put a ring on his hand, and shoes on his feet; and bring
the fatted calf and kill it, and let us eat and make
merry; for this my son was dead, and is alive again; he
was lost, and is found."

LUKE 15:21–24

The precision of Jesus' stories is astonishing. In this single
simple tale of the prodigal son he portrays a wide array of
the difficulties we encounter in family life. Moreover, the
story tells us how to face these difficulties and keep our
family sound.

Keeping the family strong and united is a fundamental concern for each of us. Nearly every psychologist

agrees that the family is crucial to our emotional well-being. A child raised in a loving family is far more likely to develop into a normal and happy adult than one who grows up in a family that is at odds. Not only do happy families suffer less from anxiety and stress, they also stay healthier and live longer than others.

But today's world works against the family. The divorce statistics are startling; add to that the tension and violence many families experience. It's parents against children and children against parents and siblings. The personal pain and suffering is devastating. How can we avoid all this? The story of the prodigal son gives us valuable suggestions.

The family Jesus describes in this brief parable is surprisingly like so many modern families. The son is spoiled, rebellious, and self-assured. He is itching to get away from home. No doubt, he has been complaining for months about how his family treats him. He's already been in a scrape or two. He could develop into a serious problem.

And yet there is something likeable about him. He yearns to be free, to go out on his own. We understand his thirst for independence because we've all experienced it. We can imagine his argument with his father about the constraints of a conservative home. He wants to have things his own way.

The father is overindulgent, perhaps. Both parents have spoiled this child by giving him everything he asked for. They are shocked and saddened and hurt by his ungrateful behavior.

Surely they have often compared him to his brother,

the good guy who has worked so hard to please them. He has always done the right thing; his brother has always been in trouble. Yet the parents have always had a soft spot in their hearts for the younger misfit.

The younger son demands his inheritance, and the father generously gives it to him. It could not have been an easy decision. The father recognized his son's immaturity and worried about the boy's trying to make his way in the world. But he also knew that keeping his son back would only make matters worse. Living away from home might be dangerous and unpleasant, and the son might fail. The boy would have to learn that for himself.

The son was chastened by his disastrous odyssey. He returned as a wiser, more humble man with a true appreciation of his parents' accomplishments. Now he realized his own fallibility and his own weaknesses.

But now the tables turn. The older brother, who appeared to be so much better, shows a dark side—a side lacking forgiveness and understanding. Perhaps he was jealous. Perhaps he too yearned to escape from the family obligations, but he had done his duty, and now he was bitter about it. Paradoxically, the younger son, learning from his mistakes and foolishness, had become the wiser of the two.

We can learn a lot from this story about keeping the family together. The father could have been angry with his young son, scolding him severely for wasting his money and preaching to him about the squalor of life in the city. But the father was wise enough to know that life teaches some lessons so much better than sermons do. By supporting his child in spite of severe mistakes, the father showed the very kind of love that binds family members together in times of crisis.

The father explains to his other son the ultimate value of acceptance and support. Love and understanding, even in the face of a child's rebellion and anger, are the same forces that can protect and strengthen a family against any threat.

FRIENDSHIP

How to Be a True Friend

> This is my commandment, that you love one another as I have loved you. Greater love has no man than this, that a man lay down his life for his friends. You are my friends if you do what I command you. No longer do I call you servants, for the servant does not know what the master is doing; but I have called you friends, for all that I have heard from my Father I have made known to you.
>
> **JOHN 15:12–15**

We need intimate friendships. We need people we can trust. We need to share our fears and hopes with others who understand how we feel and think.

But these days, intimate friendships are rare. We have lots of excuses for not having close friends—too little time, so many obligations, always on the move. We can hardly find time to spend with our family, much less to form and nurture deep and lasting friendships. But the real reason for lacking friends usually goes much deeper. Many of us are not sure what real friendship means. We worry about the obligations it brings and what we might have to give up for friendship. Jesus clears it up very well in this passage.

A few months ago Kenny, a young salesman, came to me concerning doubts he had about friendship and intimacy.

"Last week I argued with my wife, before I left on a business trip to the Midwest. I decided to take the train. You know how I hate to fly. I sat next to a woman whom, admittedly, I found rather attractive. She seemed so warm and understanding. I found myself pouring out my deepest secrets to her. I told her things I would certainly not tell my wife, not even my friends. Why can I be open with a total stranger and not with those closest to me? Is there something wrong with me? With my marriage?"

Many of us have had similar sharing experiences with total strangers. And we're likely to mistake these moments of revelation for real friendship. Jesus shows us that true friendship is quite different. Real friendship has two crucial components: The first is commitment. The second is intimacy.

A true friend is willing to lay down his life for another. That doesn't mean real friendship is only proven in moments of physical danger. Rather, that the commitment of friendship extends beyond times of joy, to times of sadness and despair. We are resolved to maintain the relationship even when things go wrong, when disagreements threaten separation, when sacrifices are required of us to keep the friendship healthy.

Jesus showed his commitment to his friends, the disciples, in both his willingness to live and teach with the full depth of his spirit, and in his willingness to die to redeem them. He filled his short time on earth with an intensity and fervor that gave his friends a radical and powerful transforming experience. Like Kenny, we often think of intimacy as a sharing of our most shameful and hidden secrets. Jesus shows us that real intimacy comes when we share the best of ourselves and what we have with our friends. He tells his disciples, "All that I have heard from my Father I have made known to you." He has given his friends his most valuable things.

When we know the meaning of real friendship, we understand why it is so rare and valuable. It takes so much courage to show who we really are. Intimacy means vulnerability. It's always possible that when we offer what is most precious to us, it will be rejected.

Jesus took such risks with his disciples. He showed us the true nature of commitment and intimacy. He also demonstrated the healing power of true friendship. It can transform and sustain us in ways we could never expect. It gave the disciples the sense of love and community they needed to overcome enormous obstacles in establishing their church. It can work similar miracles in our own lives.

The Healing Power
of Friendship
in Times of Tragedy

 Now when Job's three friends heard of all this evil that had come upon him, they came each from his own place, Eliphaz the Temanite, Bildad the Shuhite, and Zophar the Naamathite. They made an appointment together to come to condole with him and com-

fort him. And when they saw him from afar, they did not recognize him; and they raised their voices and wept; and they rent their robes and sprinkled dust upon their heads toward heaven.

JOB 2:11–12

Mary Ann visited my office to talk about her closest friend, a delightful older woman, who had lost a son in an auto accident. The woman had been a kind and loving mother and a faithful member of the church. She was charitable and generous to her friends. The loss of her son sent her into despair.

"What can I say to this woman?" Mary Ann asked. "How can I help her? She didn't deserve this. She asks me why this happened to her, what terrible thing she did to deserve this. How can I help my friend? I worry that I might make matters worse."

Many of us will also be faced with Mary Ann's problem. How can we help our friends in time of despair and deep need? What can we say to ease their suffering and pain?

The story of Job speaks directly to this issue. Job is an innocent and righteous man who loses everything—his career, his wealth, even his ten children. Understandably Job becomes profoundly depressed. Three friends come to help him, but they botch the job. Through their bad example we can learn how not to deal with tragedy and suffering.

Support the sufferer, don't blame the victim. The first mistake Job's "friends" make is to let Job think they blame him for his suffering. Job must have sinned. No just and powerful God would allow an innocent person to suffer, so Job's tragedy must be punishment for some transgression.

We know Job was innocent and just. Many make such mistakes in these situations. Well-meaning friends tell the sufferer what he might have done to avoid the situation. They use the "if only" language. "If only you had been more careful . . ." "If only you had been calm . . . " "If only you hadn't spoken when you did . . . "

Such remarks can never be helpful. We all make mistakes, and bringing them up when a person is in despair never heals. It is a theological error to presume that pain and suffering are punishment from God. It is a therapeutic mistake to remind a person of his faults and shortcomings when he is in anguish.

Attend to your friends' real needs. Job's advisors never speak to Job's needs. Rather, they look to comfort themselves. They are frightened by Job's tragedy; maybe they'll be next. They want a guarantee that Job's fate won't be theirs.

The deep crises of others can affect us in surprising ways. At times, we who come to heal and comfort discover we need to be healed ourselves. The touch and presence of fellow sufferers is often therapeutic. But we must be careful to separate our own needs from those of our friends. Is our need to be helpful interfering with the true needs of our friends? Are we burdening them with more help than they want or can tolerate at the moment? Focus on the sufferer's needs by listening closely to what they ask of us. Often in tragedy, the sufferer only needs to know that we are there, that we truly care, and that we love them. Sometimes we do more good by listening than speaking.

Face the reality of the situation. Acknowledge the pain. Job's visitors never really acknowledge the tragedy

EMENT

owder Basin Mall

an

TOP TEN Video Rentals

*Call to reserve or come
by today to pick up your
favorite video.*

Come

on

of Job's condition. They care more about discussing theology than helping Job in his agony.

We are bumblers in the presence of tragedy. To avoid confronting it we make small talk, desperately pretending nothing is wrong. Sometimes speaking of mundane and ordinary matters can be helpful. (No one can concentrate on painful grief for a long stretch.) Our minds naturally allow breaks for relief. Small talk can help. But if we use small talk to hide from our friend's pain, we lose an opportunity to help. Expressing our sorrow and acknowledging the pain of our friend establishes deep and healing contact. Simple words showing our understanding can be powerful aids to others in the worst moments of grief.

Establish contact! A hug is worth a thousand words. None of Job's advisors actually touch Job. They never make human contact. In times of tragedy, the sufferer often feels isolated. We stand apart, waiting for some indication of how much contact and what kind of interaction the sufferer wants. We don't want to intrude.

These are the times that a simple gesture of concern can bridge the icy distance. A hug or touch can communicate concern and love that is beyond words.

Be honest! In the end, we doubt the sincerity of Job's friends. They lack something crucial for healing. They reveal nothing of themselves. Their reaction is just a way to hide from their own pain and fear.

When you comfort others, be open with your own feelings. Express your own fears, pain, and confusion. Confess to your own inability to understand, your own questions and doubts. You needn't pretend to have all the answers. Few of us do.

Sharing your grief and confusion can establish a deep

bond of understanding. When you acknowledge the reality of your limitations you relieve the sense of failure sufferers often feel.

We cannot take the pain away in times of tragedy. We cannot explain why it happened. But we can show our support, and the power of love and friendship can help to heal even the deepest wounds.

How to Repair a Damaged Relationship

You have heard that it was said to the men of old, "You shall not kill; and whoever kills shall be liable to judgment." But I say to you that every one who is angry with his brother shall be liable to judgment; whoever insults his brother shall be liable to the council, and whoever says, "You fool!" shall be liable to the hell of fire. So if you are offering your gift at the altar, and there remember that your brother has something against you, leave your gift there before the altar and go; first be reconciled to your brother, and then come and offer your gift.

MATT. 5:21–24

The Bible provides masterly advice on how to deal with others. This aspect of life is so important that Jesus urges—commands, in fact—that we repair damaged relationships at once. Even before we pray!

These repair jobs are often hard to carry out—especially when we're the ones who have been mistreated or misjudged. But the Bible has an answer for even those situations.

It was just the kind of healing wisdom my friend Allen needed. I found him pacing back and forth in his office, and he was clearly upset.

"The sales manager and I had a real go-round this morning," Allen said. "I presented the figures from my project survey, and they showed his department's profits had dropped quite a bit from last year. I know I was right because I double-checked my research. He wouldn't believe my report. He told me I was incompetent. The boss was standing there listening to us argue. It was embarrassing. But that guy is in real trouble. I can prove what I said."

When I found out that this was an ongoing battle between the two, I realized the situation could be damaging for both co-workers. I suggested we sit for a moment to discuss the problem, and I mentioned Matthew's passage on reconciliation as we talked.

In the beginning Jesus quotes an old and familiar law, "You shall not kill." This is both a legal and a moral principle. It is a fundamental rule of human coexistence. Undeniably, it's a law we must obey. But how do we handle the anger that doesn't lead to murder? Jesus is way ahead of us. He knows that people often fail to live up to the standards we set. Sometimes they even fail to live up to their own.

So Jesus wisely adds another dimension. He tells us to avoid being angry with or insulting to our fellowman. Of course, we all get angry now and then. And there are times when anger is a healthy and productive emotion.

But Jesus is talking about sustained anger that can damage us if we allow it to fester and grow. The judgment and council Jesus speaks about are not legal proceedings, but the stress and emotional pain we feel as a result of holding on to our negative feelings.

"There," Allen said, "I have that fellow again. Not only is he wrong about my report, he also insulted me in public. He is doing just what Jesus said he should not do. He is going to pay double, isn't he?"

"Yes," I said, "You do have him. He is probably wrong and you are legally right. But if you persist in the fight Jesus is going to turn the tables on you."

Jesus tells us what we must do if we have been insulted or mistreated. If our brother has something against us, we must go and be reconciled. Jesus says nothing here about who is right or wrong in the dispute. Even if we are the victim of the insult, he says we are still responsible for making the reconciliation.

This seems crazy. If we were acting only by the rules of what is just, the wrongdoer should be the one to make amends. But Jesus is teaching that human relationships must be based on compassion and understanding as well as justice. We cannot expect perfection from others. All of us fail, and we all act unfairly at one time or another. If we were to judge or be judged only on the basis of absolute justice, few relationships could survive.

Jesus stresses the importance of the matter. We must perform the reconciliation before we bring a gift to the altar. In other words, a damaged relationship interferes with our relationship to God as well as to man. We must not wait to decide who is right and wrong. To allow the bad feelings to continue only makes the reconciliation more difficult. Jesus tells us to fix it now, regardless of who is in the right.

Even when Allen saw the situation from this point of view, he was reluctant to take the first step. But when he did, he found the sales manager far more willing to listen than Allen ever expected. Later, they were able to form a working relationship that was productive for both.

Jesus teaches us to mend relationships even though we are the ones who have been wronged. We must treat others with more than justice if we want to live in a world of peace. By taking upon ourselves the responsibility and task of reconciliation, we can repair a damaged relationship and make it stronger than ever.

Healing a Rift
between Friends

 So shun youthful passions and aim at righteousness, faith, love, and peace, along with those who call upon the Lord from a pure heart. Have nothing to do with stupid, senseless controversies; you know that they breed quarrels. And the Lord's servant must not be quarrelsome but kindly to every one, an apt teacher, forbearing, correcting his opponents with gentleness. God may perhaps grant that they will repent and come to know the truth.

2 TIM. 2:22–25

John and Betty found themselves in the middle of a miserable situation when a couple who were close friends went through an emotionally painful divorce.

"We love both these people. But now they're pressuring us to choose between them. Each wants us to be on his or her side. It is painful to hear them bad-mouthing each other. What's worse, they want us to settle their disputes. We can't do that! Whatever we say will offend one or the other. What can we do?" When friends quarrel, we want to find the magic words that will bring them together again. But we soon learn that there is no magic formula. So we want to withdraw from the situation, leave the two alone to fight out their problems. But if we abandon friends in need, we chance losing them forever. Maybe we can't bring both sides together in harmony and peace. But we can provide damage control.

The Apostle Paul dealt with conflicts repeatedly in the days of the early church. He knew how quickly these disputes could escalate to levels where reconciliation was impossible. He also saw how other church members could be drawn into the argument. If Paul took sides it would leave the church community fragmented. Paul gives us clear advice about handling such situations.

First, Paul tells us to "shun youthful passions and aim at righteousness . . . ." In other words, when you find yourself in the middle of a destructive quarrel, avoid the temptation to take sides. Quarrels are emotionally charged. We all have biases and prejudices that lead us to believe one side is right, the other wrong—one side is good, the other bad. But in the end, such absolute divisions are seldom correct. In most disputes, especially those concerning interpersonal matters like divorce, each person has a share of responsibility for what has happened. We need to be fair in our evaluation of the situation.

The Bible urges us to be "kindly to everyone." There are a thousand ways to be kind. A sincere offer of help, an expression of concern, a shoulder for tears and support can mean everything to someone wounded and alone.

One welcome kindness is a listening ear for each side. Some people quarrel because they lose the means to communicate with one another, so they need to tell their side of the story to someone. That may be you.

You may be uncomfortable in this role, feeling as though you are required to sympathize and condemn. But you can make clear that you are willing to listen as a friend to both parties, with hope and prayer for their reconciliation. As a good listener you can help both sides to see more clearly what they want and what they fear.

Most important, you show both sides that they are not alone and that they still have common concerns, however obscured they might be at the moment. Paul tells us to be an "apt teacher." You may find a way to help each side to appreciate the importance of those common values.

Finally, it takes patience. The process of healing a bruised or scarred relationship can be a long one. But ultimately, a mutual respect can be reestablished. Each partner who truly seeks the truth about what is best for both parties, is likely to find a new form of expression for his or her love. We can be true friends during the process. We can be a healing force in any dispute by showing we have real concern for each individual involved. We can affirm each person without attacking the other. We can emphasize the common values and concerns that all share. And we can patiently hope for God to grant them the wisdom and grace to "know the truth," to overcome the painful division and renew the love and friendship that was before.

Turn Your Back on Destructive Relationships

🌿 Then the Lord rained on Sodom and Gomorrah brimstone and fire from the Lord out of heaven; and he overthrew those cities, and all the valley, and all the inhabitants of the cities and what grew on the ground. But Lot's wife behind him looked back, and she became a pillar of salt.

GEN. 19:24–26

A serious problem we face as our lives change over the years is dealing with old relationships that turn out to be destructive. Those who truly care for us enthusiastically encourage our growth and move with us as we change. But past relationships with certain others become a hindrance to our continued well-being. They can even be ruinous. What's the best way to handle these relationships without being selfish or disloyal?

This was a problem Agnes faced. She was one of the many marvelous older students who return to college campus—some to find new careers, others to fulfill longtime dreams of earning a degree, and many just to satisfy their curiosity. Agnes was a widow whose original purpose in attending college was to brush up on her career skills. She quickly became fascinated by her courses and decided to earn a degree, perhaps to go on to law school.

Unfortunately, many of her old friends were hostile to her new ideas and her heightened aspirations. They said Agnes was becoming a snob, trying to be better than they were. She stopped socializing with many of them, partly because she no longer had the time, and partly because so few of them shared her new interests. She did invite her old friends to the plays and movies that now interested her, but most of them refused.

"Maybe they're right," she said to me over coffee. "Maybe I should give this all up and go back to being a husbandless housewife. I used to enjoy sitting around with the gang, gossiping about the latest neighborhood scandal and getting drunk on the wine over lunch. Now all that seems so wasteful to me. Still they were my friends, or I thought they were."

"Going back to that life would turn you into a pillar of salt," I said. When Agnes asked me to explain, I told her the story of Lot's wife, in which the Bible strongly directs us to leave destructive relationships behind.

Lot and his family were the only righteous citizens left in the twin cities of Sodom and Gomorrah. When God decided to destroy these cities, he sent an angel to evacuate Lot's family before the holocaust. The evil townspeople attacked the angel and nearly raped Lot's children. Still, in spite of the violence and the coming destruction, Lot's family was reluctant to desert the city.

Finally the angel took charge and forcefully led the family out of the doomed city, warning them not to look back at the devastation. Lot's wife, however, could not resist the temptation of another look at her old haunts. She turned around and instantly turned into a pillar of salt.

In symbolic terms, Lot's wife had become paralyzed by her inability to leave a situation that threatened her growth and well-being. Her story reflects the difficulties we often face in abandoning unhealthy and destructive relationships because we think they offer security and protection. Even if it's painful, a familiar association sometimes seems better than being alone or starting from scratch to find a new and healthier group of friends.

The biblical story shows us that we must give up destructive lifestyles, otherwise we risk damage to ourselves and our family. With luck, we may find any number of angels willing to lead us out of the old life and into a new and better one. This "angel" may turn up in the form of a new career, professional counseling, a new set of friends, or a renewed interest in church or charitable activities. It could even be a new hobby or sport.

Starting in a new direction is a bit frightening for anyone. We are all creatures of habit. The first steps on the path to healthier living are seldom easy. Sometimes we need an angel to lead us by the hand, even to goad us with threats. We need to be aware of what might happen to us if we continue in our old ways. Sometimes, it takes a brush with disaster to make us aware that we must change our lives.

But one thing is certain: Once the break is made, we cannot look back to our old life. This is not a warning against a comforting nostalgia for the good old days. Nor is the Bible advocating that we randomly abandon our friends whose love and concern have sustained us.

However, the Bible tells us, some relationships are beyond hope. Like the cities of Sodom and Gomorrah, some relationships result in little more than abuse and pain, and continued involvement can only lead to deeper misery. Obviously the healthiest course of action is to follow the angel's lead and never look back.

Agnes realized that she could not take up with her old friends and resume their lifestyle if she hoped to pursue her new goals and aspirations. Her new life was richly rewarding. She was able to go forward happily with never a thought of returning to the boredom and stagnation she left behind.

DEALING WITH
YOUR FELLOWMAN

How to Be Successful without Hurting Others

He was praying in a certain place, and when he ceased, one of his disciples said to him, "Lord, teach us to pray, as John taught his disciples." And he said to them, "When you pray, say:

"Father, hallowed be thy name. Thy Kingdom come. Give us each day our daily bread; and forgive us our sins, for we ourselves forgive every one who is indebted to us; and lead us not into temptation."

LUKE 11:1–4

We often repeat the prayer that Jesus taught his disciples as a matter of habit, without thinking what it means to us about conducting our life.

In fact, this prayer is a guide to improving our inner life, and our life in the world as well. It tells us eloquently what to expect from life—and what not to expect! It speaks to the problems of pain and confusion so common among those who reach their goals, but do not find in their achievements the happiness they expected.

Success carries its dangers as well as its blessings. Many feel such a need to prove themselves that they give up their sense of right and wrong to do it. If they have to hurt others in their struggle to the top, so be it. Their only concern is how to avoid being caught in any wrongdoing.

Unfortunately, this tendency is rampant among young adults today. It's an attitude they credit to imitating their older mentors. The loss of a sense of values that follows can be devastating.

I know of many stories with this tragic theme. One that comes to mind concerns a young doctor. His family, poor and determined, literally saved their pennies to put him through medical school. He became the chairman of the department of neurology in a major university hospital. To all appearances, he was successful. But by the time he was forty, he had divorced his wife, had allowed himself to get into heavy debt, and had become addicted to recreational drugs. Then the hospital cut back its budget and found it necessary to slash the young doctor's salary by a third, and his crisis became acute.

"It is not just the loss of money," he said to me. "But I'm no longer practicing medicine in the way I wanted. Now I have to be concerned with hospital budgets, administrative costs, and lawsuits. I never have contact with a patient. I haven't touched a patient in months. I thought I was a successful human being. Now, I am not sure at all. I sacrificed my marriage and my friendships for this career. Now I have nothing I really wanted."

The prayer that Jesus gave his disciples is simple. But it can help to heal the tragedy that comes from damaged expectations and blighted hopes for happiness. Let's look closely at what it says.

Jesus asks us first to pray for our daily bread. He recognizes the need for basic necessities of life. We have to provide for ourselves and for those who depend on us.

However, the "bread" that Jesus speaks of here is not only material or physical goods, but emotional and spiritual necessities as well—self-esteem, love, a sense of security, the respect of others. The fulfillment of these spiritual needs is just as vital as the fulfillment of physical necessities.

It is right that we ask for all these from our Creator. Each of us deserves to have both kinds of requirements met. Success is more than material wealth; we need spiritual and emotional fulfillment too. Without it no amount of money in the bank, no houseful of possessions, will satisfy us.

Jesus also recognizes that in fulfilling our material and spiritual needs, we are bound to become indebted to others.

We don't live in this world alone. Our lives are intertwined with others' lives. This intertwining implies interdependence. Each of us owes much to others, and we can never fully repay it. Think of the sacrifices made for us all by our friends, our parents, our ancestors, and the human race as a whole.

When Jesus asks us to forgive and be forgiven our debts, he is asking us to recognize how much we owe others for our happiness and success. He wants us to realize how interconnected we are with others in the world.

Finally, Jesus tells us to ask that we not be led into temptation. Temptation is a natural human weakness. Who hasn't flirted with the idea of cheating to get to the top? Yet the success that comes in this way is no success at all. It can lead to misery and despair.

Keeping tight hold on our sense of right and wrong might slow us down, it's true. It might also cost us in material wealth. But the spiritual returns will more than compensate for the loss.

The next time you pray the Lord's Prayer, think of it as a prayer for "success" in the broadest sense of the word. It is a prayer for a life of harmony and balance. It is a prayer for satisfaction and for the comfort of being with others in peace.

The Healing Power of Forgiveness

Then Peter came up and said to him, "Lord, how often shall my brother sin against me, and I forgive him? As many as seven times?" Jesus said to him, "I do not say to you seven times, but seventy times seven.

"Therefore the kingdom of heaven may be compared to a king who wished to settle accounts with his servants. When he began the reckoning, one was brought to him who owed him ten thousand talents; and as he could not pay, his lord ordered him to be sold, with his wife and children and all that he had, and payment to be made. So the servant fell on his knees, imploring him, 'Lord, have patience with me, and I will pay you everything.' And out of pity for him the lord of that servant released him and forgave him the debt. But that same servant, as he went out, came upon one of his fellow servants who owed him a hundred denarii; and seizing him by the throat he said, 'Pay what you owe.' So his fellow servant fell down and besought him, 'Have patience with me, and I will pay you.' He refused and went and put him in prison till he should pay the debt.

"When his fellow servants saw what had taken place, they were greatly distressed, and they went and reported to their lord all that had taken place. Then his lord summoned him and said to him, 'You wicked servant! I forgave you all that debt because you besought me; and should not you have had mercy on your fellow servant, as I had mercy on you?' And in anger his lord delivered him to the jailers, till he should pay his debt. So also my heavenly Father will do to every one of you, if you do not forgive your brother from your heart."

MATT. 18:21–35

This description of Jesus' teaching about forgiveness is one of the most paradoxical in all of the Gospel. Yet it holds profound wisdom about the importance of loving and creative human relationships. Jesus wants to teach us how deeply we depend on others for our own spiritual and emotional health. It is essential that we keep the flow of support and love open among ourselves. Jesus' story explains how it's done.

It opens with Peter's question about how many times we should forgive. Jesus betters Peter's original suggestion

of seven times when he answers, " . . . seventy times seven."
Then Jesus tells a strange parable. A king forgives his
servant's debts. But when that same servant fails to forgive
his own debtors, the king throws the greedy man into jail,
refusing to forgive again.

Like most of Jesus' parables, this one sets our minds
reeling. Why was the king so unforgiving the second
time? Shouldn't he too forgive his servant "seventy times
seven" times? Will God not forgive us when we make
more than one mistake? On first reading, the story seems
to be inconsistent with the moral teaching of forgiveness
the story is supposed to support.

When we seek for deeper meaning, however, the
power of the story to show us the dynamic power of
forgiveness in our lives becomes clear.

In the story, Jesus shows us the effects of our refusal to
forgive both on ourselves and others. First, Jesus reminds
us that none of us are without debt and blame for some
fault or failure. The unforgiving servant is deeply indebted
to his lord. Like him, each of us wants and needs forgiveness of our debt from others.

Unfortunately, we are often unmindful of our need
to forgive. Even though we rely on compassion from
others, we often refuse it to those who have wronged us in
some way. In our worst moments, we imagine ourselves to
be morally superior. We act self-righteous and are
condescending. We demand payment, usually in guilt
or shame.

The second point Jesus makes is that such demands
for payment seriously damage our chances of closeness
with others. Like the servant of the story, when we refuse

to forgive others, we strangle our own friendships. The mental and spiritual barriers we erect starve us as much as they impoverish our friends.

We all need others to depend on for support and understanding. People who have strong relationships with others deal with stress and crisis better. They are less likely to experience emotional crises. They are more creative and flexible in solving their problems and achieving their goals.

People who are unable to tolerate others' faults, and who would rather punish than help, finally become miserable themselves. They shut themselves off from the healing power of loving relationships.

Jesus wants us to know that God forgives mistakes. Helpful and forgiving attitudes are essential for our own well-being. So learn to forgive often and freely, and receive the gifts of mutual love and support in return.

A Healthy Attitude toward Sex

 Then God said, "Let us make man in our image, after our likeness; and let them have dominion over the fish of the sea, and over the birds of the air, and over the cattle, and over all the earth, and over every creeping thing that creeps upon the earth." So God created man in his own image, in the image of God he created him; male and female he created them.

GEN. 1:26–27

If asked to choose one topic that separates the teachings of the Bible from modern psychology, most people would say, "Sex." The Bible has an undeserved reputation for being prudish and even antisexual. In fact, the Bible gives sound advice on healthy and responsible sexuality.

The Book of Genesis tells us that the gift of sexuality is a fundamental part of creation. As such it is good. This goodness continues throughout time.

For humans, having a child is our most creative act. Nothing else can match the magic of bringing another person into the world. Sexuality finds its fulfillment and sanctity as a part of this magic. Sexuality is a divine gift, and "very good."

Some religious thinkers miss this point. They argue that sexuality is connected to the physical. The physical is not the spiritual, and therefore it is at best inferior, and perhaps, evil. Consequently, sex, too, must be evil.

This argument is simply wrong because it ignores the biblical insistence that God's creation is good throughout. The notion that physical creation or any part of it is ugly, disgusting, or evil clearly contradicts the text. Only if creation were essentially evil, could we accept this point of view. Genesis tells us just the opposite.

This argument can be severely damaging psychologically. It can destroy a healthy sexual relationship. People who see the body as impure often have difficulty accepting the pleasure the body can give in the sexual act. They might link pleasure with guilt and pain, or they might idealize love to exclude sexuality altogether. In either case, a joyful and satisfying sexual relationship is impossible.

The Bible shows us that responsible sexuality arises

from reverence for creation and reverence for ourselves. Again, the Bible provides sound advice. In religious terms, the Bible asks us to recognize that we and our partners are beings created in the image of the Divine. As likenesses of God, we are obligated to treasure each other in the sexual act. In psychological terms, we know that mutual respect for each others' needs, both physical and emotional, are essential. Any other approach to sexuality only results in abuse.

To use another person selfishly is to exploit creation. It is the same misuse of creation as a violation of our dominion over the earth's other resources. If we squander the natural gifts of this world, we face a self-inflicted extinction. If we squander the gift of sexuality, we lose the value and splendor that sex can offer us.

For many, the counseling of the Bible about sex suggests that only within marriage is sexuality permissible or healthy. Certainly, the Bible offers a stern prohibition against adultery. Family therapists tend to agree that promiscuity in marriage is nearly always destructive. The notion of the "open marriage" is now generally acknowledged to be unworkable.

On the other hand, the Bible harbors few illusions concerning the weaknesses of men and women on this score. Many biblical heroes succumbed to sexual temptation repeatedly. For those who are quick to condemn others, Jesus reminds us that anyone who "looks at a woman lustfully has already committed adultery in his heart." For Jesus, the inner thought is as effective and telling as the outward act. His observation condemns us all, as anyone who is honest within himself will acknowledge.

Furthermore, Jesus was quick to forgive sexual mistakes and soothe the suffering that such mistakes caused.

The crucial issue is not promiscuity. The mistake we must avoid is to abuse the gift of sex in such a way that we cause pain to others and ourselves. To do so is a waste of the best of what creation has to offer. We must learn to use the gift of sexuality to realize its full potential for giving joy and life.

Keeping Your Commitments

And God said, "This is the sign of the covenant which I make between me and you and every living creature that is with you, for all future generations: I set my bow in the cloud, and it shall be a sign of the covenant between me and the earth. When I bring clouds over the earth and the bow is seen in the clouds, I will remember my covenant which is between me and you and every living creature of all flesh; and the waters shall never again become a flood to destroy all flesh."

GEN. 9:12–15

Students in my classroom love to talk about the "sixties generation." You're probably not surprised. It's part of the classic picture: college students exchanging views on sex, drugs, and dropping out. But those things aren't really central to our discussions. It's the sense of commitment those sixties students showed that captures the imagination and admiration of today's young people. I'm reassured by their interest in a concern that is as important today as it was a generation ago. These youngsters want to understand what it means to make a commitment. Can we get through life without making commitments? How can we sustain the commitments we make when others care so little about their own?

Students say their elders give the impression that a commitment is in force only as long as it's convenient to carry out. As soon as a commitment becomes a burden we can throw it in the trash.

The Bible view is far different. God's promise to mankind in the story of Noah is a model of genuine commitment. It reveals the nature of commitment and assures us that commitments are essential to the human spirit. It also shows us how to keep our commitments to ourselves and to each other.

The notion of commitment troubles us. On the one hand, we sense a need for the dedication and direction serious commitment brings. On the other, we worry that our commitments might trap us in causes that abuse our trust. The causes that seek our support in terms of time or money once fired our emotions, but now disappoint us.

On a personal level, many of us find it hard to sustain commitments. In frivolous matters it may not mean so much. All of us cheat on diets and forget New Year's resolutions by February. But to break a commitment to marriage, to friendships, to our children, or to our deepest principles, is serious business. In fact, people who cannot keep commitments at all must be counted as emotionally impaired. The devastating emotional cost to themselves and those around them indicates the need for professional counseling.

In the story of Noah, God makes a commitment or "covenant" with mankind and all earthly creatures. Never again, he says, will the world be destroyed by flood. The rainbow is to serve as an eternal reminder of this commitment made to "all future generations."

This wonderful narrative shows how commitments preserve our relationships with others. It assures us that the relationship between God and man is guaranteed. The covenant shelters us against his justifiable wrath toward human wrongdoing. Without it our relationship with him might shatter.

This is true of relationships between people, too. If a relationship is to endure, it requires commitment. Without it the family will crumble and friendships will dissolve. Without a reliable promise to keep agreements and contracts, commerce would be impossible. Our communities would fall apart if we failed to honor the rules that guide them. The ability to make and keep commitments is essential to our personal and social life in the widest possible sense.

The story of God's covenant with Noah also teaches us that our commitments give us an identity, determine our character. Commitments result from the choices we make. When we find commitments difficult to make or keep, it suggests that we don't really know who we are or what we want to be. Those who lack commitment entirely have no center to their existence. They resemble a rudderless ship sailing in a storm.

This means that we need to make and keep commitments. They are a path to psychological and emotional health. We choose to be strong and effective by making responsible commitments to ourselves and others. Lasting promises give our lives stability and bring the rewards of strong and caring relationships.

What are the secrets of making and keeping commitments? The story of Noah shows that we must choose carefully when we commit ourselves. God based his covenant on experience with the evils of mankind and the catastrophe of the flood. We can make effective commitments too, if we learn from our experience. Committing to impossible goals or making commitments without considering what might change in the future is dangerous. We must take into account what we know about ourselves and others before we make any promises.

Another help in keeping commitments is to establish a symbol of that commitment and keep it visible. Don't underestimate the importance of symbols. As the story of Noah shows, commitments depend on memory and even God set up a reminder of his promise—the rainbow. We, too, need reminders of our commitments. This is why we wear a wedding ring on our finger or keep family pictures on our office desk. These symbols keep us aware of our commitments to family relationships. We can remind ourselves of other commitments in similar ways.

As God gives us an example of firm commitment in the story of Noah, we must give examples of strong and enduring commitment to our children and to future generations. The choices we make and the way we keep our promises influence the character of those we touch.

Young people watch what we do and compare it to what we say. Just as human existence depends on God's keeping his covenant, the endurance of our society depends on what our own actions teach our children.

What Envying Others Says about Your Life

🌿 Neither shall you covet your neighbor's wife; and you shall not desire your neighbor's house, his field, or his manservant, or his maidservant, his ox, or his ass, or anything that is your neighbor's.

DEUT. 5:21

Much American advertising urges us to ignore the tenth commandment. Television and radio ads get us to buy things we don't need or want by telling us our neighbors have them. The ads encourage us to make our neighbors envious. What fun to flaunt our good fortune and make them sick with jealousy!

Given this contemporary tendency, it is worth exploring the significance of the tenth commandment. How and why is it important to our well-being?

Common sense provides one answer. Coveting our neighbors' possessions, especially a spouse, is simply the path to conflict.

We can tell ourselves that harboring secret illegitimate desires for someone or something is all right so long as we don't act on them. In fact, we put ourselves in danger of losing the battle, forgetting the consequences, and following our desires wherever they lead.

The commandment advises that we deliberately direct our desires toward more beneficial and accessible objects. Temptation is thwarted and we live on good terms with our community.

But the issue is deeper and more serious. The commandment points to a problem that threatens everyone when life isn't fulfilling. The intensity of unlawful desire is a symptom of an emotional privation that should be attended to as soon as it appears.

That becomes obvious when we question the source of our desire for someone else's possessions. Why do we want what is out of our reach or forbidden? Why is the attraction so strong? Are those possessions really necessary to us? Are they so much better than anything readily available to us?

Probably they are not. The only thing that distinguishes them is that they belong to someone else. Our fascination with other people's possessions is really a fascination with the people themselves and the life they lead. When we feel empty and harbor profound doubts about our own worth, we envy what appears to be a fullness in our neighbor's existence.

When we covet our neighbors' possessions we are really trying to fill our own emptiness by becoming someone else. We want to take on their identity or at least the part of it we lack ourselves.

Naturally, we cannot steal such intangible qualities as happiness and joy, so we try for what seems to be the nearest substitute, material goods. We want to believe we can find meaning and identity in the outward trappings of another's life.

Failure is inevitable. The tenth commandment warns us that we can never find the path to our own development by appropriating someone else's. We can learn from others' successes; we can also avoid their mistakes. But we must live our lives and win or lose our own battles.

How to Overcome Rejection

And behold, a Canaanite woman from that region came out and cried, "Have mercy on me, O Lord, Son of David; my daughter is severely possessed by a Demon." But he did not answer her a word. And his disciples came and begged him, saying, "Send her away, for she is crying after us." He answered, "I was sent only to the lost sheep of the house of Israel." But she came and knelt before him, saying, "Lord, help me." And he answered, "It is not fair to take the children's bread and throw it to the dogs." She said, "Yes Lord, yet even the dogs eat the crumbs that fall from their master's table." Then Jesus answered her, "O woman, great is your faith! Be it done for you as you desire." And her daughter was healed instantly.

MATT. 15:22–28

The story of the Canaanite woman is one of the most painful and baffling of the Gospels. It shows us the humanity of Jesus and his disciples, and the inevitable mistakes that come as a result of this humanity. At the same time, it is poignant and healing. It can help us deal with one of the most upsetting emotional problems in life—rejection.

The Canaanite woman comes to Jesus with a real and desperate problem. Her daughter is possessed by a demon. (We would say, today, the girl was mentally ill.) We know from the woman's persistence how desperate she was to find a cure. We can be sure the whole family felt the painful effects of this illness. The helplessness they experienced, the social stigma attached to this sort of disease, the practical difficulties of caring for someone who cannot cope with reality—these are enormous even in modern society. Imagine how bad it was for the family in ancient times.

We sympathize with the mother. Her need is real and her motives are the best. The gospel writers do not allow easy excuses for what happens next.

We hope that a woman who comes to Jesus and his disciples for healing under these circumstances will find a sympathetic and kind reception. We pray that if we were ever burdened with this same kind of problem, we would find others to help us. The woman expected compassion from a man of God and his disciples, perhaps even a cure for her daughter.

But all expectations are shattered. Instead of compassion, the woman is rebuffed.

First the disciples try to send her away. They are traveling in a foreign country. Perhaps they have had a difficult time and everyone is tired. Perhaps they are not willing to help a woman who does not share their faith. Still, we are startled. Shouldn't these men at least have given the woman a hearing?

The woman persists. She is desperate. She will be as annoying and obtrusive as necessary to get help. She does not allow the rejection to stop her.

The disciples don't want to deal with this woman any longer. They turn to Jesus for help in getting rid of her.

At last, we think, the mother will find help with Jesus, the master therapist and healer. Certainly, he will be able to treat the girl. He is compassionate and loving. He will not reject this woman.

We are shocked and disappointed. Jesus first refuses to speak with her. Then she breaks through the protective circle of disciples and pleads with the Rabbi on her knees.

Instead of help, Jesus insults her. "It is not fair to take the children's bread and throw it to the dogs."

We cannot know why Jesus said such cruel words. We hope he had a healing motive that even the gospel writers did not comprehend.

But we must accept the possibility that this gospel merely shows the humanity of Jesus. Perhaps he, too, was momentarily blinded by the prejudice and bigotry of his culture. Perhaps, for an instant, he did not realize that the woman who knelt before him could have the same faith and devotion as any of his disciples. Perhaps Jesus made a mistake.

Whatever we think of the case, Matthew (and Mark as well) are absolutely honest in telling the story. They do not attempt to give excuses.

Most of us would have crumbled at Jesus' words. Facing this sort of rejection would be unbearable. We all need acceptance and love from those around us. We all need to be told we are worthwhile human beings. We need praise for our achievements and sympathy for our failures. Most of all, we need to know that support and aid are available when we face severe trials.

The woman did not crumble. With enormous strength and courage, she rose from the pain and anguish she felt, and responded with a precision and dignity that no one, including Jesus, could deny. "Yes, Lord, yet even the dogs eat the crumbs that fall from their master's table."

The power of her response lies in her unwillingness to accept any rejection as absolute and final. She knows, deep within, that her mission is one of love and caring. With this inner assurance, she can tolerate rejection and refusal to acknowledge her value and her suffering. Nothing can turn her from her basic faith in her own humanity and the humanity of others.

Her faith is universally healing. Jesus immediately recognizes its power and rewards her. The woman's courage in the face of rejection brings healing to her daughter.

We can learn the healing power of this faith. It is based on a simple, unswayable determination to look beyond all external differences, to the humanity of all. With this kind of faith, we can face any rejection, no matter what the source.

How to Stop Trying
to Control Others

🌿 Afterward Moses and Aaron went to Pharaoh and
said, "Thus says the Lord, the God of Israel, 'Let my
people go, that they may hold a feast to me in the
wilderness.' " But Pharaoh said, "Who is the Lord,
that I should heed his voice and let Israel go? I do not
know the Lord, and moreover I will not let Israel go."

EXOD. 5:1–2

The Pharaoh in the story of Exodus symbolizes the unhealthy
emotional response many people have when they are
threatened or challenged. Pharaoh is so addicted to author-
ity and control of others that he destroys his family and
risks his nation to maintain power over the Jewish people.

It's hard to admit it, but we all have a bit of the
Pharaoh in us. Each of us feels vulnerable and protective
about some part of our life. If that "territory" is threatened,
we are quite likely to act as the Egyptian ruler did.

Of course we need some control over ourselves and
our environment to live. But when the need to control
becomes an addiction, and we try, inappropriately, to
extend our power over others, we risk serious damage to
them and ourselves.

The trouble is that we can easily persuade ourselves
that we want control and power for legitimate reasons.
We are only doing what is necessary to help ourselves,

only making it easier for others by giving them helpful advice.

At first, Moses requests only that his people be allowed to go to the wilderness to worship God. Pharaoh's immediate refusal of this simple request illustrates his fears that he will lose control of his slaves when they are out of sight. A Pharaoh secure in his might could have decided, rationally, that the Israelites would work better once their need to worship had been satisfied.

Pharaoh's most significant remark in his conversation with Aaron and Moses is "Who is the Lord that I should heed his voice . . . ?" Pharaoh is in the position of all those who allow their insecurities to dominate them. He can only alleviate his deepest fear by demanding absolute power over life. As long as there is anything or anyone to harm or challenge him, he will not rest easy.

Pharaoh is unrealistic. Psychologically and emotionally mature people recognize that life is always somewhat uncertain. To pretend otherwise is to delude ourselves with the idea that we have godlike powers, that we are greater than anything in the universe.

The way to overcome the harmful desire for absolute control over our lives is simply to accept the reality that such control is impossible. Pharaoh learns this lesson through a series of horrible plagues. We can avoid paying such a high price for addiction to power by anticipating the personal tension and broken relationships it can cause. The impulse to abandon our addiction follows naturally.

We soon feel the benefits of our new attitude. We escape the tension of trying to force the world to be "right" according to our criteria. We find a renewed sense of relationship when we allow others to be themselves.

The Danger of Judging Others

🌿 And as he sat at the table in the house, behold many tax collectors and sinners came and sat down with Jesus and his disciples. And when the Pharisees saw this, they said to his disciples, "Why does your teacher eat with tax collectors and sinners?" But when he heard it, he said, "Those who are well have no need of a physician, but those who are sick. Go and learn what this means, 'I desire mercy, and not sacrifice.' For I came not to call the righteous, but sinners."

MATT. 9:10–13

Jesus repeatedly shocks the sensibilities of those around him. He heals on the Sabbath, he speaks against dietary laws, and, in this story, he eats with tax collectors and sinners.

Jesus has a motive behind what he does. Not only does he heal the people he is with, he surprises and confuses his disciples, his critics—and us! He goads us into throwing away old prejudices and putting ourselves and others into a fresh perspective. By looking in this new way, we may come to recognize and understand a healing truth.

This time, Jesus is trying to introduce us to a new notion of what it means to be "righteous." In biblical times, righteousness was more than a moral concept. It was a pattern for living that sustained a person on every level, from the social and ethical to the spiritual and psychological. In Jesus' day, the concept of right-eousness was the concept of the right way to live every waking moment.

As you read this story, imagine yourself in the Phari-sees' position. Consider for a moment whom you admire as good, upstanding people. Each of us has a set of stand-ards we would apply in choosing this group. It's our sense of righteousness we use in such a situation.

When the Pharisees challenge Jesus on his choice of supper companions, they are really asking him if he shares their standards of righteousness. If so, why is he associating with the dregs of society? Doesn't he know how bad these people have been? Isn't he excusing their past behavior by socializing with them?

At first, Jesus seems to be placating the Pharisees. In effect, he tells the Pharisees, "Someone is sick here. Some-one needs therapy. I am a physician and a therapist. I am only doing my job."

Of course the Pharisees assume Jesus is speaking of his dinner companions at the table, as we do, unless we read carefully. These wretched sinners must be sick, the Phari-sees think, look how different they are from us good folks.

But Jesus turns the Pharisees and our own presump-tions on their head. "Go and learn what this means, 'I desire mercy, and not sacrifice.'"

With these words, Jesus challenges the standard notion of righteousness. Jesus tells the Pharisees that righteousness is not a matter of performing the correct ritual sacrifices. In modern terms, simply living up to the outward stand-ards of conduct is not the whole story in how to behave. First, we must live by the rule of mercy.

Jesus subtly leads us to wonder who in this story needs a physician most, the sinners at the table or the Pharisees who don't recognize their own sickness in refusing to allow mercy to govern their attitudes and actions.

Now our impulse may be to condemn the Pharisees. What self-righteous hypocrites they are. What pompous merciless sinners.

Again we are caught up short. We are reacting exactly as the Pharisees did.

Jesus ultimately asks us to question ourselves. How often have we shut mercy out of our own life? How often have we condemned others for not living up to our standards of right and wrong? How often have we condemned ourselves?

The Pharisees need healing far more than the sinners at the dinner table. They need it so desperately because they are unable to see how spiritually ill they are. Eating at the table, the communion with others, is the symbol for healing companionship and understanding. As long as we hold ourselves aloof from this healing community, as long as we fail to see our own shortcomings, we can never begin to grow and recover.

Jesus teaches us that any notion of righteousness that allows us to condemn and reject others will ultimately lead to sickness. We must understand that all of us are sinners, all of us are imperfect, all of us fail to meet the standards we set for ourselves and for other people.

True righteousness means that we will be merciful equally to ourselves and all others in the world. As a community of sinners, we can all sit at the table together in loving understanding.

Turn Unfairness into a Blessing

 For the kingdom of heaven is like a householder who went out early in the morning to hire laborers for his vineyard. After agreeing with the laborers for a denarius a day, he sent them into his vineyard. And going out about the third hour he saw others standing idle in the marketplace; and to them he said, "You go into the vineyard too, and whatever is right I will give you." So they went. Going out again about the sixth hour and the ninth hour, he did the same. And about the eleventh hour he went out and found others standing; and he said to them, "Why do you stand here idle all day?" They said to him, "Because no one has hired us." He said to them, "You go into the vineyard too." And when evening came, the owner of the vineyard said to his steward, "Call the laborers and pay them their wages, beginning with the last, up to the first." And when those hired about the eleventh hour came, each of them received a denarius. Now when the first came, they thought they would receive more; but each of them also received a denarius. And on receiving it they grumbled at the householder, saying, "These last worked only one hour, and you have made them equal to us who have borne the burden of the day and the scorching heat." But he replied to them, "Friend, I

am doing you no wrong; did you not agree with me
for a denarius? Take what belongs to you and go; I
choose to give to this last as I give to you. Am I not
allowed to do what I choose with what belongs to
me? Or do you begrudge my generosity? So the last
will be first, and the first last."

MATT. 20:1–16

It's certainly no news that life is unfair. In fact, almost
anyone you ask can talk for ten minutes on the unfair
experiences of any given day. But the Bible teaches us how
to turn the unfairness we encounter so often into a blessing.
My niece, Jennifer, and I learned this together.

She called me in tears. She had written what she
thought was an excellent term paper. But the professor
had given her only a B. "It just isn't fair," she said. "I'm not
going back to that class. I'm dropping the course. Mine
was far better than anything Jody ever wrote and she got
an A. I stayed up two nights in a row finishing that paper.
Jody handed in her first draft. Even if mine weren't a great
paper (and I think it is), it would still be better than hers."

I asked Jennifer to come over and bring the paper, so
we could sit down together and talk. During our conversation we checked the Bible for some advice on this matter,
and I headed straight for the Book of Matthew and the
parable of the laborers in the vineyard. Here Jesus tells the
story of a householder who pays the same wages to workers
who are hired an hour before quitting time as he does to
workers who spend the whole day doing the identical job.

"You know," Jennifer said, "I have to admit that
those early workers have a point. Is Jesus asking us to

accept economic injustice? People who work longer hours should be paid more."

I explained to Jennifer that Jesus' parables are often surprising paradoxes that catch us when we aren't looking. It is this "catch" that so often gives us the healing insight. I asked Jennifer to join me in a game I often use to find the deeper meaning of biblical stories.

"Pretend you're one of the early workers," I said. "How does it feel?"

"He must have felt just like I feel now," she said. "Angry and hurt."

"Now," I said. "Pretend for a moment you are one of the latecomers. How does that feel?"

"I feel great. Just like the time I found that ten dollar bill in the park."

I told Jennifer that Jesus knows we will, in all probability, identify with the worker who feels sorry for himself. So often we are sure that the world is against us, that we are not getting what we have coming. For some people this sense of tragedy is a way of life. The chip on their shoulder will never come off. This self-pitying attitude threatens to interfere with their ability to relate to others or to function in the world.

But the other side of Jesus' story is the worker who had the good fortune to be hired late. He too was treated unfairly. In his case, the unfairness worked to his advantage. We would say he was lucky. Jesus wants us to consider this side of the issue too. We never complain when the world's unfairness works to our advantage. Ethiopians are starving and we have plenty to eat; auto workers get laid off and we work steadily; our son is a football star, theirs is killed by a drunk driver. We rarely notice how lucky we are—or how unfair our good fortune really is.

Jesus wants us to realize that we often receive far more than we deserve. It's good therapy to consider how often we have been the workers who arrived late and were paid well anyway. Most of us have gotten much more out of life than we ever dared hope for. It's so easy to forget those times when some lucky happening turned an impossible predicament into a piece of good fortune. We can, of course, concentrate on the negatives and ignore the positives of life. We can nurture resentment about the unfairness in the world, and refuse to be happy in the face of it. But this is hardly what Jesus has in mind.

Jesus makes the point that we must try to see the unfairness we encounter as a challenge. Rather than use it to excuse failure or indulge in self-pity, Jesus teaches that the healthy way to cope with unfairness is to change these experiences around. See unfairness as a signal that something needs improvement, as a golden opportunity to change our lives and the world we touch for the better.

This is exactly what Jennifer did. She decided to take her paper back to the professor and ask for suggestions for revising it. He was so impressed with her interest, she later told me, that he invited her to publish the revised version in the school's literary magazine.

An experience of unfairness can be an opening for us to make a change where one is needed. Accepting the challenge of unfairness is the best kind of healing medicine.

Mature Love Embraces Everybody

🌿 Joseph, being seventeen years old, was shepherding the flock with his brothers; he was a lad with the sons of Bilhah and Zilpah, his father's wives; and Joseph brought an ill report of them to their father. Now Israel loved Joseph more than any other of his children, because he was the son of his old age; and he made him a long robe with sleeves. But when his brothers saw that their father loved him more than all his brothers, they hated him, and could not speak peaceably to him.

GEN. 37:2–4

The romantic picture of love leaves out the hardships we encounter in learning to love one another. Mature and responsible love is the product of experience and of the wisdom that experience brings. It does not necessarily come naturally to us.

The story of Joseph takes up more than the last third of the book of Genesis as it explores this issue. It is a story of estrangement and reconciliation. It shows how immature love can separate and isolate us, and how responsible love can bring us back together.

When Israel gave his favorite son, Joseph, a multicolored coat, he must have known it would cause trouble.

The story tells us clearly, the father loved his youngest more than his other children. He did not hide the fact. Quite the contrary, he made it painfully clear to everyone.

We would never doubt that the love Israel felt for his son was real. But we would question the maturity and wisdom of his love. It was exclusive and selective. He loved Joseph so much that he loved the others less.

The brothers wanted and needed their father's love as much as Joseph did. But it was not there for them. When Joseph reported their misbehavior to his father, it only made the gulf wider. It seemed that Joseph was trying to cut them off entirely from what little affection they had.

When love excludes others from intimacy and caring we must question its wisdom. Sometimes, this exclusivity is legitimate. The love of man and wife, for example, does not allow that same kind of love to extend to others. The marriage vows consciously exclude others from this kind of intimacy. But when the love of man and wife disallows other kinds of love, say to children and friends, that love is a prison for each partner.

Joseph's brothers came to hate the love between him and their father. They hated Joseph for having that love; they hated the robe that symbolized it. When they sold Joseph into slavery and smeared his robe with blood, their hatred had overcome their moral consciousness. Their hatred created a gap in the family structure that might never be reconciled.

Joseph learns the lesson of mature love during his years in Egypt. His first painful experience with sexual love and its potential for deceit and violence is devastating. His master's wife attempts to seduce him, and when Joseph rebuffs her, she accuses him unjustly of attempted rape and has him jailed. Again Joseph survives. Slowly, Joseph is educated through dreams and through overcoming obstacles and bad fortune. He learns how to predict abundance and famine in life. He learns to recognize the need for nourishment and caring that we all have. He becomes the caretaker of all Egypt. By now, he has learned to love in a way that includes all people. His mature love will sustain them all through hard times.

When his brothers come to Egypt to be fed, Joseph is able to bridge the separation caused by his father's exclusive love. Joseph's reconciliation with his family demonstrates how well he has learned to include all human beings in his love. Even those who once tried to take his life!

The story shows us that mature love nourishes and sustains relationships in spite of devisive forces. Mature love includes all others, and it only grows in power as we bring more people into its field.

A Joiner's Guide to Finding the Right Group

 As he walked by the Sea of Galilee, he saw two brothers, Simon who is called Peter and Andrew his brother, casting a net into the sea; for they were fishermen. And he said to them, "Follow me, and I will make you fishers of men." Immediately they left their nets and

followed him. And going on from there he saw two other brothers, James the son of Zebedee and John his brother, in the boat with Zebedee, their father, mending their nets, and he called them. Immediately they left the boat and their father, and followed him.

MATT. 4:18–22

We wonder how Zebedee felt, watching his sons leave the boat to follow this strange new rabbi. Was the father infused with the same zeal and faith as his sons? The gospel writer never tells.

Imagine how you might feel if these were your children. They're leaving their jobs for this new teacher? How do they know he is genuine? What if he exploits them? What if he turns them against you? These days, there are plenty of opportunities to join one community or another. We have hosts of religious denominations to choose from. And there are political movements, service clubs, sporting groups; the list is long.

Though the benefits of a community are enormous, there are dangers. The inclination to become part of a larger group of like-minded people is basic. But which are the good communities? Cults and hate groups crop up on the scene far too often. We worry that our children might join a religious or political cult that exploits them. Have we taught them how to discriminate wisely?

Jesus recruited his followers by showing them possibilities far beyond their original vocations. They were ordinary fishermen, working for a daily wage, and Jesus offered to make them "fishers of men." He showed them a new vision of what they could become and what life could mean for them. Jesus would teach them a new path and show them how to solve the problems of Israel and, in a broader sense, of all humanity.

Jesus promised a community that would bring all men and women together, not isolate them from the world. Rather, they would be closer to others than ever before.

This is the mark of healing communities. They bring people together rather than separate or isolate. Communities that foster exclusivity and suspicion of nonmembers nearly always damage their members, as well as their supposed enemies.

With caution, we can find wonderful groups for support and healing. Like Jesus and his disciples, we want communities that teach care and concern for others. Accept nothing less.

How to Help Someone Lonely

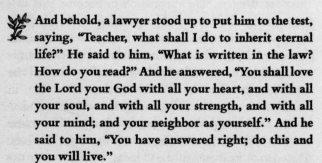 And behold, a lawyer stood up to put him to the test, saying, "Teacher, what shall I do to inherit eternal life?" He said to him, "What is written in the law? How do you read?" And he answered, "You shall love the Lord your God with all your heart, and with all your soul, and with all your strength, and with all your mind; and your neighbor as yourself." And he said to him, "You have answered right; do this and you will live."

But he, desiring to justify himself, said to Jesus,

"And who is my neighbor?" Jesus replied. "A man was going down from Jerusalem to Jericho, and he fell among robbers, who stripped him and beat him, and departed, leaving him half dead. Now by chance a priest was going down that road; and when he saw him he passed by on the other side. So likewise a Levite, when he came to the place and saw him, passed by on the other side. But a Samaritan, as he journeyed, came to where he was; and when he saw him, he had compassion, and went to him and bound up his wounds pouring on oil and wine; then he set him on his own beast and brought him to an inn, and took care of him. And the next day he took out two denarii and gave them to the innkeeper, saying, 'Take care of him; and whatever more you spend, I will repay you when I come back.' Which of these three do you think, proved neighbor to the man who fell among the robbers?" He said, "The one who showed mercy on him." And Jesus said to him, "Go and do likewise."

LUKE 10:25–37

Jesus' genius as a therapist is breathtaking. One example is his response to the lawyer in the text that includes the parable of the good Samaritan. In this story, Jesus diagnoses and heals a stranger in the blink of an eye. At the same time, he provides us with invaluable wisdom in dealing with common problems in the modern world.

The story begins with a lawyer who puts Jesus to the test. The lawyer's question shows how much pain he feels. "How can I find eternal life?" he asks. Jesus senses the hidden torture. Why is my life so miserable? Why I am so afraid and alone? Where can I find what I need to be happy?

Jesus saw the root of the problem immediately. The lawyer lacked the ability to relate to other people. He craved human contact, but his arrogance blocked him from finding this contact. The lawyer wanted to ask Jesus for help. But he tried to pick a fight instead. We can be sure this was a pattern for his whole life. Rather than asking for and giving love, and thereby making himself vulnerable to the possibility of hurt and disappointment, he protected himself with the facade of intellectual superiority. We can only imagine how successful he was in pushing others away. He managed to isolate himself and deny the very sustenance he most needed.

Modern psychologists would say that the lawyer suffered from "alienation." It is one of the foremost problems we face in the modern world. Many people feel cut off from real relationships with others. They often lack a sense of trust and fellowship. Some people, perhaps like the lawyer, have been so hurt by others they unconsciously destroy all possibility of real love. Unaware of what they are doing, they isolate themselves by hiding behind a facade of arrogance, intellectual distance, pride, or prejudice. They are caught in a trap of loneliness they have created themselves.

Jesus' response to this sad and desperate man shows profound insight. Most of us would respond to the lawyer's challenge with a counterattack. We would have played his game and he would have left convinced that his pain and isolation were inevitable. Jesus does the opposite. Instead of attacking, he gives the lawyer support. He asks a question the lawyer most certainly can answer. He affirms the lawyer's answer. He compliments his knowledge. He allows the lawyer to be right.

The support Jesus gives this man is the first step to a healing relationship. Jesus breaks the pattern of hurt and defensiveness. The lawyer begins to see that here a possibility for love exists. He finds the hope that he can have contact with another person that will not be damaging and fearful.

The lawyer also experiences a moment of profound insight into his own spiritual sickness. He realizes, through the answer he gives to his own question, that he does not know how to build lasting and real intimacy with other people. "Who is my neighbor?" he asks. How can I learn how to trust and open myself to others? How can I find a community where I can allow myself to be open to others, and be myself without fear?

Jesus knows that he has opened an avenue for real communication with this man. Now he begins to provide him with the insight and wisdom that hold the cure he craves. The parable of the good Samaritan gently reminds the lawyer of the isolation he has created in his own life. In one sense he is the victim. He has been hurt by others. His former relationships have left him half dead. This was his state when he met Jesus. This was the reason he had separated himself from those around him.

At the same time, the lawyer is also like the priest and Levite. In his pain he has created a barrier of pride and disdain which insures that he will journey alone on the path of life.

Jesus shows the lawyer, and us as well, that only

when we are able to give and receive support and love can we break through the walls of isolation and alienation we build around ourselves. Jesus' message is, in the end, very simple. Our neighbors are those who need love and compassion. We know we all have these needs. Our neighbors are those who have been hurt and disappointed. We have all been hurt and disappointed.

Isolation and alienation can be cured through our recognition that we are all part of the human community, neighbors to each other and ourselves. Through our loving compassion and concern for the pain and needs of others we can establish God's kingdom on earth.

Some People Are Never Satisfied

 To what then shall I compare the men of this generation, and what are they like? They are like children sitting in the market place and calling to one another.

> "We piped to you, and you did not dance;
> we wailed, and you did not weep."

For John the Baptist has come eating no bread and drinking no wine and you say, "He has a demon." The Son of man has come eating and drinking; and you say, "Behold, a glutton and a drunkard, a friend of the tax collectors and sinners!" Yet wisdom is justified by all her children.

LUKE 7:31–35

Sometimes, Jesus became exasperated with his followers. He listened to their problems and he healed their physical, spiritual, and emotional wounds. But occasionally the complaints got out of hand. People always found some reason to be dissatisfied. They always had something critical to say about others. It is as true today as it was then. Why do we complain so much? Why is it so difficult for us to be satisfied? Is there something wrong with the world? Or is it us?

Jesus compares his complaining followers to children who want constant attention. When they play a flute, they want you to dance. When they weep, they want comfort. This is the way children are. A young child thinks primarily of his own needs and wants, even in play. If he is entertained, he is pleasant. If a child gets bored, he whines and cries.

We willingly deal with children this way. But not adults. In extreme cases, an adult who acts this way has a serious problem in relating to others.

Most of us are cranky or dissatisfied occasionally. Nothing seems right in our lives. We wish the world would be a little more accommodating. Usually, these feelings pass in a few days. Perhaps someone becomes annoyed with our behavior and tells us to grow up.

However, some people adopt this kind of critical dissatisfaction as their prevailing attitude toward life. Nothing is ever right for them. A meal at a restaurant always becomes a battle over the food and service. The minister's sermon is never long enough, or always too long. The cleaning at home is never properly done. The job they have is too hard, or pays too little.

Leveled at John the Baptist and Jesus himself, the immature complaints of the people of Israel became a serious, even lethal attack. In fact, when Jesus refused to meet his followers' childish demands that he become a militant Messiah, many of them turned against him.

Wisdom helps us rise above this immature and dangerous way of dealing with life. Jesus tells us that, "Wisdom is justified by all her children." Wisdom means the ability to cope with the problems in life with maturity and compassion. It means the ability to tell the difference between childish whining and reasonable criticism. We all have the right and even the obligation to complain and criticize when a situation is unfair or wrong. Jesus himself challenged the prevailing religious attitudes and practices in his time.

Mature criticism is accompanied by a clear and workable solution. The solution must be offered seriously and in good faith. Good faith implies satisfaction once the solution is put into effect, if it is successful. Seriousness means that if our solution fails, we will acknowledge the failure and work with others to find a new solution.

Without seriousness and good faith, criticism is merely a plea for someone else to solve our problem for us. We want to be taken care of as children are. But childish wants are infinite, so we can never be satisfied by what others do to please us.

Wise people face the true problems in their lives honestly. The "children of wisdom" are real solutions to difficult situations. And they come from a healthy faith in our own competence to make the world workable for us and others.

ONE-ON-ONE WITH GOD

The Healing Power of Finding Your Soul

> And he told them a parable, saying, "The land of a rich man brought forth plentifully; and he thought to himself, 'What shall I do, for I have nowhere to store my crops?' And he said, 'I will do this; I will pull down my barns, and build larger ones; and there I will store all my grain and my goods. And I will say to my soul, Soul, you have ample goods laid up for many years; take your ease, eat, drink, be merry.' But God said to him, 'Fool! This night your soul is required of you; and the things you have prepared, whose will they be?' So is he who lays up treasure for himself, and is not rich toward God."
>
> LUKE 12:16–21

Do you ever think of your soul? Maybe you deny its existence altogether, as many people do. Or perhaps you think of it as an abstraction that somehow makes a person immortal. But, probably, like most of us, you go through your days with hardly a thought of your soul. Carl Jung, the great psychologist, titled one of his books, *Modern*

Man in Search of a Soul. Jung's title implies that, in this technological civilization, we must go in *search* of our souls because we have lost them. Like the rich man in Jesus' parable, we are so intent on accumulating material wealth we lose sight of the inner self and its condition.

I often ask my students if they know where their soul is. If God were to require their soul of them today, would they know where to look for it, or whether it's healthy or sick? Has it had proper nourishment and attention? Or has it been neglected entirely? Many cannot answer at all!

Imagine for a moment what you would feel if your soul were truly lost. You might feel you had lost all sense of purpose or direction in your life. Perhaps you would feel that you had lost the capacity to feel deeply about yourself or others. Perhaps you would feel cut off from something within you that was divine or holy.

It is interesting that such feelings reflect the very problems psychologists encounter most in treating their patients. The most common and damaging distress people feel is the sense of being cut off from the depths of their own being and from other people, of not having a strong identity or sense of themselves, of lacking purpose or meaning. Like the rich man in Jesus' parable, many of us have neglected and lost our souls. And we spend millions of dollars every year in therapy trying to find them again!

Jesus' parable emphasizes the dangers of this neglect of our souls. Suppose God were to ask us for an accounting of our souls on a moment's notice. We need to be prepared. And this is not just good theological advice; it is profoundly important for our psychological health as well. Jesus presents a valuable lesson in preventive mental health: Taking care of our souls is one of our most important tasks in life. It is more important than taking care of bank accounts or cars. Our happiness and sanity depend on it.

How can we find our souls again? How can we learn whether our souls are healthy or not? Jesus' parable tells how.

First, don't let yourself lose sight of your soul. Don't become complacent because you have achieved a level of worldly success. It doesn't mean you have taken care of your spiritual and emotional needs.

How do you truly feel inside? Are you honestly happy with yourself and your relationships? Have you found a satisfying spiritual path? Or do you feel something lacking in your life? Is your life outwardly luxurious and inwardly barren? If it is, you need to make contact again with your soul.

Second, learn to *listen* to your soul. In Jesus' parable, the rich man makes a terrible mistake. He *tells* his soul how things are going. Do you ever try to convince yourself that everything is wonderful when you know it's not? Worse, do you put on a show for others and then pretend to yourself that you're showing the real you?

Instead, learn to ask your soul quietly how it is doing. Then wait patiently for an answer. This may feel silly at first, but you'll be surprised at how quickly and honestly your soul responds. The answer may come as a feeling, or an inner voice. It may come in an image or even a dream. Your soul will tell you what it needs and what to do to keep this inner self happy and healthy.

The time you spend on this internal inventory will be more than repaid. You will be replenished spiritually and your psychological health will benefit for as long as you live.

Listening
to That "Still Small Voice"

🌿 And he said, "Go forth, and stand upon the mount before the Lord." And behold the Lord passed by, and a great and strong wind rent the mountains, and broke in pieces the rocks before the Lord, but the Lord was not in the wind; and after the wind an earthquake, but the Lord was not in the earthquake; and after the earthquake a fire, but the Lord was not in the fire; and after the fire a still small voice. And when Elijah heard it, he wrapped his face in his mantle and went out and stood at the entrance of the cave. And behold, there came a voice to him and said, "What are you doing here, Elijah?"

1 KINGS 19:11–13

Linda was a scrappy, bright, teenager who, unlike many her age, took an interest in political and social issues. Her friends described her as "deep." She came to my office one afternoon needing to talk.

"I just don't know who to listen to anymore. So often, people I thought I could trust betray my faith. Everyone pretends to have the answers. But few people really do. I try to listen to all sides. There are so many different points of view. My parents say one thing, my friends say another, my boyfriend something else.

"I want to understand what is going on in the world.

So I read the newspapers and watch television. Political leaders, social leaders, religious leaders—they all claim to have the truth, but many of them disagree on what the truth is. I'm so confused. I hardly know what I believe anymore."

Like Linda, most of us are confused by the contradictory things we see and hear. In our search for the truth we ache for a moment of quiet clarity.

The story of Elijah teaches us how to find that clarity. And its message is as practical and useful now as it was three thousand years ago.

Elijah was one of Israel's great prophets. His mission was to turn the sinful Israelites back to the ways of God. But the Israelites were totally unreceptive. Elijah was in despair.

To cope with his problems he went to a place where he could be alone. He needed to find out what God wanted him to do next.

The confusion of his world is reflected in the turmoil of nature—wind, rain, earthquake, and fire rage all around Elijah. But he does not find God in any of these distracting events. Then, the prophet hears a "still small voice," the voice that tells him he is in the presence of God.

We can use this healing strategy in times of turmoil and trouble. Just withdraw to a silent place and listen to that still small voice. Each of us can find it—if only we take the time to listen.

As soon as we learn to pay attention, its healing qualities become apparent. Even if its message is not what we want to hear, we sense its rightness and we are relieved from our confusion.

Making us aware that this voice exists is one of the Bible's most important therapeutic gifts. Psychologists of today tell us the voice connects to the most primeval and ancient layers of our psyche. The same voice often provides guidance to both therapist and client when the usual therapeutic measures fail. Medical doctors sometimes use it to diagnose and treat medical problems that defy more traditional procedures.

The world is so full of distractions, it's easy to ignore the simple steps it takes to listen well to the healing voice. All that's necessary is a quiet place and a bit of free time. Then silently ask the question, and wait patiently for an answer.

The answer may come as a voice, or as a feeling of right or wrong. We often find our body responding in small ways to these feelings. We might sense a gentle infusion of energy and spirit; our muscles might seem to realign themselves and a sense of inner comfort might take over.

I must warn you that the voice does not always give the answer we expect or hope to hear. More often it presents a challenge which we may or may not choose to answer.

The decision is always ours. The "still small voice" does not compel or nag; it is not a manifestation of guilt or obsession. Its power lies in the healing quality and the sense of truth and rightness it carries. Its answer may not be direct; instead it may reveal something we should know about ourselves. Then we can use that knowledge, if we choose, to become a better person, make a better world.

Moments of Moral and Religious Uncertainty Are Signs of Healthy Faith

🌿 Jesus then said to the Jews who had believed in him, "If you continue in my word, you are truly my disciples, and you will know the truth, and the truth will make you free."

JOHN 8:31–32

Every believer, no matter how strong and determined, passes through moments in which moral religious faith is challenged. It may arise from emotional pain and tragedy, or from deep doubt about how capable we are of ever really knowing the truth.

We may also find the challenge in another's failure. When a loved and respected religious leader shows himself to be far less than perfect, his followers may experience a crisis in their own faith. Closer to home, perhaps a friend we respect disappoints us.

In moments of doubt, whatever their source, the best thing to do is to accept these doubts as a challenge and an invitation to grow. See them as an invitation to find new meaning and a deeper understanding of our faith and of ourselves. It takes effort. It may even be uncomfortable. But in the end, facing the challenge and accepting the invitation is the healthiest approach.

People who staunchly refuse to face their doubts may find the battle against these inner uncertainties exhausting. They become so fragile and sensitive that a small criticism will overwhelm them. They become extremely defensive. Any one who disagrees with them is seen as evil. They won't listen to or associate with anyone who holds a different viewpoint. In the worst cases, they simply cut themselves off even from friends and relatives who don't agree completely with their beliefs.

When we feel weak and insecure about our doubts, it helps to remember that Jesus was always ready to debate with the scholars and religious experts of his time. He openly invited their questions and their criticisms, and these debates were public. It is interesting to note that Jesus did not always convince the crowd of his position. In this reading from John's Gospel taken from a debate, Jesus was forced to hide and run from the temple because the crowd was threatening to stone him.

Our faith is not a matter of how well we convince others of what we believe, but our own resolve to find the truth. This search seldom proceeds easily. We often have to backtrack and rethink our view of ourselves and the world. We must always be willing to admit that we might be mistaken.

Being open to correction and to further examination is not a sign of weakness or lack of faith. Quite the opposite, it confirms our faith that the truth can and will be known, in spite of our own shortsightedness and ignorance. We're open to criticism and challenge because that's the way error—our own or that of another—can be exposed and corrected.

Jesus promises that we shall know the truth. Moments of doubt and uncertainty are evidence that the process of finding the truth and learning more about ourselves and God is ongoing. There is always more to learn. When we doubt, it is a signal that we are about to discover something new about ourselves and what we believe. Welcome the challenge and feel the excitement of anticipating what the world will show us next.

Spiritual Housecleaning: A Daily Task for All of Us

Now as they went on their way, he entered a village; and a woman named Martha received him into her house. And she had a sister called Mary, who sat at the Lord's feet and listened to his teaching. But Martha was distracted with much serving; and she went to him and said, "Lord, do you not care that my sister has left me to serve alone? Tell her then to help me." But the Lord answered her, "Martha, Martha, you are anxious and troubled about many things; one thing is needful. Mary has chosen the good portion, which shall not be taken away from her.

LUKE 10:38–42

When Julienne sobbed and shouted angrily at her husband, David, "You just don't love me anymore," and ran to their bedroom, it was clear to all the guests that the party was over. David simply did not understand. Everything was going so well. The food was perfect. The guests were happy. He had no idea why Julienne was angry.

Later the couple came to my office to talk. "It's not that David doesn't help out," Julienne said. "He's very good around the house. But I wanted everything to be perfect for the party. Then I found myself cooped up in that kitchen and everyone outside enjoying themselves. I was so angry and frustrated I just lost control."

Julienne was suffering from a condition so common I have to call it the "Martha syndrome" from the story in the Book of Luke. In this syndrome we lose ourselves in the details and minor obligations in life and feel so resentful and frustrated because of it that we take it out on the people around us. It strikes men as well as women. Most of us are susceptible to it at some time or another, especially these days, when there are so many details to take care of in our lives.

In the milder form of the Martha syndrome, days seem to be taken up with one boring task after another— writing checks, cleaning the house, taking the car for repairs, shopping for groceries. We want to do the jobs right and they all need to be done. Yet we feel that these tasks just get in the way of more important matters. Then someone makes one more "small" request and we unload our frustration. This form of the Martha syndrome is easy to take care of. We finish a day of tiresome trivia and recognize that the frustrations we are feeling are only temporary. Tomorrow we can get to the more important matters.

But the Martha syndrome can become a way of life for some people. They feel overwhelmed by day-to-day details and the frustration and anxiety of it can turn into a sense of being trapped by life. From there they can slide into a long-lasting depression. As the emotional pain builds, these people blame their conflicts on others around them, destroying relationships.

Like Julienne, Martha in Luke's Gospel had been working in the kitchen trying to make sure that her important guests would be well fed and comfortable. She was probably a good cook and an immaculate housekeeper. It was an important day. She wanted everything to be just right. Meanwhile Mary, her sister, was in the next room listening to the Great Teacher, just what Martha wanted to do too. But Martha wanted to make a fine meal, which meant staying in the kitchen. She couldn't cook *and* sit at the Master's feet at the same time!

Finally, out of frustration, Martha went to Jesus to complain. Jesus recognized that Martha's impatience with Mary could easily develop into something more serious between them. Jesus' advice cuts right to the root of the problem and helps Martha to calm down.

Jesus reminds Martha that she's been so busy taking care of everyday housework that she's forgotten to do her spiritual housecleaning. She needs, he says, to learn to "choose the good portion." In other words, Martha was so caught up in taking care of the details of this special occasion, that she neglected the extraordinary opportunity she was offered. She should have realized that learning at the feet of the Messiah would be far more important at that moment than preparing the meal.

I advised Julienne and David to do some spiritual housecleaning. I told them to ask themselves every day, "What is truly important? What do I really want to accomplish? What are my highest goals and values?" I also suggested that they take time to consider the extraordinary opportunities the day can bring. It's so easy to lose these opportunities because we fail to prepare for them. Our everyday routines are allowed to blind us to the grander possibilities that lie at our doorstep.

This task of inner housekeeping helps in setting priorities. If we are aware of the "good portion"—the most important goals and tasks—we can plan to take care of them first, allotting the time they deserve. The other matters can be handled more quickly, or put off to a more convenient time. We need to ask ourselves, "Must the dishes be done at this moment?" "Must the oil in the car be changed today?" "Is cleaning the garage really worth doing to perfection?" "Do other matters deserve more of our time and attention?"

This daily spiritual housecleaning can free us from the sense of being trapped by trivial details in life. It can also keep us attuned to the values and aspirations that make life worth living. Most important, it can free us from the unfair resentment we often feel toward others when we don't have the time to meet our own crucial needs.

You Are Never Truly Helpless

Ask, and it will be given you; seek and you will find; knock and it will be opened to you. For every one who asks receives, and he who seeks finds, and to him who knocks it will be opened. Or what man of you, if

his son asks him for bread, will give him a stone; or if
he asks for a fish, will give him a serpent? If you then,
who are evil, know how to give good gifts to your
children, how much more will your Father who is in
heaven give good things to those who ask him!

MATT. 7:7–11

Psychologists find that depression, anxiety, hostility, and
loneliness all stem from a sense of helplessness, a feeling
that we have no control of our lives. Where does this
feeling come from? We are not born with it. We must
acquire it, but how?

Jerry, a good-looking, pre-law student in one of my
classes, was an example of someone who anguished over
losing control of his life. His life was rich with promise,
then one day he noticed an unusual stiffness in his shoulder.
It persisted and worsened, and turned out to be cancer.
Luckily, it was caught in the earliest stages, and the prog-
nosis was excellent. Still, Jerry was stunned.

"I thought I was going to be a big shot. Now I realize
I have absolutely no control in my life. No matter what I
do, I may die tomorrow. Why should I work for good
grades or law school? What difference does it make?"

Many victims of disease or tragedy feel as Jerry did. It
is perfectly natural. But this way of thinking can put us
into a vicious cycle. First, we feel that nothing we do can
make a difference. So we do nothing. Consequently, we
never change or improve, and our original feelings are
confirmed. Our conviction of helplessness becomes greater.
This cycle can make us depressed and miserable to the
point of becoming truly disabled.

The Bible provides an escape hatch from helplessness-thinking. Jesus shows his disciples how to overcome the feelings of powerlessness and despair that can arise from failure or tragedy.

He tells them that they must take charge of their lives. They are to "seek" and "ask." When we feel helpless, this first step is crucial, for it's easy to feel so damaged that we lose our sense of direction. But we can't let this continue. No matter how helpless we feel, we can, at the very least, decide for ourselves what we want. We can reestablish our goals and direction. It may seem futile at first. But this first step is absolutely necessary.

Jesus is emphatic about this matter. He repeats his advice in the second verse, this time with a stronger assurance. "For every one who asks receives." Jesus is not promising we will get all that we want, whenever we want it. Rather, he tells us that we will receive some benefit. It may be small at first. It may not resolve every problem. But it's a start.

The best beginning is to set reachable goals. We can wash the dishes or vacuum the carpet. We can return a library book, call a friend, or pay a bill. Small accomplishments can provide a renewed sense that we do have control over our lives. They can counter the irrational idea that nothing we do matters.

Next, Jesus tells his disciples to go to others for help and support. Helplessness-thinking often leads us to cut ourselves off from friends or from others who can offer useful advice. We forget how many people truly want to help. One of the best ways to accomplish our goals is to find others who have the same goals and work together with them. We know psychologists find support groups best for healing a variety of psychological, and even physical problems. The sense of community and sharing can be immensely beneficial in exchanging information and combining efforts to conquer common problems.

Jesus' third antidote to helplessness is stronger and more profound than the first two. He tells his disciples to trust that the whole universe is conspiring *for them!* Jesus reminds his disciples that even evil people are good to their children. Certainly, God will ensure the best possible outcome for his children.

Notice that Jesus' advice applies also to those who are not religious in the traditional sense. A pessimistic attitude makes life nearly impossible. Ultimately, logic itself points to the conclusion that the universe is good to us in much the same way that parents are good to their children. We are fragile and we need its gifts—the air we breathe, the water we drink, and the food we eat. As Jesus points out, they were given to us in abundance from the beginning.

Follow Jesus' advice to overcome helplessness-thinking and resume the trip toward fulfillment and happiness. Of course, the path may not be entirely free of obstacles, but we are on the road to success with God's gifts always there for us to use and enjoy.

GET THE FULL BENEFIT
OF THE BEATITUDES

Through the centuries, Jesus' Sermon on the Mount has been a source of consolation and hope for all people. In it Jesus assures us that God will not neglect our spiritual and psychological needs. No matter how deep our suffering, our prayers for healing will be answered.

Jesus' sermon contains more than just a promise. It provides a model for spiritual growth and transformation. It offers a program for healing with principles to follow for effecting a positive change in the future.

When we first read the sermon, we might miss these principles. Jesus' words are paradoxical in places. Sometimes his advice seems impractical, and even impossible to carry out.

However, as we explore the depth and mystery of the sermon, we find an unsurpassed wisdom in these words. We also discover a set of rules that are valid for all situations in every age.

Now let us look at each beatitude in turn.

Wealth Comes to the Poor in Spirit

> Blessed are the poor in spirit, for theirs is the king-
> dom of heaven.

MATT. 5:3

Jesus begins by telling us that the poor in spirit are blessed. We wonder why? What does Jesus mean by "the poor in spirit?" Why are they blessed? Wouldn't the rich in spirit be even more blessed? Isn't spiritual richness the goal we all seek?

The first principle of healing, which I call the Law of Psychological Reversal, explains it all.

This law says: *In order to enjoy the heights of spiritual and psychological growth we must experience the depths of spiritual loss.*

Times of spiritual poverty do lead to the greatest inner transformations. Once we hit rock bottom in our spiritual lives, we start to turn around, to move upward toward a better life.

I have often seen this principle at work. People find the courage and resolve to change their lives at just those moments when despair is deepest and energy and life are virtually extinguished.

This is the spiritual miracle Jesus speaks of in the first

beatitude. But among the most inspiring examples of it are the victories of those who win the battle of alcoholism. John, a forty-five-year-old executive, tells how he found the courage to fight this disease:

"I was a social drinker from the age of fifteen or sixteen. But I got into it seriously when my life got tough. My father died suddenly, and we were very close. Two weeks later, I got laid off from a job I held for twelve years. I couldn't find work for six months. Then I found another job, but was laid off soon after. I couldn't find the energy to go out and look for work again. My self-esteem was crushed. I sat around the whole day drinking alone and crying like a baby.

"Finally, my wife Julie couldn't take it anymore, and she walked out. I never felt pain like that. I was ready to take my life. But suddenly something deep within me changed. A voice said, 'You are going to beat this disease.' At that moment I made the most important decision of my life—to go on living."

John went on: "I went for treatment. It is a long process, but now I know I will win. Julie and I are back together. I have a good job again. But I would never have made this new beginning without hitting bottom like that. I never want to go that low again, but my despair taught me a valuable lesson."

The first beatitude teaches us that even those times of deep spiritual and psychological pain can be beneficial. Jesus promises that our darkest experiences can provide the impetus toward the highest form of inner peace. In these anguished moments, we experience the greatest transformations for good.

The sense of spiritual poverty is often necessary as a first stage of interior development. Too often, people fail to take this first step. They deny their own inner hunger, believing they should know only happy times.

We must experience the full range of emotions. To know only the good without the evil, the light without the darkness, is to be deprived. Those who confront the worst life has to offer learn how to revere the good things.

THE SECOND BEATITUDE

The Rewards of Change

Blessed are those who mourn, for they shall be comforted.

MATT. 5:4

Jesus gives his second blessing to those who mourn. Who are the mourners? What are they mourning? What loss is the cause of this grief?

In the first beatitude, Jesus assures us that the spiritual poverty we feel is often necessary to move us into action. In the second beatitude, Jesus addresses a surprising response we will have as we start the journey to a new and healthier life — grief.

In this second stage of spiritual growth, we make the decision to change. The old way of living and feeling is no longer satisfying for us. Worse, it is damaging and hurtful, so a new beginning is essential.

But the decision to change brings a twinge of grief. We realize that we must give up much of our past—all of our old identity. What we mourn, then, is the loss of our old self and our old way of life.

The second beatitude articulates another psychological law: *In order to change, we must give up part of our past life.*

As we pass through life, we experience a series of losses and gains. It is necessary to give up something of the past to progress to the future. Jesus assures us that we will be compensated for these losses.

Jesus often refers to this law in his teaching: "For whoever would save his life will lose it, and whoever loses his life for my sake will find it."—Matt. 16:25. "And every one who has left houses or brothers or sisters or father or mother or children or lands, for my name's sake, will receive a hundredfold, and inherit eternal life."—Matt. 19:29.

It is natural to feel sad for what we leave behind as we grow. Even if the old life failed us, the old way held its attractions at least for a time. It satisfied some of our needs and desires. It held the solution to our life's problems during that period. The sense of mourning is a sign that the changes are real and we are serious about the task of growing.

We must not allow our nostalgia for the old ways to obstruct our transformation. Of course, we must sacrifice to change. But, as most therapists know, the first thing we give up if we want to change is, surprisingly, our personal pain.

It is amazing how we sometimes cling to our suffering. For some, a familiar situation, no matter how bad, is preferable to an unknown future, no matter how good it might be. The unknown is frightening. We often hide from current problems by retreating to pleasant memories of a past that no longer meets our needs. Jesus is assuring us that the benefits accompanying the movement toward growth are worth any risk involved.

The promise that we will be comforted has a foundation in the reality. Once the change is made, we see that the stage we gave up so reluctantly was actually confining. It held us back. It would have been dangerous to continue there too long. We are comforted in the knowledge that our forward leap opened us to a happiness we barely hoped for when we first began.

THE THIRD BEATITUDE

Be Meek, Be Strong

Blessed are the meek, for they shall inherit the earth.
MATT. 5:5

Another paradox. Common sense tells us that the ambitious and aggressive are the successful ones. Fearlessness and strength are the best characteristics for living in this brutal age. A meek person is bound to lose in the struggle for any earthly values, when pitted against these tough guys.

As in the first and second blessing, Jesus is speaking in spiritual terms. To him, meekness is not a personality flaw. Jesus uses the term with a special focus, as he gives us the third law of psychological development: *Healing happens in its own time. We cannot force ourselves or others to change.*

The meek are willing to observe this law, a necessary stage in the process of self-understanding. It can only happen when we move our ego out of the way. If we lack meekness we bully our way through life, trying to force our thoughts and emotions into some preconceived pattern.

For Jesus, meekness is a collection of the following traits we must foster in ourselves if we are to progress spiritually.

First, we are willing to wait patiently for change in ourselves or in others. This can be difficult. Once we set out on the spiritual path and feel the first indications of strength and renewal, we want to move forward as quickly as possible. At times we may become frustrated that we are not advancing more rapidly. Even worse, we become annoyed with others if they don't show the proper enthusiasm for our new attitude and gains.

Pushiness like this has a negative effect. We have to be tolerant of our limitations and those of others. We have to accept the pace of change our minds and souls can tolerate. Healing often takes time, and we can't skip any of the steps.

Second, meekness suggests an openness to life. It means accepting the risk of being hurt or disappointed. At times, of course, toughness is called for. But too often, we overprotect ourselves against hurt, and, in the process, block the possibility of change. Refusing to allow anyone or anything to affect us only cripples our chances of progress.

Finally, meekness indicates a willingness to be led, led by the inner voices often muffled by anxiety or ambition. We tend to think of a meek person as a follower, someone who takes orders. Jesus, however, speaks of a spiritual meekness, which calls for us to surrender the pretense of absolute power over our lives. We acknowledge that our conscious egos do not have the full answer to our problems. We must search in quiet prayer for the meaning and direction we need.

The answers to our prayers usually come as a gentle nudge rather than a tidal wave of powerful emotion. The most significant transformations come when we meekly follow the gentle urgings of the best parts of ourselves. These promptings are subtle, but they are persistent. They do not so much demand that we change, rather they show us how to change.

Is Jesus right? How can the meek really inherit the earth? I believe that those who are truly meek, in the way Jesus meant, are remarkably effective in the world. There is power and strength in meekness. I have seen it.

During my term as a VISTA Volunteer some years ago, I worked in a poverty-stricken neighborhood in North Philadelphia. It was a community with serious problems: crime, drugs, unemployment, juvenile delinquency, racial tension. A man named Calvin lived there. He was quiet and reserved. I never heard him raise his voice. He was not physically imposing. He was certainly not rich or politically strong.

His house was small and he had three children of his own. Nevertheless, he took in his brother's family when they lost their own home in a fire. In spite of all the bustle and noise in that crowded house, I never heard Calvin threaten or complain. Most people would agree that Calvin was "meek."

But Calvin had a power as deep as any I have ever

seen. He spoke quietly when he was angry, but he was heard. I once saw Calvin come between two gangs, one black the other Hispanic, who were close to fighting. Calvin simply spoke softly to each of them. As I watched from a safe distance, I saw members of both groups nod their heads; some even smiled. Soon, they went their own way.

Afterwards, I asked Calvin what he told them. He smiled and said, "The truth."

Calvin's meekness was a force that could compel others to hear the truth, do the right thing. We can only pray that world leadership will use the power of such meekness to preserve and defend us all.

THE FOURTH BEATITUDE

Common Obstacles to Spiritual Goals

Blessed are those who hunger and thirst for right-eousness for they shall be satisfied.

MATT. 5:6

The fourth psychological law is: *A deep desire for spiritual insight is a crucial factor in healing and growth.*

It seems obvious that we should long for spiritual "righteousness." Do we really need to be reminded of this fact? Jesus seems to think so—he makes it the central and pivotal point of his Sermon on the Mount. Why is this matter so significant?

Jesus speaks here to an aspect of the spiritual journey everyone must travel. Each of us goes through life attempting to grow toward our goals of happiness and spiritual fulfillment. And each of us will surely meet obstacles as we go.

We wish the journey could always be easy. But unfortunately, we all have to overcome experiences that stand in our way. If you feel blocked in your efforts to understand yourself and find spiritual and psychological health, Jesus is talking directly to you.

What sort of blocks can we expect to meet? It is impossible to list them all, since everyone's path is unique. But some problems are common. Here are a few:

Distractions. When we are in crisis, hitting the depths of spiritual poverty, we make wonderful resolutions to change our life and work to achieve our purpose. Then, when the immediate crisis is past, and life is back to "normal," we become strong candidates for distraction from our new resolves. We need to find a new job, work on the house, or take a vacation. Quietly, the resolutions are forgotten, and the valuable lesson we might have learned is lost.

Temptations. No matter what the stage of our journey to healing and salvation, temptation is always with us working to hold us back. Those who conquer their addiction to a bad relationship, alcohol, drugs, or gambling know they must always guard against regressing to these self-destructive behaviors. But other temptations are there for all of us—the temptation to give up on ourselves; the temptation to use others or to ignore their needs; the temptation to pretend to ourselves or others we are better in some way than we actually are.

Failures. Nobody is perfect. Everyone makes mistakes. Sadly, all of us will give in to some temptation at some point of our journey. Failure, however, is never the end of the journey. Failure never means defeat, unless we see it that way.

Successes. At times, success is a worse obstacle than failure. Success always seems to be wonderful. But if we allow our success to convince us that we have nothing more to accomplish, or that we need not try anymore, we risk losing our direction altogether.

Boredom. One of the most dangerous obstacles on our spiritual road is boredom. We all know periods in life when nothing seems to be happening. Our inner battles seem to have quieted, and we hear no call to move forward. We feel stuck right where we are forever. I can assure you such periods pass, but often we think we are lost in the darkness, and lose interest in the struggle to achieve new heights.

Jesus' assurance, in this blessing, is both simple and powerful. He promises we can overcome every obstacle as long as we have the deep desire to succeed.

The first important fact to remember is that every journey has these blocks. No one escapes them. Don't feel guilty or inadequate when you encounter them; above all, never allow them to stop you. The absence of these obstacles is never the reason for spiritual success. True success lies in learning to overcome them.

Second, be forewarned. Once you know these blocks will crop up at some point, you can prepare yourself to meet them. The process of healing and growth has moments of pure spontaneity. Sometimes, our accomplishments seem to happen on their own as gifts of God's grace. Take the gifts and be grateful. There are also times when the process requires effort, planning and plain old hard work. These times call for a discipline that arises from a fundamental desire to understand and follow the healing inner path.

Finally, this deep desire to move toward inner healing is, as Jesus points out, our strongest help in overcoming obstacles. Jesus promises that fulfillment will come. This is not a vague hope, but a psychological fact.

Within us there is a motivation for spiritual improvement that is as powerful as physical hunger and thirst. When we exploit this potent need for growth and healing, all obstacles melt away.

THE FIFTH BEATITUDE

The Crucial Skills of Mercy and Forgiveness

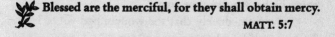 **Blessed are the merciful, for they shall obtain mercy.**
MATT. 5:7

In this blessing, Jesus shows us one way to find and strengthen the powerful inner motivation that gets us over the hurdles blocking the path to spiritual fulfillment. The law he gives us is: *Spiritual progress only comes when we forgive the faults and failures of ourselves and others.*

Since we know mistakes and faults are unavoidable, we all must learn the crucial skills of mercy and forgiveness. The alternative is a constant sense of guilt and shame, even hate. These negative emotions are never productive or helpful.

Guilt and shame over past failures and sins can only drain our energy and smother our hope.

A number of years ago, a young woman consumed with guilt over the death of her mother came to me. The daughter cared for the mother throughout a prolonged illness, but secretly, perhaps even unconsciously, resented giving her time. When the mother finally died, the woman felt a sudden burst of elation. Finally, she was free! Then, realizing how strong her resentment had been, she was overcome with shame at her own selfishness.

Since that time she had never stopped mourning her mother's death. Years after, she still cried herself to sleep. Worse, she was unable to make any significant decisions about her own life.

My first question to her was, "What is standing in the way of your mercy? Why are you punishing yourself like this?"

She thought for a while, then said, "I am afraid God has seen how I really am. How can I forgive myself unless I know he has forgiven me first?"

I saw immediately that the woman had yet to learn the power of Jesus' message of mercy.

Jesus makes it clear God is always ready to show his infinite compassion. The question is, are we able and ready to forgive ourselves? And just as important, are we ready to forgive others?

This young woman did not forgive herself for her imperfections. She wanted to be absolutely pure and good. Of course, like all of us, she was not. She was not willing to forgive herself her natural shortcomings.

But there was a deeper problem too. The young woman also needed to be merciful to her mother. She had loved and needed her mother, but she was angry at her as well. The young woman had yet to really forgive her mother for becoming sick and then dying and abandoning her.

As she told me how lost and deserted she felt when her mother died, the young woman again found herself in tears. She had desperately wanted her mother to recover. The woman blamed her mother all these years for the loneliness and sorrow that consumed her life.

Later in our conversation, the woman was willing to speak to her mother as if she were in the room. She told her all she felt in the last few years. She asked for mercy and forgiveness for her resentment, then she forgave her mother for leaving her. Then she said good-bye.

The wave of grief she felt at this moment was overwhelming. But its effect was cleansing and freeing. Quietly she looked at me and said, "I know I am forgiven. I am finally free."

Don't Ignore God's Energy

🌿 **Blessed are the pure in heart, for they shall see God.**
MATT. 5:8

A divine energy is all around us and within us. Its presence is nearer to us than we are to ourselves. Creation continuously sings its praise and glory. Every movement in the cosmos shows the wonders of this energy at work.

And we miss it!

Day after day, we ignore the joyful presence of this energy. We blindfold our eyes with fear and worry. We stuff our ears with anxiety and self-centered concern. We numb our hearts to the possibility of truly touching and being touched by those we love.

All around us, the world is calling out, "Wake up! Wake up! Can't you see the magnificence of creation? Can't you hear it? Can't you feel it? The wonder of creation is here beside you. Just look! You don't need to go on vacation. You don't need to do anything special. You certainly don't need to be famous or rich. Just look!"

And we rarely open our eyes and ears to the bountiful glory within our reach. We mope and groan our way through life, like spoiled children, feeling sorry for ourselves.

There is so much more to life. In the sixth blessing,

Jesus reveals to us a wonderful secret and a delightful promise. He tells us that once we have learned forgiveness and fulfilled our desire to follow the path of inward healing, we will find ourselves able to see God ever more clearly throughout our daily life.

It is his sixth principle of psychological and spiritual progress: *As we grow and mature inwardly, we become ever more aware of the Divine presence, within us and among us.*

Millions have experienced the truth of this principle. You can see this promise fulfilled even in the earliest stages of your spiritual and psychological path. You can experiment yourself to test it. Here's an exercise to try sometime soon.

One evening, when the weather is good and the sky is clear, take a bit of time for yourself. Turn off the television and go outside.

Now close your eyes and make a deal with yourself. Allow yourself, just for a few minutes, to put aside all your problems and cares. Give yourself a psychotherapeutic holiday. For just a minute or two put away every one of your troubles and worries.

After you've cleaned out the emotional darkness, imagine this to be your first night in God's creation. Pretend you are a child who has never seen the world before. Inwardly and outwardly you are pure of all the burdens life has offered. Try to feel yourself completely new, completely reborn. Can you feel it?

Now slowly turn your gaze upward to the stars!

What a magnificent vision you will find there! Words can never approach the splendor of the night sky filled with stars. Consider as you look upward the full reach of creation. Realize that our eyes, even at their best, can only see the smallest portion of the totality of the cosmos.

This vision is here for all us every evening. And it is only one possibility for sensing the wonder and beauty around us. The child asleep, the snowflake melting on your finger tip, the loving concern of a friend, the beauty of a tree in autumn—in all these and in so much more, we can find a spiritual presence in our life.

Jesus shows us that as we progress along the path and conquer our inner anxieties and fears, we will be able to see and feel God's presence in every facet of our lives. The healing we experience will open our vision.

This new vision is a sure sign that we are traveling in the right direction. It is one of many inward confirmations that we are forging ahead in the path of righteousness. The capacity to find the divine presence everywhere around us, surprising us daily with its beauty and power, is the result of our progress.

The increased awareness we gain is also a source of encouragement and energy that urges us onward and helps shield us from the temptation to backslide or become distracted. Once we experience such visions, we can know without doubt that we are surrounded by an infinite and undiminished love, always there for us, even when we cannot see it.

Inner Peace
Is Unbounded Energy

🌿 **Blessed are the peacemakers, for they shall be called the sons of God.**

MATT. 5:9

One goal of spiritual and psychological growth is inner peace—"the peace that passes all understanding." Jesus places this achievement near the end of his sermon on spiritual growth. It is a most precious and lofty attainment and one that comes only after great effort.

To find inner peace is to be so attuned with the divine power of love and concern as to be counted among those closest to God in our actions and attitudes. What exactly is this inner peace? How can we find it? Jesus' sermon answers these questions.

In this part of his sermon Jesus reveals the seventh principle of psychological and spiritual growth: *The most powerful and effective actions in bringing God's Kingdom of Heaven to the world begin with spiritual peace.*

I often use this principle in explaining the concept of inner peace to my college students. Students often find the notion challenging.

One student asked recently, "Why is there so much

talk of peace in the gospels? From what I can understand, Jesus caused disturbances wherever he went. He challenged the religious authorities. He debated the sages. He even overturned the tables of the money changers in the temple. He doesn't seem all that peaceful to me."

I admitted the young man's picture of Jesus was accurate. But his notion of peace was off the mark. The student had accepted the common idea of inner peace as passivity and relaxation. He thought of peace as a state of low energy and rest. He imagined that people who made peace with themselves and the world would avoid any exertion. Their favorite pastime would be, perhaps, quiet meditation.

In fact, the opposite is true. Inner peace brings with it enormous energy. It is an emotional state from which our most effective actions flow, a state of mind that provides maximum energy for whatever we choose to do.

One of our first discoveries as we begin our spiritual journey is how much we are at war with ourselves. We are angry at ourselves for our mistakes. We oppose the urge to violate our ideals and standards. We resent our weaknesses. We struggle to overcome our resistance to fulfill our obligations. We work so hard to avoid seeing ourselves as we truly are.

All this takes enormous effort. This inner conflict drains our resources. We get so caught up in resolving this warfare, we have little energy left to do anything more in the world but get by. At times, even getting by is difficult.

The real problem is not that we lack energy, even though we feel bone-tired. The energy is there. But it's scattered and fragmented.

This state of inner conflict is so common and all-pervasive, we hardly notice it. We discover it, usually, only in moments of inner truce where we allow ourselves to rest from this raging battle. Then we realize how we have exhausted ourselves.

The realization also helps us understand that our emotional conflicts are not eternal. As the inner conflicts recede, the energy that fueled the battle now becomes accessible for use in daily life. Our energy level skyrockets. We are prepared for action in the world.

The increase in usable psychic energy is one of the most significant rewards for attaining the kind of spiritual growth the Bible urges on us. Not only do we have more energy, but we can use it far more efficiently. We are less likely to waste our inner resources with regret or indecision, less likely to blame others for our failures.

We often marvel that the biblical heroes and heroines accomplished so much, often against odds that would have daunted anyone else. Abraham, Jacob, Moses, Esther, David, the disciples of Jesus, and Paul were effective and powerful in their actions because they knew an inner peace that allowed them to concentrate their energies on doing God's work. They were known, in Jesus' words, as "sons of God" because they carried on his divine plan.

As you progress along the spiritual path taught to us in the Bible, you will feel this same inner energy. As you use this inner energy for good, it will increase to meet all your needs, and flow to help others. It is the energy that can heal the world.

Self-Improvement Is Always a Work in Progress

🌿 Blessed are those who are persecuted for righteousness'
sake for theirs is the kingdom of heaven.

Blessed are you when men revile you and persecute you and utter all kinds of evil against you falsely
on my account. Rejoice and be glad, for your reward
is great in heaven, for so men persecuted the prophets
who were before you.

MATT. 5:10–12

Here at the end of the spiritual journey we are ready for
our reward. We have suffered through spiritual poverty
and the grueling transitions we have made. We have
found a deep desire for healing and growth, and we have
accepted our failures and mistakes. We have felt the divine
energy around us and have gained the power that comes
from inner peace. The journey has been long. Now we are
ready for the reward.

What does Jesus offer? Can we rest? Can we have a
vacation? Are all our problems resolved? No! Jesus tells us
we will find persecution. We will encounter false accusations.

Wait a minute! We expected something different.

Again, Jesus, like any good therapist, turns our expectations upside down. He now offers us the final law of psychological progress: *The spiritual journey is a process of a lifetime. It is never finished.*

We often expect psychological healing to be like the physical healing our family doctor provides. We think of our sick bodies as machines that are broken down. The doctor does the necessary repairs and we can go about our business.

This model of healing doesn't work well for the physical body. It certainly does not work for the mind and spirit. Our consciousness is not a machine that breaks down; it is a spiritual unity. It is a personality that understands and worries, an awareness that reflects upon itself and the world. More than anything else, it is a seeker that sets goals and grows toward those goals.

Jesus' final blessing teaches us that we do not relax and quit when we achieve a goal. Quite the contrary, we seek new goals, new ways to grow and meet life's challenges. This is especially true of our spiritual life. We never finish the process of personal development.

To many psychologists life is a series of stages in growth and progress. Each stage has its own tasks and its challenge. Our goals in our youth are quite different from those we strive for as mature adults. As we meet the needs of each stage in life, we grow to find a new set of needs and goals to replace the old ones.

The blessing of Jesus is that we need never stop growing and learning. There are always new vistas and new levels of maturity. The increasing maturity we acquire in this process gives us more spiritual power and emotional strength.

Jesus sees these new challenges in terms of "persecution and scorn." These are hard words, but Jesus does not want us to underestimate the task. The harshness Jesus speaks of here refers to both the inward conflict that is yet to come, and the resistance we will be sure to meet as we carry our new-found wisdom into the world. The inward conflict will come as we begin again the process of growth to meet the challenges of our newly won maturity. The outward conflict will arise as we apply our wisdom to meeting the needs and healing the pain of others.

In the end, it is in applying and testing our insights and spiritual maturity by helping others that we prove their merit. We must risk the possibility that our insights are mistaken. We may find that our vision was obscured or that we only saw part of the picture. This process of correction and revision is also necessary to the process of spiritual healing.

Most important, inner healing always leads to the "righteousness" so often mentioned in the Bible. A spirituality that is purely self-serving is immature and useless. True spiritual progress means we find intimacy and love with others. It means we can accept other's faults and understand their mistakes. We have met these same faults and mistakes in our own struggle.

In the end, our spiritual search makes us stronger and more resilient. We meet challenges that would have paralyzed us before. We face opposition we would have avoided at all costs. Our new strengths and insights lead us to more effective living and greater joy, both for ourselves and for the world.

Index